Learning from case studies

Learning from case studies

SECOND EDITION

GEOFF EASTON
University of Lancaster

PRENTICE HALL
New York · London · Toronto · Sydney
Tokyo · Singapore

This edition published 1992 by
Prentice Hall International (UK) Ltd
66 Wood Lane End, Hemel Hempstead
Hertfordshire HP2 4RG
A division of
Simon & Schuster International Group

Typeset in 10/12pt Palacio
by MCS Limited, Salisbury, England.

Printed and bound in Great Britain at
BPC Wheatons Ltd, Exeter

Library of Congress Cataloging-in-Publication Data

Easton, Geoff.
  Learning from case studies / Geoff Easton.
    p. cm.
  Includes bibliographical references and index.
  ISBN 0-13-528688-3
  1. Management—Study and teaching. 2. Case method.
  I. Title.
HD30.4.E27 1992   91-24397
658′00722—dc20   CIP

British Library Catatoguing in Publication Data

Easton, Geoff
  Learning from case studies.–2nd ed.
  I. Title
  371.3078

  ISBN 0-13-528688-3

---

4 5 96 95 94

To
Helen, George, Jonathan, David

Contents

Preface to the Second Edition

It is over ten years since the first edition of this book was published. In preparing the second edition I have been thinking about the changes that have taken place with respect to the use of case studies in the intervening time period. I have done nothing in the way of formal research but I have detected a number of trends which lead me to believe that writing a second edition is not likely to be wasted effort. There has, for example, been a continuing expansion in people-centred, vocationally oriented education in such areas as management, social and public administration, architecture, medicine, law and so on. Unfortunately there has not always been a corresponding increase in the resources devoted to teaching. Thus, while there has been an increase in the training of teachers and lecturers in simulation learning experiences such as the case study, there still remain a large number who are unable to help students learn from the experience in an effective way. As a consequence I think that the need for a book of this type has not significantly diminished over time. Whether this particular book actually fulfils that need is up to the reader to judge.

Students continue to be very receptive to methods of learning which allow them a glimpse of the world they will be entering. These methods attempt to simulate reality in the classroom. They include projects, exercises, games, role playing and, of course, case studies.

The introduction of these new learning methods has not been wholly successful. A number of major hurdles stand in the way. In particular, the case method continues to suffer from a student backlash in each new generation. This can be attributed to a number of factors. Simulation learning methods are prodigal of resources, difficult to schedule, organize and control, and raise many assessment problems. In short, they do not integrate well with existing teaching methods. Of these methods, however, the case study is the least radical. It has therefore been a favourite addition to existing courses. 'Let's give them a case or two – that should keep them happy', has too often been the response to students' demands for relevance. This has sometimes resulted in excessive and inappropriate use of the case method. In addition, many case instructors learned to 'lead' cases by being thrown in at the deep end. This inclines too many of them to believe that their students should receive the same treatment. It is even possible to rationalize this approach: 'Students must be given room to explore' ... 'Students mustn't become too dependent on teachers' ... 'They're always wanting to know the "right" answer; the case method has no right answer. It's my job to keep them confused.' All these comments may be valid in particular circumstances. Too frequently they hide a basic problem. Case instructors know how they analyze cases but cannot, or will not, pass this knowledge on to their students.

Cases involve a lot of hard work for students. They often stimulate students to efforts far beyond those devoted to more conventional learning methods. Unfortunately much of this effort is wasted. If this were true only of the first few cases in a case course, then there would be no problem, but it is frequently true that students are no nearer understanding what cases are all about at the end of the course than they were at the beginning. Is it any wonder that they become frustrated, bored, unhappy and finally disenchanted with the case method? Add to this the need to pass a case examination, and the disenchantment of students with case courses can be understood.

Yet these problems can be solved. No teacher would wish to prevent students from exploring, but they should not be asked to do so without the necessary equipment. Thrust back on their own resources most students learn some of the necessary skills, but do so rather inefficiently; some students learn no skills at all. Put another way, the gap between conventional and simulation learning methods is too great: conventional learning methods require students to accept and learn the concepts, principles and techniques that the teacher thinks will be useful; simulation learning methods ask students to invent their own concepts, principles and techniques. This gap can and should be bridged.

This book sprang originally out of an increasing awareness that case studies, as they are normally used, are inefficient teaching vehicles. My experience since writing the first edition has not led me to change my mind. Indeed, if anything, it has confirmed my original judgement. As a result of the publication of this book I have been invited to give a number of seminars dealing with the use, and abuse, of case studies. The participants, mostly teachers or lecturers who have had some experience of the case method, have been at once excited and frustrated: excited over the possibilities and frustrated because they are unsure how the learning process should be managed and have too little time for training or experimentation. They find it particularly difficult to know how to help their students to learn since simply analyzing the case and discussing it takes so much time. What is offered here is a way around these problems.

Beginning case analysts require guidelines to help them negotiate the first few obstacles to learning. These guidelines are not intended to be, and indeed they could not be, a complete guide to action. They are a base from which to develop a personal approach. I have used these guidelines on case courses on which I have taught several hundred students, and they have usually (but not always !) resulted in much improved case performances. Discussions have been more sharply focused and the gap between the expertise of the case leader and the students has been narrowed. Yet this has not stunted creativity: rather, creativity has been stimulated towards more specific ends.

Case analysis is meant to provide practice in problem solving and decision making in a simulated situation. The guidelines were therefore developed from some of the current principles and theories of problem solving and decision making. These have been interpreted and simplified in order to create a set of practical rules which can be followed in one specific situation – the case analysis. This book therefore goes beyond what is normally found in a student guide to case analysis: it may even make a modest contribution to the field by integrating a number of different approaches. The main criterion in writing this book was always, 'Will it work in a case analysis situation?'

My experience over the last ten years has led me to make some minor modifications and changes in emphasis in the methods described. In particular, I now tend to take a 'softer' line. By that I mean that I am more and more convinced that we tend to create our own social reality and that data are always less concrete than we might hope or expect. However, we must learn to live in this social reality when we work with others so it is entirely sensible that the case method should prepare us for it.

One major change in exposition has been made. Rather than have a series of cases which illustrate particular aspects of the case guidelines I have decided to use only one. Reviewers and users of the first edition pointed out that it was rather discouraging for students to have to analyze a series of case studies, and that seeing one through from beginning to end would be much more helpful. I cannot but agree.

This book is aimed at students at a number of different levels. I have used it successfully with undergraduates, postgraduates and post-experience students. Perhaps the most important conditions for success are that the users should want to learn rather than be concerned solely with earning bits of paper and that they should be doing enough case studies so that the 'lessons' can be learned.

A step-by-step approach is described. Within each step a number of more sophisticated and therefore more effective techniques are discussed. Beginners may feel that they can only cope with the most basic steps; more experienced case analysts could proceed much further and employ many more of the techniques and concepts on offer. The choice is left to the individual: it is a question of balancing time and effort against the rewards of acquiring more skills. Use anything that is helpful and discard the rest. You must learn to learn in your own way though you should know what choices are open to you.

A number of people helped me in the twin tasks of clarifying my ideas on the case method and of putting those ideas on paper for the first edition. My major debt is to Professor Ken Simmonds of the London Business School. He was my first case instructor and, in the light of experience, the best. The impetus this gave to my interest in the case method has kept me enthusiastic ever since. The late Jackie Marrian, the first director of the MA in Marketing Education at Lancaster, contributed a great deal to my understanding of management learning experiences. Our discussions were always interesting, usually enjoyable and sometimes hilarious. As a particular tribute to her I have tried to avoid sexist language in my writing. Past MA in Marketing Education students must also be thanked for the part they have played as guinea pigs, sounding boards and leg-people. Members of the Department of Marketing at Lancaster have continued to give me help and advice, particularly George Long and Peter Spillard. The Management Learning Department at Lancaster has provided an atmosphere in which the questioning of theories of teaching and learning is always encouraged and I thank them for that. Numerous individuals including seminar participants and reviewers have given me helpful and constructive feedback and I have tried, not always successfully, to accept it graciously.

Much of the first edition was written in Honolulu at the University of Hawaii on an exchange visit I made there in 1979/80 and I have residual debts to acknowledge to Ed Faison, Laurie Jacobs and Gladys Kuwata. More recently I have been greatly obliged to my secretary at Lancaster, Angela Bidle, who has protected and supported me and helped to create the time necessary to write the second edition.

Finally, my wife Helen, and sons Jonathan, George and David, by heroically resisting the temptation to invade my study too often, helped me to complete both editions sooner than I had a right to expect.

Geoff Easton

The Case Method

1.1 THE CASE

The word 'case' comes from the Latin *casus*, meaning 'occurrence'. Freely translated, it is something that falls out, occurs, happens. More particularly, it is used in this book to mean a description of what has occurred. Even more particularly, the word is used in educational circles as shorthand for case study. A case study is different from a case history, which is simply a description of what has happened, with no specific purpose in mind. A case study, by contrast, is, or should be, designed as a learning vehicle with specific educational objectives in mind. Those objectives are broader than simply to provide information, data or a description which can be used to demonstrate the application of certain concepts or techniques, for example accounting principles. I would prefer to use the term 'case example' in these instances. The educational objectives of case studies are, in general, broader and more ambitious as we shall see later in this chapter. Finally, it is important to distinguish the use of the term 'case study' in learning and research contexts. Social scientists use the term to describe the intensive study, description and analysis of a person, group, or organization from which theory can be derived or by which theory can be tested. Bromley (1986) provides a useful summary of its uses in this setting. In practice you will usually have little problem in knowing what a case study is. It will be given to you by a case instructor with the directive, 'Analyze it for next Tuesday'.

The typical case consists of a number of pages of written description of an actual situation facing an organization. It will usually describe how the current position developed and what problems key personalities in the case are currently facing. Tables of data, diagrams and photographs may be necessary to help provide a more complete picture. Appendices are normally used to include large amounts of data that would otherwise clutter the text.

1

There are many variations on this basic theme. Cases may be a few sentences or hundreds of pages long. Students taking their first case course usually associate length with difficulty. This is a dangerous principle: many short cases prove to be very taxing. All of the insignificant detail has been stripped away and the student has to tackle basic issues head on. By contrast, some long cases provide challenges in organizing material rather than practice in solving complex problems. It is never wise to judge a case by its length.

Cases are normally written, but there is no reason why this should be the sole form of communication. Film, video and audio tapes and tape/slide sequences have all been used as vehicles for case descriptions. These all serve to make the case more realistic for the student. However, they also create problems. Written information is easier to work with and analyze than the information contained in, for example, a film. It becomes necessary to summarize the information from the film in written form. This is not only time-consuming but can also lead to all sorts of errors. Multimedia cases are for students who have already mastered the written case.

There are relatively few multimedia cases available because they are expensive to prepare. This leads to a general point about all case studies which is worth making early on in this book. There is a dearth of good case studies for case instructors to choose from. Good cases studies take a long time to prepare, write and test. In addition they bring little academic or financial reward to the case writer. There may be a temptation to cut corners and produce cases which appear to be superficially interesting but which don't work in learning terms. The warning I would offer is not to assume that all case studies are well constructed; conversely, you should not assume that they are all badly put together.

Although cases normally involve organizations, they need not do so. Cases describing the problems of individuals, couples, groups, social institutions or even nations may be used in particular educational situations. Cases are not confined to use by business or management students. They are used in social administration, psychiatry, architectural studies, education, engineering and have potential in any discipline where the skills of solving complex unstructured problems are required. After all, the case method has its origins in the methods used to teach Harvard lawyers. In this book the case study used as an example is drawn from a business setting. However, the basic principles put forward are general enough to apply to any situation where the case method is used.

Cases may be attempts to provide accurate descriptions of real situations or they may be works of fiction. Most cases fall somewhere between these two extremes. Organizations frequently require that their identities be disguised for fear of revealing information which might be of use to competitors. This may simply mean that a fictitious name is used. In other cases many of the data fundamental to an understanding of a case are changed. This can have unfortunate results. One technique is simply to multiply all the figures by a constant factor such as 3.4. This maintains the relationship within the particular set of data. However, it distorts the relationship between this set of data and the data in the rest of the case. For example, inflating profit and loss account figures may suggest that a company has the resources to do things which in reality it would not be capable of doing. Case writers may also 'rewrite history' to suit a specific educational objective.

A case is not the truth, the whole truth and nothing but the truth. For reasons mentioned above it may be partly a work of fiction. There is also a more profound philosophical point. All descriptions of human situations are necessarily partial and incomplete. All of us, including case writers, construct our own versions of reality even when we strive to be as 'objective' as possible. If you accept that idea you will, I believe, be able to make more of your case learning experiences. You should, as a result, approach cases with a sceptical attitude about their fundamental 'truth' while recognizing that you can learn a great deal from working in the setting that they provide. In Chapter 3 we shall look at the kinds of information a case contains and try to assess how valid the information is.

Some cases are entirely fictitious. This may occur when access to real-life situations is restricted or where the case writer wishes to explore a particular problem. In these instances you are relying on the literary talents and experience of the case writer to produce a consistent and believable situation. Many students do not like fictitious cases. They do not get the profound sense of involvement that comes with knowing that they are examining the workings of a real situation. Nevertheless, fictitious cases can be very important and useful when the alternative is having no satisfactory case at all which fits the bill. A colleague of mine once remarked, 'It doesn't matter whether it is true or not, only whether it could be true'.

1.2 WAYS IN WHICH CASES ARE USED

The case method in most people's minds is the method used to teach MBA students at Harvard Business School. At Harvard, students are given a case study to prepare and they discuss their analyses in large open classes with an instructor leading the case by asking questions of individuals, promoting class discussion, summarizing, prompting and controlling the learning experience.

Harvard may represent the most obvious current protagonists of the case method but it has been argued that case teaching has been around for a long time. Parables may be regarded as cases, for example. For those interested, Masoner (1988) provides a well-referenced summary history of the case method. A look at history confirms what is only too obvious anyway. There are a vast range of alternative ways in which cases can be used. There isn't just one case method.

It is useful first of all to distinguish between the case method and an exercise. An exercise may superficially resemble a case in that it uses a description of an actual or fictitious situation which I earlier called an example. However, the objectives of doing an exercise are different. An example provides the material for a student to learn to apply a particular concept, technique or principle. A case is used to help students learn a broad range of skills. An exercise has a solution and one way of reaching that solution. A case has many solutions and many alternative pathways to reach them.

There is a middle ground. Many cases are written to allow students to practise particular analytical techniques or to approach problems in a particular way. Students may even be directed to use certain techniques or given specific questions to answer. While this gives them some of the flavour of an exercise, we are still talking of the case method; they still remain cases. The central function of the case method, as I will argue in the next section, is to teach students to solve complex unstructured problems. There are no analytical techniques or approaches which can solve these kinds of problems. Some can help, but in the case method their use will usually be subsidiary to the central purpose of learning high-level complex cognitive skills. If a student is confused about whether a case is being used as a case or as an example, it is well worth discussing the problem with the instructor involved. It is always possible that the instructor has not clearly made the distinction in his or her own mind.

Cases can also be 'dead' or 'live', or somewhere in between. A 'dead' case is one in which all the case information is presented to students at the start of the case analysis. To make a case 'live' a way has to be found to inject further information into the case over time. This allows a case to develop in a more realistic way. Some cases have a number of versions which describe different problem situations in the same organization at the same time. Students can build up their knowledge of the organization and its problems and develop increasingly sophisticated answers. Other cases allow for additional units of information to be added to the case over time. Sometimes this information is given; sometimes it has to be specifically asked for.

The truly 'live' case can take one of two forms. In the first form a member of the organization describes an existing situation in outline. Students must then ask questions in order to create for themselves a sufficiently full picture of the organization and its problems. Clearly such a case will be different each time it is taught. The second form involves a written description, as in the conventional case method. However, students are then allowed to become involved in the actual situation, collecting further information as they see fit. In this form the live case comes close to another learning method – the project. The main difference lies in the nature of the relationship between the organization and the students. A project would normally involve a student group recommending a course of action to members of the organization. A live case would tend to use the organization mainly as a source of information. The more 'live' a case becomes the more realistic it appears. Its potential for effective learning also increases, largely as a result of increased motivation. In addition it provides learning in the skills of information acquisition and evaluation. However, 'live' cases require a level of skill that the beginning student will not usually possess. Most case instructors prefer to use this kind of case instruction as a bridge between a traditional case course and real-world projects.

Even using a conventional written case there are a number of ways in which cases may be used. Figure 1.1 illustrates some of the alternatives. Examinations using cases are becoming more and more

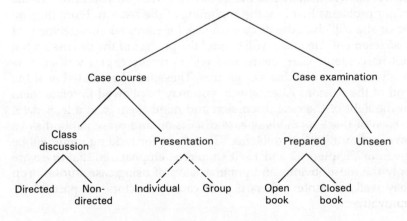

Figure 1.1 Alternative methods of using cases

popular, not only to assess case courses but also to evaluate the overall performance of students graduating from a course. In most situations cases are distributed some time before the examination. Students then analyze the case and bring their notes to the examination where they are required to answer previously unseen questions. Occasionally students may be asked to analyze a very short and straightforward case that they have not seen before in the examination room.

Case courses usually make use of one of two methods in the classroom. The traditional Harvard method, as already described, is an open class discussion. An alternative approach is to ask individuals or groups to make formal oral presentations of their case analyses and recommendations. This may or may not be followed by a general discussion. This method is easier to control than open discussions and fits the conventional timetable rather better. It also allows you practice at communicating your thoughts clearly. Unfortunately it tends to be less dynamic than the traditional Harvard method. Most learning takes place outside the classroom. It also allows some students to minimize the effort they put in since they will usually only be involved in one or two presentations per course.

In the class discussion a major factor is the extent to which the case instructor directs the discussion. This direction may begin when the case is handed out. The case instructor may ask you to direct your attention to a number of questions he or she would like answered. He or she may even specify which analytical techniques are to be used. A directive case instructor will control the flow of the discussion and ask specific students for their contributions. He or she may finish by outlining a solution to the case. A non-directive case instructor will usually ask the question, 'What do you think are the major problems here?' at the beginning of the session. From then on he or she will chair the discussion, ask for clarification, agreement or disagreement. He or she will control the process of the discussion but not its content. Case instructors will normally expect written case analyses from individuals or groups. These may be handed in at the end of the session. Alternatively you may be allowed to refine them in the light of the case discussion and hand them in at a later date.

Each of these methods of case discussion and presentation has its own communication problems. Guidelines for tackling them will be given in Chapters 12 and 13. It should be emphasized that these are only the most obvious and popular ways of using case studies. You may well encounter others if your case instructors are particularly innovative.

1.3 SKILLS DEVELOPED BY THE CASE METHOD

The case method is a vehicle for developing a wide variety of behavioural outcomes. These can roughly be divided into three categories: knowledge, skills and attitudes. However, these attributes, by themselves, are not sufficient to make a good decision maker. Harvard MBAs have been criticized, on occasions, for treating real-world problems like case studies. There are major differences. Cases are one way in which instructors can provide a simulated environment in which to practise and develop skills. There is little at stake, so students are free to experiment and learn. This is the strength of the case method, but also its weakness. Be aware that there is a difference between simulation and reality.

As well as knowledge and attitudes there are nine major skill areas that the case method can help to develop. Together they can be described in one phrase: creative problem solving.

1. *Knowledge*

   Acquiring specific knowledge is not a central objective of the case method. Other learning experiences are better designed to achieve this end. But it is an incidental benefit and it is often surprising how much you pick up that turns out to be useful in another context. Far more importantly, you create your own knowledge. You build useful frameworks, maps and general models of particular kinds of situations which you can draw on when faced with similar situations in the future. The components of such structures are often concepts and theoretical ideas which come from learning on parallel or previous courses.

2. *Analytical skills*

   There are a number of analytical skills which the case method can promote. Case studies comprise information or, more properly, data. Data do not become information until they have meaning and relevance for the analyst. One of the analytical skills developed by the case method therefore is that of information handling. You learn to classify, organize and evaluate information. You learn to recognize when vital information is missing and how it might be obtained.

   To solve problems you need to be able to find them. What the problems are and how they can be defined and interrelated are issues which have to be faced and resolved. You will find that solving a problem already identified, and one that is not, needs very different analytical skills. Using information you attempt to understand the situation as described. You learn to build models.

In doing so you practise thinking clearly and logically. You also learn what works and what does not work. You develop your own best practice from the process.

3. *Application skills.*

At a slightly lower level of difficulty the case method provides you with practice at applying concepts, techniques and principles. For example, techniques like discounted cash flow, decision theory and multiple regression can be used to help you in your analysis. The key word is 'help'. Techniques like these cannot provide a solution by themselves. In addition you learn to judge which techniques are appropriate, when they may be used and how they fit in with less precise methods of analysis.

4. *Creative skills*

Cases cannot be unravelled by logical processes alone. Creativity is vital to good quality case work. This is not widely understood. Many students who are afraid of quantitative methods but who nevertheless pride themselves on their creativity are frightened of cases. They must realize that they have a vital skill necessary to good case work. They should have the courage to play to their strengths while remedying their weaknesses. Creativity is particularly important in generating alternative solutions to the problems uncovered by logical analysis. But it is also vital in finding the problems in a case and building models which help you to comprehend what is going on. Creativity helps when trying to predict the outcome to a particular course of action and when communicating the results of all your work.

5. *Decision-making skills*

Case studies are above all action-oriented. They demand that you make choices and do something. Decision making is concerned with judgement. Thus, while analysis and creativity are important, so too are the cognitive and emotional processes which lead to decisions. They involve skilled reasoning and a deep understanding of the nature of values and how they affect choices.

6. *Communication skills*

What communication skills are developed will depend on the way in which the case instructor chooses to run his or her class. You can learn to plan your communication, present findings orally, use visual aids and other media, co-operate in group presentations, defend your own viewpoint, convince others of your arguments and write clear and well-constructed reports. One outcome of successful learning in this area is often an increase in overall self-confidence.

7. *Social skills*

Case discussions are essentially social processes. You can learn to communicate, listen, empathize, support, argue, guide and control yourself. Above all you should gain a better understanding of your own behaviour and that of others in a loosely structured social situation. Many students have said that in case courses they learned more about human behaviour than about problem solving. This is particularly true if the class is split into work groups which give separate, competitive presentations.

8. *Self-analysis skills*

Frequently disagreements occur in case discussions over value judgements rather than analytical judgements. Cases provide a useful forum for analyzing your values. Would you really dismiss someone if you knew he could not get another job? If a bribe were necessary to get a foreign contract, would you pay it? It is certainly better to decide what you believe in before you get into the firing line. You may be surprised how much moral and ethical issues complicate what would otherwise be simple decisions. Your instructor may deliberately use a case the central issue of which is an ethical dilemma. This type of case often generates the most active, and heated, participation.

9. *Attitudes*

Because the case method is such an involving learning experience it has a great potential for forming and changing attitudes. One such attitude is a belief that analysis should lead to action and not be an end in its own right. Another is to value the contributions of others. A third is to be comfortable with the notion that there are many possible solutions to a case. Attitude outcomes are usually the most controversial learning objectives that can be stated. However, attitude change of some kind will occur. It would be helpful to you if your case instructor shared such goals with you and your class mates rather than leaving them unstated and perhaps unrecognized.

Instructors, by the way in which they teach, can emphasize certain learning objectives at the expense of others. That is their right: they see the educational priorities. However, you should be aware of what it is possible to learn – by doing so you are likely to make case analysis a richer experience for yourself.

1.4 LEARNING PROBLEMS WITH THE CASE METHOD

The list of skills that can be learned by means of the case method is impressive – perhaps too impressive. It is clear that the case method is very different from traditional teaching methods: the lecture, seminar or tutorial. Many students find the transition between the two very difficult to achieve. Below are some of the problems that typically occur:

1. *What are we supposed to do?*
   There are three aspects to this dilemma. Firstly, students are not told what the problem is. They have to find it for themselves. Previously, it had always been clear what their goal was: learn a fact, apply a technique. Now they have to define their own goals. Worse still, even when they get an answer they are told that there is no unique solution. They cannot tell whether they are right or not. To cap it all, the information they have to work with is not cut and dried. It is sometimes ambiguous, sometimes irrelevant and sometimes it is not there at all. Students often describe their first few case discussions like being in a fog without a compass. All their hard-won study skills are no longer applicable. It can be a disheartening experience.

2. *What are we learning?*
   After a lecture you know that you have learned some facts. You know that there are more facts in your notes that you can learn. You feel that you have achieved something: you have learned. After a case discussion students may feel that they have learned nothing. They may despair at the rambling and seemingly inefficient discussion process. They may feel they are no further forward. This is mainly due to the fact that improvements in the higher level skills that the case method promotes are difficult to detect. Individuals may not be aware that they are progressing. Only by taking a longer-term view will it be possible to be really sure that results are being achieved. Unfortunately, students may drop out, at least in terms of commitment to case analysis, before this occurs.

3. *Why doesn't the teacher teach?*
   Students frequently find the role of the case leader hard to understand. In their previous experience teachers taught and lecturers lectured. In a case discussion case instructors appear to refuse to do either. In particular, they refuse to tell students what is correct and what is incorrect, though they do provide varying degrees of guidance. Nevertheless, students are left much more to their own judgement or that of their peers.
   Alternatively, case instructors guide students to a predetermined answer while denying that such an answer exists, leaving

students in the dark about how they might repeat the process when the case instructor is not there. Argyris (1980) describes how 'star' case instructors from leading US business schools taught cases. Each had rather complete action maps for understanding the case but kept them secret until towards the end of a session. 'Why were the key questions not given ahead of time?. Because, as one faculty member put it, "That would blow the whole game".'

The combination of these problems can be a devastating one. Students may feel helpless, disoriented, demotivated, and ultimately bored and resentful. Yet this need not be the case. Case instructors feel, quite rightly, that students should have to face complex, ambiguous situations and learn how to cope with them. They should not, however, be asked to do so without any help or outside guidance as to the processes that might be involved. That is not to say that they should be drilled in mechanical procedures to produce standard case analyses: there is a happy medium. Providing students with broad and flexible guidelines helps them to get over the initial shock of total immersion in the case method. It also provides a base from which they can build their own personal case analysis style. The rest of the book sets out such a system of guidelines. They have been tested and they appear to work. Read on and see how they can improve your case analysis skills.

A Step-by-Step Approach

2.1 RATIONALE

In order to understand each step of the approach the whole process is described in this chapter in outline. In addition, suggestions for learning to use the approach are discussed. Before doing this, however, it might be worth describing where this approach originated. Most papers and books on complex problem solving describe a similar approach. The basic ideas in different combinations have been around for a long time. The approach is often described as the rational problem-solving approach. However, two important adaptations have been made.

Firstly, an attempt has been made to develop the approach into a set of practical guidelines. This wasn't an easy task. It may be that in the process some ideas have been distorted: that isn't too important. If the guidelines are relevant and practical, then that justifies what has been done. Secondly, the approach has been specifically tailored to the case method. Complex problems differ in all sorts of ways. By concentrating on the kinds of problems that arise in case studies, a more specific and therefore useful approach is possible.

It has been argued that people don't actually solve problems in this way. There are limits to human information-processing capacity, especially when the data are 'soft', which lead to short cuts, heuristics and sub-optimal or even unsatisfactory outcomes. Rational problem solving is beyond our capabilities. I have a great deal of sympathy with this view. How I suggest you cope with this problem is set out in section 2.3.

2.2 THE SEVEN STEPS

1. *Understanding the situation*
   The basic meat of a case study is information. In the first step you must become familiar with this information and begin to work on

it. The goal is to build a descriptive, almost certainly qualitative, model of the situation. The information should be organized to help you understand it and help you locate it easily later on. The information contained in the case also needs evaluation. Not all of the information is valid, precise, or relevant. Vital pieces are missing. You will need to extrapolate from what is given if you are to make any decisions at all.

2. *Diagnosing problem areas*
   A problem is defined as the difference between what is (or will be) and what we would like the situation to be. In this step you will be attempting to uncover these differences in the case situation. You already know what is happening in the organization. What is or will be wrong with it? This is not altogether an easy task. Sometimes problems are simply symptoms of more fundamental problems. Sometimes problems are caused by a number of factors. Sometimes basic problems can lead to any number of symptoms. In this step you will be attempting to unravel these relationships. You will state the problems as precisely as you can and will relate them to each other. Not all problems are equally important. As your last task in this step, you will have to decide which problem (or problems) gets priority and why.

3. *Generating alternative solutions*
   This is a creative step. You need to understand, however, the nature of alternative solutions before you begin to use a variety of methods to think them up. This process could produce an enormous number of alternatives. There must therefore be some process of ranking the alternatives. Major strategic alternatives must be examined first. When a decision has been reached concerning them, it then makes sense to examine tactical alternatives. This may involve cycling through steps 4, 5 and 6 a number of times.

4. *Predicting outcomes*
   The first stage in choosing among alternatives is to predict what would happen if a particular solution were put into action. Two particular warnings are important here. The first is to be sure to predict most of the possible important outcomes. It may be that a particular solution solves one problem only at the expense of creating another. Secondly, predicting is a difficult and uncertain business. Not all outcomes are equally likely to occur. You should be aware of the techniques which attempt to cope with the risk and uncertainty associated with a particular action.

13

5. *Evaluating alternatives*
   In this stage you will choose among the alternatives. This starts with the listing of pros and cons for each. In a series of stages these may be elaborated, qualified, and quantified to allow direct comparisons to be made. The choice is then made.

6. *Rounding out the analysis*
   Step 6 forms a bridge between the case analysis and communication of its results. It involves making a decision about how many times you wish to cycle through stages 4 to 6 or, in other words, how much detail you wish to include. Events may not always turn out as you hope. A way of coping with this is contingency planning. It helps to add breadth as well as depth to your solution.

7. *Communicating the results*
   Your task does not end with a successfully completed case analysis. You must be prepared to undertake quite a bit more work planning how to communicate it. Chapters 12 and 13 cover oral and written communication using a traditional communication framework. Suffice it to say that there are more factors to take into account when designing a case presentation than most students realize.

2.3 USING THIS APPROACH

At this point it seems a useful idea to give some general advice on how to use this approach even before you fully understand it. One important psychological point to start with: it takes more time to read about the approach than to apply it, so don't be discouraged by the amount of material facing you. Once you have grasped the main points, the detail will fall into place.

My position on learning complex skills is that they can only be acquired incrementally. You have to start from what you can do now and improve bit by bit. Thus I would not advocate that the reader attempt to 'learn' the approach, in detail and in total, as set out below. I suggest it can be used in two ways. Firstly, as a bank of separate ideas and concepts upon which to draw. Secondly, as an overall, rather general, framework to give shape to case analysis. Most important of all is to experiment and try out the ideas. If they do not work for you abandon them, but not the quest for the skills that they seek to provide. Start by reading Chapters 3 to 11 fairly quickly to get an overall appreciation of the ideas being presented. Try to grasp the essentials rather than worry about the details. You may not be ready for this degree of complexity yet. To help you, at the end of each chapter or pair of chapters there is a section called 'Guide to use'. This section discusses which procedures are more fundamental and which may be regarded as optional, at least in the early stages of learning the case method.

Choose a short case and try out the procedures described. In each chapter read the 'Guide to use' first and decide which procedures you think will be most useful at your next stage of development. Compare your results with the examples given in the text to make sure you can apply the ideas correctly. As your case experience increases try out the optional procedures. You should find that they help you to continue improving your skills.

While you are still a beginner, you may find that you have to cycle back to earlier steps in the process because you missed a problem or failed to see a particularly attractive solution. Don't worry too much about this. However, you should beware of missing out steps if you are using the approach as a framework only. This is a 'building up from the foundations' approach. You may find that your finished work does not stand up to criticism if you have not laid the ground-work well. You may also notice that different cases will make varying demands on different steps of the process. This is only to be expected. In recognizing this you are beginning to develop as a case analyst.

In the long term, the aim must be to develop your own approach. It is important to emphasize that the approach described here is not meant to be a mechanical set of procedures to be followed *ad nauseam*. It is meant to bridge the gap between the complete novice and the skilled practitioner. Your own personal case work style might incorporate elements from this approach or it may be completely different. The objective of this book is simply to get you over the initial learning hurdles so that you can develop in your own way.

Step One: Understanding the Situation (I)

Step one involves trying to understand the case situation without prejudgement. This is achieved through the processes of organizing and evaluating the information and then building a model to describe it.

3.1 CASE EXAMPLE

There is no better way to understand the application of a principle or concept than by concrete example. For this reason each step in the case analysis process is illustrated by means of a case study – Wolverhampton and Dudley Breweries – which is set out in the next section. It is a long and relatively complex case which encompasses a number of issues relevant to various management disciplines. On the other hand it exemplifies a number of problems that organizations of many types face. It is an interesting case study, but it is by no means perfect as a teaching vehicle. This was another reason why it was chosen, as we shall see later.

In effect what follows is an analysis of the case, but an incomplete one. It would take too much time and space not only to describe the processes of analysis but also to go through them for every aspect of the case. What is offered is a series of illustrations or examples of the way in which the step-by-step approach can be carried out.

It is recommended however that *you* attempt a full case analysis. It is the best way to understand what follows. In other words, when a particular piece of the analysis is described as an illustration, you should continue the process until you are satisfied that you understand how to do it. At the very minimum you will need to be reasonably familiar with the case as you read the chapters that follow. In addition you will need to refer back to the case whenever data from the case are used so that you can see how they occur in context.

3.1.1 Wolverhampton and Dudley Breweries *(Copyright M. Jalland, 1983)*

On 25 May 1983, Wolverhampton and Dudley Breweries (WDB) finally abandoned its contested takeover bid for neighbouring Birmingham brewers, Davenports. Its offer, valued at £26m, had been rejected by Baron Davenport's Charity Trust which owned 29.9% of the shares. The takeover attempt had also been influenced by Whitbread investment which took a 5.68% holding in Davenport's brewery following its policy of 'helping smaller groups retain their independence'.

The failure of the bid left WDB holding a 15.7% stake in Davenport's and forced it to reconsider its expansion plans. For several years the company had been regarded by stockholders as 'an extremely sound investment' in the brewery sector, due to the steady growth in sales and profits. In 1983, sales reached £86.4m, with a 10% increase in profits to £12.5m (details of recent financial performance are shown in Tables 3.1, 3.2, 3.3). However, the continuing slump in beer sales and the limited opportunities for further growth in the Wolverhampton area raised questions about the ability of the widely admired regional brewer to continue its rate of growth through the mid-1980s.

Early history

The Wolverhampton and Dudley Breweries Ltd was formed on 14 May 1890 from an amalgamation of three local businesses: Banks and Co. which had been brewing at Park Brewery since 1875; George Thompson and Sons, Dudley and Victoria Breweries, Dudley, established maltsters since 1840 and brewers since 1878; and C. C. Smith's brewery, the Fox Brewery, Wolverhampton. An early aim of the company was to preserve the traditional flavour and quality of Black Country beer.

Other local firms in Stourbridge, Blackheath, Oldbury and Brierley Hill were included in the group at an early stage. Later acquisitions were breweries in Stourbridge (1909), Netherton (1912), Kidderminster (1914), Lichfield (1917), Worcester (1928) and Shifnal (1960), which included the Crown and Raven Hotels Ltd. Julia Hanson and Sons Ltd was acquired in 1928.

Mr G. Thompson, of George Thompson and Sons, had a son, Edwin John Thompson, who had acted as a manager since the formation of the company in 1890, becoming managing director in 1894. His grandson, Mr E. J. Thompson, is the current chairman and managing director.

The name of the beers brewed at Park Brewery was originally 'Banks and Co.' before 14 May 1890, and thereafter 'Banks'. The two names currently in use — 'Banks's' and 'Hanson's' — are noted for traditional draught beers naturally conditioned in the cask.

Brewing and beer wholesaling activities

Brewing activities accounted for some 75% of profits in 1983. The company operated two breweries, the main one located in Wolverhampton, the other less

17

Table 3.1. *Wolverhampton and Dudley Breweries Plc: profit and loss account – historic basis*

Year ended Sept. 30	Turnover £000	Net profit before tax £000	Net profit after tax £000	Depreciation £000	Bank interest £000	Average total	Employees Number part-time	Remuneration £000
1973	18,524	3,845	2,145	553	—	3,643	NA	2,997
1974	19,815	3,425	1,645	677	1	3,870	NA	3,490
1975	26,496	4,213	1,997	797	96	4,122	NA	4,713
1976	34,857	5,185	2,473	905	72	4,433	NA	5,882
1977	41,762	5,770	2,735	1,104	169	4,742	2,935	7,260
1978	48,886	7,124	3,411	1,662	290	4,960	3,108	9,747
1979	56,368	8,167	5,482	2,182	341	5,146	3,259	10,514
1980	63,403	9,054	5,577	2,540	398	5,429	3,441	12,505
1981	73,540	10,216	5,408	2,893	325	5,443	3,885	14,387
1982	80,105	11,342	6,314	3,189	295	5,620	4,208	15,604
1983	86,424	12,512	6,649	3,495	213	5,663	4,270	16,560

Table 3.2. Wolverhampton and Dudley Breweries Plc: balance sheets (historic basis) 30 September (£000)

	1978	1979	1980	1981	1982	1983
Sales	48,886	56,368	63,403	73,540	80,105	86,424
Current Assets						
Stock	4,334	4,710	5,100	6,160	6,799	6,974
Debtors	1,593	1,970	2,130	2,843	3,947	4,069
Cash	664	400	410	586	885	1,031
	6,591	7,080	7,640	9,589	11,631	12,074
Current Liabilities						
Creditors	5,515	7,187	7,464	8,825	9,337	7,096
Overdrafts	3,437	679	1,671	886	707	2,267
Deposits	152	131	141	114	87	79
Tax	532	2,522	2,793	3,578	4,328	7,792
Dividends	740	971	1,132	1,246	1,375	1,471
	10,376	11,490	13,201	14,629	15,834	18,705
Net current assets	Dr 3,785	Dr 4,410	Dr 5,561	Dr 5,040	Dr 4,203	Dr 6,631
Investments	2,575	2,897	3,765	2,877	3,538	5,500
Fixed assets	33,967	38,220	43,387	48,698	52,837	59,051
Act recoverable	—	416	485	534	589	630
	32,757	37,123	41,986	47,069	52,761	58,550
Capital	4,112	4,112	8,149	8,149	8,149	8,149
Reserves	19,226	30,702	30,842	34,711	39,996	45,091
Debenture stock	165	134	129	129	—	—
Corporation tax	2,084	2,175	2,866	3,780	4,316	5,010
Deferred tax	7,170	—	—	300	300	300
	32,757	37,123	41,986	47,069	52,761	58,550
Freehold properties	22,619	24,876	28,225	31,691	34,666	39,899
Leasehold properties	192	179	176	593	816	1,593

Table 3.3 *Wolverhampton and Dudley Breweries: source and application of funds (£000)*

Year ended 30 Sept.	Source of funds				Application of funds							Increase/ decrease net liquid funds
	Operations	Sale of assets	Total	Dividends	Fixed assets	Taxation	Debenture stock	Investments	Working capital*	Total		
1979	10,924	1,058	11,982	1,145	7,263	735	30	1,212	(918)	9,467		+2,515
1980	11,824	130	11,954	1,457	7,836	2,596	6	778	272	12,945		−991
1981	13,485	122	13,607	1,667	8,326	2,992	—	(798)	412	12,599		+1,008
1982	15,300	253	15,553	1,828	7,490	3,638	129	752	1,232	15,069		+484
1983	16,689	528	17,217	2,120	9,906	4,415	—	2,294	(112)	18,623		−1,406

Note. * Excluding net liquid funds.

than ten miles away at Dudley. The total output of the breweries was around 600,000 barrels (1 barrel = 288 pints) including small quantities of beers of other brewers. Some three-quarters of production was accounted for by the Wolverhampton site and was sold under the Banks's name. Beers brewed at Dudley were marketed under the name Hanson's. Both brands had established a separate consumer identity and were regarded as different products even though the prices charged tended to be the same. The taste differed in part because of variations in the mix of raw materials and partly because water supplies differ. Mild and bitter were sold under both names.

The company placed considerable emphasis on the quality of its beers and believed that control over malting was necessary to maintain standards. Since the early days it had owned its own maltings and could supply more than 50% of its needs. Steady investment in storage and processing facilities meant that it had the capacity to buy raw materials in bulk on good terms and could ensure reliable supplies.

Both breweries operated at high levels of efficiency and wastage levels were reputed to be among the lowest in the industry. Around 1,000 full-time employees were employed in production, packaging and distribution giving levels of productivity which were good by industry standards and probably only exceeded by a few very large breweries in the UK. Labour relations were good, with few disputes, and both tied and free trade customers were able to rely on regular supplies. Other larger competitors had suffered in recent years from strikes which disrupted supplies for weeks at a time.

Mild beer accounted for over half of production with sales of bitter at around 20%. The limited product range meant that operations were relatively uncomplicated, with fewer changes between beer types than in the case of many competitors, and easier quality control. A limited range of bottled beers was also produced. Considerable investment in new production facilities had taken place over the past five years which had not only increased brewing capacity but significantly added to WDB's packaging capabilities. (See Table 3.4 for details.)

Steady improvements had been made to work-place conditions by the installation of air-conditioning for example. The new packaging hall, which opened in 1977, replaced the old, out-of-date bottling plant. In 1983 further additions to packaging plant were being undertaken to cope with the growth in demand. Although it also produced cans, operations were concentrated on bottling and WDB had become an important contract bottler and canner for other brewers. The kegging plant had also been updated progressively and was used to fill Harp and Kronenbourg lagers supplied by the Harp consortium which WDB had joined in 1979.

Product range

For many years cask-conditioned mild had been the most important beer in the product range. It represented 70% of WDB sales in 1983, while nationally, mild accounted for a declining share of about 10% of beer sales. Mild was seen as a low-quality, low-priced product in much of the UK. In contrast, WDB's mild

Table 3.4 *Investment in production, 1977–83*

Year	Park Brewery	Dudley Brewery/Maltings
1977	New packaging hall (canning and kegging) Extra fermenting vessels	New automatic cask washer 12 new fermenting vessels
1978	Transfer of bottling Air conditioning of cask storage and fermenting rooms in old bottling hall	New yeast collecting plant
1979	New malt intake and storage system 2 extra mash tuns 16 new fermenting vessels New cask and keg store Second bottling and can filler on packaging line	Covering of brewery yard Air conditioning of fermenting rooms and cellars
1980		New maltings floors at Langley New malt storage bins at Langley and Lichfield
1981	Improved cellar storage facilities and additional fermenting space	
1982	New garage/transport facilities Office consolidation New keg and draught filling plant	New capacity extensions

had a good reputation. This was partly due to the company's attention to quality in production, distribution and in the public house. This received national recognition in 1980 and 1981 when Hanson's and Banks's Draught Mild Ale won the championships for the best traditional mild ale in the country at the Great British Beer Festival in successive years. In addition WDB's mild beers had a relatively higher gravity (1036°) than the mild sold in other areas of the country which ranged between 1028° and 1033°. Relatively 'strong' beers have a gravity of 1040° and above. 'Weak' beers are those below 1030°. The average gravity for all UK production in 1982 was 1037°.

Another factor contributing to WDB's success was the level of beer consumption in the Wolverhampton area which was well above the national average. As a result the company had a higher proportion of heavy beer drinkers than its competitors (the national average was six pints per week). The low carbon dioxide levels in the cask-conditioned beer also aided consumption.

The pricing policy adopted by WDB was to maintain prices at a level some 3–5p below competitors'. This policy came about originally as a result of restrictions imposed by government price controls during the early 1970s when margins could not be increased. The price differential was thought to be important to customers and thus the company's freedom to adjust margins was restricted.

WDB's bitter beers were relatively less important, but had price and strength advantages over some competitors' who were marketing bitter beers below the national average gravity. (Since tax was levied according to gravity level, lower strength brands could be more profitable.) Although famous for its cask-conditioned bitter the company made a break with tradition in 1982, and launched 'Lion' bitter, a keg beer 'for free trade customers who lack the facilities necessary to keep traditional draught beer in peak condition'. This was followed in 1983 by 'Lion mild', also for the free trade.

WDB had no production facilities for lager. Recently, in a deal with Ansells Wrexham, lager had been introduced into 30 of the company's Welsh pubs. However, WDB relied primarily on its membership of the Harp consortium for products and both Harp and the premium Kronenbourg lager were packaged and distributed. WDB had a 10% share in Harp Ltd, whose other shareholders were Guinness with a 70% holding and Greene, King and Sons with 20% of the ordinary shares. The major capital asset of Harp Ltd was a lager brewery at Park Royal, North London, and its main functions were the brewing of lager and the provision of marketing and technical services for the Harp Kronenbourg and Salzenbrau Diat Pils brands. Harp Ltd also had franchise agreements with Courage and Scottish and Newcastle breweries to brew and market Harp products. WDB's earnings from the consortium were a combination of sales rebates based on sales volume, interest on loan capital and dividends.

WDB's investment in marketing and promotion was relatively low, although it maintained strong links with its tenants and managers and was active in sponsoring local sporting events. Local posters were used and a Banks's hot air balloon was a familiar sight at local festivals. The company also received favourable publicity from the Campaign for Real Ale (CAMRA) for its traditional ales and the way they were served. However, the aim was to provide a full range of products in public houses including mild, bitter, lager and Guinness which WDB also packaged.

Trading area and public houses

In 1983 WDB operated some 750 licensed outlets which included 13 hotels and 19 off-licences. Three-quarters of the company's outlets were within 20 miles of the two breweries and many of the others were sited within easy reach of major highways. Distribution was therefore direct and no distribution depots had yet been set up.

The trading area was increasing, however. New pubs had recently been opened as far away as Rugby, Leicester and Bristol. (See Table 3.5 for recent new outlets and refurbishings.) The area covered by the company extended therefore from the Potteries to Bristol and from Aberystwyth to Leicester. WDB policy was to move into towns less affected by unemployment. In addition the failure of the Davenport bid meant that WDB was free to move into the neighbouring Birmingham territory which it had previously avoided.

Table 3.5   *Public houses: new outlets and refurbishing, 1979–84*

	New pubs	Refurbishing
1979	5	2 pubs taken over from Whitbread–Leamington Spa and Hereford
1980	—	7 + major alterations
1981	6 Newtown, Powys Bushbury, Wolverhampton Tettenhall, nr Wolverhampton Penkridge, nr Stafford Crackley Bank, nr Telford (purchased) Darlaston (purchased)	6 + major alterations
1982	4 Redditch Darlaston Leicester Tamworth	8 + major alterations
1983	5 Shard End, Birmingham (2) Kidderminster Perton, Wolverhampton Nuneaton	10 + major alterations
1984 planned	7 Derby Burslem Five Ways, Birmingham Bristol Coalville Droitwich Rugby	9 + major alterations

One advantage of the concentration of outlets in the Wolverhampton area was that the number of licensed premises per 10,000 population was 17.18 which was well below the average for England and Wales of 24.84 per 10,000. Potentially therefore the company was less vulnerable to pub closures at a time of falling demand. Throughput per outlet was also likely to be higher than in other parts of the country. It had been suggested (by Buckmaster and Moore) that average beer sales per outlet were over 600 barrels per annum, nearly three times the national average.

Around 50% of WDB's public houses were managed (rather than tenanted), a relatively high proportion by industry standards. This was partly due to a local tradition of managed houses. It allowed more control over pub activities but required greater management effort than in the case of an estate dominated by tenancies. In order to overcome some of the problems of recruiting and keeping good managers WDB operated a package deal which put the manager on commission, giving an incentive to boost turnover. Considerable attention was paid to standards of decoration in pubs and a series of major renovations had been undertaken in recent years. Consistent with changing customer expectations food was provided in most outlets and much effort had been directed at improving standards. There was no 'standard formula'. Rather, the combination of drinking, eating and entertainment facilities was tailored to suit the location and the customer mix.

An increasing proportion of company sales were through free trade outlets, reaching some 25% by 1983. (A strike at Ansells' Birmingham brewery, and its subsequent closure, had provided several new outlets in 1981, in particular in clubs which had been shared with Ansells.) Historically WDB had limited its sales to exclude pubs which might not be able to handle and dispense its traditional beers properly. The saturation of existing markets and the cost of opening new outlets made the acquisition of free trade outlets an attractive route to increased sales. However, this involved WDB in servicing and providing technical advice and drew them into the difficult and potentially expensive arena of loan and grant competition. It was common practice in the industry for improvements in pub facilities which would increase throughput to be financed by the provision of loans by brewers at relatively low rates of interest. Since there was keen competition in the free trade for new business, smaller competitors with weaker brand franchises were potentially at a disadvantage when accounts became available. Trade loans and investments increased from £1.0m in 1980 to £1.7m in 1983. The launch of the Lion range of keg beers was aimed at extending the free trade franchise by providing an alternative to traditional beers.

Other activities

Unlike other companies in the industry WDB had not expanded in hotel or off-licence and wines and spirits activities in recent years. Profits had been steady but small at around £0.5m a year. The hotels served the business and 'function' trade rather than the tourist trade, and the largest had 34 rooms. Some had achieved strong local reputations and were heavily booked for weddings, exhibitions and the like. (See Table 3.6 for a list of hotels and locations.) Similarly, off-licences relied on local catchment areas and did not compete with the supermarket and multiple wines and spirits chains. The company had own brands in the major gin and whisky spirit markets but these were not extensively promoted.

The bid for Davenport's

For several years WDB had a holding of just under 5% in Davenport's Brewery, a smaller neighbouring brewery with 120 public houses located mainly in the Birmingham area. Davenport's had established off-licence sales to the free trade in recent years and had a unique house delivery service of beers, wines and spirits. The company had also pioneered the packaging of $1\frac{1}{2}$ and 2 litre PET plastic bottles as a result of its flash pasteurising technology. These had

Table 3.6 *Wolverhampton and Dudley Breweries: locations of hotels*

Talbot Hotel, Stourbridge
Bell Hotel, Stourbridge
Stewponey Hotel, Stourton
Royal Victoria, Newport
The Briars, Kidderminster
The Star, Worcester
Garth Hotel, Stafford
The Vine, Stafford
Station Hotel, Dudley
Ward Arms Hotel, Dudley
Ravensholt Hotel, Wolverhampton
Fox Hotel, Wolverhampton
Eaton Lodge Hotel, Rugeley

---

been enthusiastically adopted by grocery multiples (instead of glass) and several major brewers were using Davenport's as contract packers.

In February 1982, WDB increased its holding to 6% and subsequently to 8% of the ordinary shares. This was intended 'as a statement of long-term interest'. 'If ever the Davenport board lost its enthusiasm for independence, WDB would be very happy to move in', said Mr. Bob Houle, WDB's finance director. However, WDB did not see itself as an aggressive predator.

Almost 30% of the shares belonged to the Baron Davenport's Charity Trust, which was founded by its deed to act for the benefit of Davenport's workers. There was no question of being able to accept a bid that would cause redundancies. Britannic Assurance held a further 9.3% and directors' and pension fund shareholdings amounted to 8.5%.

On 9 March 1983, after a rejection of their soundings, WDB launched a full bid. Their opening offer was 230p cash plus one of its own shares for every two Davenport shares, effectively valuing the company at £21m. This was improved on 22 March to £23.5m and on 27 April a final offer of £26m was made after a series of rejections by Davenport's board, who emphasized that the company preferred to remain independent. The trustees, among them the Mayor and City Treasurer, also rejected WDB's offer although Mr E. J. Thompson accused Davenport's chairman of 'clutching at straws' to keep the company independent. In Birmingham community leaders were particularly conscious of the impact of the recent Ansells closure. Meanwhile, Lord Cockfield, the Secretary of State for Trade, had decided not to refer the takeover bid to the Monopolies Commission.

On 9 May, Davenport's announced a sharp rise in interim pre-tax profits from £0.6m to £1.12m and an increased dividend. Beer production and sales had increased, in contrast to the decrease in beer sales nationally. In a defence circular the directors had forecast trading profits for the year to October 1983 of about £2.1m to which would be added the surplus on property sales of more than £600,000. By 12 May WDB owned 12.69% of Davenport's ordinary and 50.2% of its preference shares, and had received acceptances for a further 21.03% of the ordinary shares. The bid was extended to 25 May. On 13 May WDB announced interim net profits of £3.6m (vs £3.14m) and an increased dividend. City opinion was divided in its advice to Davenport's shareholders, recognizing the company's desire for continued independence but conscious of the 'generosity' of WDB's bid. However, on 24 May Whitbread Investment, 49.9% owned by Whitbread, took a 5.68% holding in Davenport's as part of its policy of 'helping smaller groups retain their independence'. Whitbread held similar long-term investments in Morland, Marston, Devenish and Boddingtons.

A possible further increase in WDB's cash bid was not sufficient to influence Davenport's merchant bankers and on 25 May WDB conceded failure. It was left with 15.75% of Davenport shares and Mr Houle conceded that the stake might not be easy to dispose of.

Trading performance and future prospects

During the late 1970s WDB's sales of beer increased steadily and at a rate faster than the national average. UK beer consumption grew by 6% between 1975 and 1979 and WDB achieved a growth in national market share of nearly 25% to reach approximately 1.5% by 1979. During the more difficult trading conditions of the 1980s sales in the West Midlands suffered. For the first time the region experienced extensive unemployment with levels rising about 15% as the automotive and engineering industries declined rapidly. WDB was forced to seek new outlets in a wider trading area, particularly in the free trade. Turnover was also boosted by the growth in packaging activities. As a result the rate of annual growth slowed from 16.0% in 1981 to 8% in 1983. Similarly, profits increased 10% in 1983 versus 13% in 1981. However, it must be noted that the growth in sales revenue was partly due to price rises and was also strongly influenced by a duty increase of 4p a pint in 1981. Thus, during this period volume fell, although less than the national average of 10%.

In 1983, like many other companies WDB initiated reviews of procedures and working methods in order to maintain tighter control of costs. The spending on new outlets in new trading areas was continuing and pubs had been purchased as far south as Bristol. The reaction of Mr Houle, WDB's finance director, to the failed bid for Davenport's was stoical: 'We are not planning any other acquisitions. We are not that sort of company. For the time being we will look upon our shareholding in Davenports as an investment and forget about it.' Similarly, Mr E. J. Thompson, the chairman commented: 'We regretted that our bid for Davenport's last spring proved unsuccessful as we continue to believe it would have been in the best interests of both companies. However, it resolved a situation which was beginning to inhibit our plans for expansion.'

There were signs that the trading circumstances which had favoured regional brewers during the 1970s had now disappeared for ever. The growth of lager, the imminent decline in the important 18–25 age group, the changes in the patterns of drinking towards greater home consumption including sales in plastic bottles, combined with the effects of unemployment, were dramatically threatening brewers' sales. As the *Investors Chronicle* commented, 'There are serious doubts over the future of beer drinking.' 'The best (share) buys at the moment are those companies which have started to diversify away from beer following the nationals and whose ratings are nearer to the industry giants.' Against this background observers of WDB were beginning to wonder whether the trading formula which had served the company so well was still appropriate for the 1980s.

3.1.2 The UK brewing industry *(Copyright N. Campbell)*

The UK brewing industry is not only a major industry in the UK, but is the third largest in the world after the USA and West Germany. However, in the early 1980s the industry was preoccupied with a decline in demand. Table 3.7 records beer consumption from 1960 to 1982 and shows that the underlying decline in demand started in the mid-1970s. In 1974, this three-year moving

Table 3.7 *The UK brewing industry: UK beer consumption*

Year	Million barrels	% change on previous year	3-year moving average
1960	27.24	—	—
1961	28.61	5.03	—
1962	28.61	nil	—
1963	28.69	0.28	1.8
1964	30.07	4.81	1.7
1965	30.30	0.76	2.0
1966	30.82	1.72	2.4
1967	31.52	2.21	1.6
1968	32.02	1.59	1.9
1969	33.39	4.28	2.7
1970	34.42	3.08	3.0
1971	35.78	3.95	3.8
1972	36.65	2.43	3.2
1973	38.25	4.37	3.6
1974	39.09	2.17	3.0
1975	40.10	2.61	3.1
1976	40.65	1.37	2.1
1977	40.26	− 0.96	1.0
1978	41.42	2.88	1.1
1979	41.67	0.60	0.8
1980	40.02	− 3.94	− 0.2
1981	38.08	− 4.85	− 2.7
1982	36.98	− 2.88	− 3.9

Source: HM Customs and Excise.

average showed a growth of 3.0%, but by 1982 it had fallen to a decline of 3.9%. In 1982, 36.9 million bulk barrels were consumed compared with 41.7 million in 1979.

Growth in consumption of wine and spirits

Several factors were thought to be contributing to this decline in demand. First was the growth in consumption of wine and spirits (see Table 3.8). It is clear from Table 3.8 that consumer tastes were changing, with more people opting for light wines and vodka in preference to beer. Many of the non-beer drinkers were new drinkers and this was worrying for the beer industry in that it indicated that it would no longer be possible to rely on a steady influx of new drinkers to expand or even stabilize the existing market. International comparisons were also worrying. The growth of beer consumption in other countries had slowed and the share of the total alcoholic drinks market held by beer had declined in West Germany and Australia.

Economic factors influencing demand

A number of specific economic influences can be added to changing drinking habits as causes of the decline in consumption. In early 1980, when beer consumption fell heavily, consumers experienced heavy increases in the price of 'essentials' such as mortgage and interest payments (up to 50% on a year earlier), petrol and oil (up 50%) and postage (up 42%). Thus discretionary expenditure was squeezed. At the same time the Chancellor imposed steep increases in duty leading to beer price rises between May 1979 and May 1982 of 81% compared to rises in the Retail Price Index of 49%. (see Table 3.9).

Against this background of escalating prices came rising unemployment. Moreover, some of the biggest increases in unemployment came from those regions of heavy industry where beer consumption was traditionally high. Those in employment also suffered from reductions in overtime and from an increase in short-time working. The economic uncertainty facing many families also led to an increase in the savings ratio, bringing another reduction in disposable income.

Imports and exports

Fortunately for the UK industry, this decline in domestic consumption was not accompanied by a rise in imports. Imports from Scandinavia and Europe accounted for about 4% of UK consumption in 1980 and had been at this level for a number of years. By contrast, exports represented only about 1% of UK consumption.

Changing drinking habits

More varieties of beer — bitter, mild, stout, lager — are brewed in the UK than anywhere else in the world. Lager is the main type of beer in most countries,

Table 3.8 *Consumption of beer, wines, spirits and cider in the UK*

	Percentage increases in volume			
	Beer	All wine	Spirits	Cider
1950–80	57	797	366	136
1970–80	26	147	144	48

Table 3.9 *Increases in beer prices and the RPI*

	May 79	May 80	May 81	May 82	% increase 1979–82
Pint of non-premium bitter in the pub	41.4	44.6	67.5	75.3	81.0
Analysis of price					
Excise duty	7.5	9.2	12.6	14.3	91.0
VAT	2.3	5.2	6.3	7.0	20.4
Government	9.8	4.4	18.9	21.3	117.0
Brewer and retailer	21.8	25.8	29.7	32.7	50.0
Retail Price Index	216.0	263.0	294.0	322.0	49.0

although in 1981 it accounted for only 31% of UK consumption. The volume of beer sold in draught (79%) is also much higher in the UK than elsewhere. In West Germany only 30% of beer is sold in draught, while in the USA the proportion is as low as 12%. Trends in consumption by type of beer are given in Table 3.10. While the split between draught and packaged has remained much the same, sales of lager have grown from 10% in 1971 to 23% in 1976 and 31% in 1981. (Packaged means in bottles or cans.) Research in 1979 showed that lager was the most popular drink among 16–24-year-old men and among 34% of women who drink beer.

The leading lager brands in 1982 were Heineken (Whitbread), Carlsberg (United Danish Breweries), Carling Black Label (Bass), Skol (Allied), Hofmeister (Courage), Kestrel (Scottish and Newcastle), and Harp. Within the bitter market the national brands such as Bass Toby, Watney Special, Courage Best Bitter, Tartan, etc. had a dominant position. However, the demand for 'real' ale had caused the brewers to resurrect a number of local brand names and offer an increasing variety of 'premium' bitters. The Campaign for Real Ale (CAMRA) was started in 1971 and it had a noticeable success in forcing the large brewers to move away from keg beer despite its longer life and easier handling.

Table 3.10 *The UK brewing industry: the UK beer market by product (% of volume sales)*

	1978	1979	1980	1981	1982
Draught					
Bitter	31.8	31.5	32.2	33.0	32.6
Lager	20.6	22.1	23.0	23.2	23.2
Premium bitter and stout	13.8	13.2	12.3	12.0	13.3
Mild	11.9	11.4	11.3	11.2	10.9
Total	78.2	78.3	78.8	79.4	79.0
Packaged					
Lager	6.2	6.9	7.7	7.8	8.4
Light, Pale, Export	8.5	8.1	7.5	7.3	7.2
Stout	3.7	3.5	3.2	3.0	3.1
Brown	1.9	1.8	1.6	1.4	1.3
Others	1.5	1.4	1.2	1.1	1.0
Total	21.8	21.7	21.2	20.6	21.0

Source: Brewers Society.

Table 3.11 *Sales by distribution channel*

	1970 %	1975 %	1980 %	% change 1970–80
Pubs	77	70	63	−5
Clubs	15	20	25	+95
Take home	8	10	12	+75
Total	100	100	100	+16

Pubs, clubs and the take-home market

Changes in what to drink were accompanied by changes in where to drink. As Table 3.11 shows, drinking at home and in clubs became more and more popular. This change in drinking habits reflected a change in the proportion of licensed premises. The number of off-licences and clubs grew dramatically so that by 1980 there were 76,260 on-licences, 21,970 restricted on-licences, where alcohol could only be consumed with a meal or sold to residents, 33,110 clubs and 42,300 off-licences. Many supermarkets now had off-licences and it was estimated in 1982 that they accounted for about half of the total take-home trade.

The declining sales of beer through pubs was linked to a change in the role of the pub. It was becoming more of a social centre and the family was being attracted as hard-drinking beer consumers declined. Many pubs now offered food, and electronic games and fruit machines proved popular. Public houses were the brewers' principal assets, accounting for between 50% and 75% of capital employed. Curiously the retail margin on beer was not as good as that on other products, as a 1980 survey reported (see Table 3.12).

Packaging trends

Until the 1960s the vast majority of UK brands were packaged either in wooden casks and barrels or in returnable half-pint or one-pint bottles. The market in 1981 was completely different. Draught beer accounted for 79%, bottled beer 10% and cans 10%. The growth of canned beer could be traced to the advent of off-licences and supermarkets and other sources of supply. A major new development in packaging in 1981 was the introduction of the PET (polyethylene terephthalate) bottle. PET bottles were aimed at the off-licence trade and were normally sold in the large two-litre size. Since they are reclosable, the consumer was quick to realize that his beer would not go flat.

Industry structure

By 1983, the number of UK brewers was half the total in 1960, and had decreased dramatically since the beginning of the century when nearly 6,500 brewing companies were active. In 1981, apart from the 50 or so small brewers, there were 80 brewing companies.

The market was dominated by the 'big six': Bass, Allied-Lyons, Whitbread, Watney, Scottish and Newcastle, and Courage. Together they controlled about 75% of the market. Next came the seven regional brewers. In order of size they were Greenall Whitley, Vaux, Wolverhampton and Dudley, Greene King, Marston, Thompson and Evershed and Boddingtons. Comparative sales and financial figures are given in Table 3.13.

Table 3.12 *Margins by product in public houses, 1980*

Product	Retail margin (%)
Draught beer	31
Draught lager	38
Spirits (sold in nips)	52
Wines	57
Minerals	47
Food	50

Source: *Accountants Weekly*.

Table 3.13 *The UK brewing industry: financial data—some national and regional brewers*

Brewer	Year end	Sales £m	Pre-tax profit £m	Profit to sales	Return on capital %	Stock turnover %
Bass	9-81	1,713	133	7.8	10.8	9.4
Allied	3-81	644	52	8.0	7.5	10.3
Whitbread	2.82	842	73	8.7	7.6	7.0
S & N	5-81	588	33	5.6	8.4	8.6
Courage	3-81	644	46	7.3	14.3	7.2
Guinness	9-81	127	5	3.9	10.5	18.8
Greenalls	9-81	195	22	11.5	10.9	8.5
Vaux	10-81	86	10	11.5	10.1	8.8
W & D	9-81	73	10	13.9	23.6	11.9
Industry average	—	—	—	8.8	10.1	8.3

Note: Figures for Watney Mann (part of Grand Metropolitan) are not available.
Source: Company reports.

Bass, the giant of the UK industry, was formed in 1967 by the merger of Bass Mitchells Butler with Charrington United Breweries. In 1982, company brands totalled over 80 and the market share was 21%. The 'Allied' in the name of Allied-Lyons refers to the three-way merger in 1961 of Tetley, Ansells and Inde Coope. The company's 50 or so brands claimed a share of approximately 15%. The 1958 merger of Watney and Mann, and their later incorporation into the Grand Metropolitan Group, was the foundation for Watney Mann and Truman, a group which brewed roughly 12 out of every 100 pints of beer consumed in the UK, and which controlled 8.5% of all public houses. Whitbread's impressive growth from a large southern brewer to national status was achieved by buying minority stakes which later became majorities in small brewers. Whitbread had about 13% of the market by volume. Scottish and Newcastle was formed from the merger in 1960 of Scottish Brewers and Newcastle Breweries. Finally, Courage, now part of the Imperial Group, assumed its present size following mergers with Barclay (1955) and Simonds (1960) and the takeover of John Smith in 1970. Courage believed that it had about 8% of the market.

The big six were characterized by their control of distribution through tied estates — brewers owned 64% of on-licences in 1980 — and by their wide range of other activities in wines and spirits, off-licences, restaurants and hotels. Some details of these other interests are given in Table 3.14. They reflect, in part, the different philosophies of the big six. Bass wanted to increase its leisure side to 25%; Grand Metropolitan said it saw itself as a pub operator; while Whitbread's philosophy was to go for down-the-throat leisure.

Table 3.14 The UK brewing industry: major brewers – range of activities

Brewer	Tied estate	Hotels	Restaurants	Off-licences	Wines and spirits	Other interests
Bass	7,800	104 Crest Hotels, 67 in UK	48 Toby Inns	928 Galleon	Hedges and Butler	Coral Pontins
Allied	7,600	42 Embassy Hotels, Mainly Midlands and North	69 including 30 London Steak Houses	930 Victoria Wine	IDV Harveys	Lyons
Whitbread	7,080	6 Hotels	111 in-house Beefeaters	647 Threshers	Stowells Julius Wile Calvet (France)	Biotechnology at Leicester University
Watney Mann Truman	7,750	Intercontinental*	291 Berni Inns	553 Westminster Wine	International Vintners	Dance halls Bingo Casinos
Scottish & Newcastle	1,470	40 Thistle Hotels		225 Gough Bros	Waverley Vintners	
Courage	5,350	35 West Country	19 Happy Eaters	407 Arthur Cooper and S. E. Roberts	Saccone & Speed	Holiday business

Note:* Grand Metropolitan, the parent company, owns the Intercontinental hotel chain.
Source: Company reports.

Before coming to the regional brewers it is necessary to mention three companies with wide national distribution but no tied estate: Guinness (a subsidiary of the Irish Group), Carlsberg (a subsidiary of the Danish United Breweries) and Harp (a consortium).

Regional and small breweries

Greenall Whitley was the largest regional brewery group. It was based in Warrington and has three breweries as well as 1,600 public houses. With the purchase of Arrowsmith Sunshine Holidays in 1982, Greenall Whitley seemed keen to become a mixed leisure group like the national brewers. Vaux had also pursued diversification, prompted by its depressed home base in Sunderland. The company had bought hotels and it had interests in Australia, Belgium and the USA. Wolverhampton and Dudley, on the other hand, had concentrated on its beer business. With 700 public houses its style was summed up in the advertising slogan, 'Unspoiled by progress'. In keeping with this image WDB concentrated on selling mild beer which was given less importance by other companies. The other four regional companies have pursued policies more in tune with WDB than Greenall and Vaux. They all enjoyed high reputations for their beers and, with the exception of Marstons, they operated in restricted areas.

The balance of brewing companies was made up of small independents like Eldridge, Pope, Shepherd Neame, G. Ruddle, Tollemache and Cobbold. Their output ranged from 60,000 to 200,000 bulk barrels. Finally came the very small craft brewers whose output was less than 10,000 barrels a year. Interestingly, a 1982 report by the Intermediate Technology Group found that there were four economies of scale in brewing. Beer-making savings in larger plants were offset by higher selling, distributive and administrative costs. The report said: 'In practice both large and small brewers have different though valid roles to play, one providing cheap bulk beers and the other distinctive 'real' beers'.

The tied and the free trade

Tied estates were an important feature of the industry, although the number owned by the brewers had declined by 16% since 1967. The big six brewers controlled 76% of the 48,958 tied pubs in 1980, and the three largest regional companies — Greenalls, Vaux and Greene King — controlled another 6%. Most tied public houses were tenanted, although the pattern differed between companies, as shown in Table 3.15.

The anomaly of Scottish & Newcastle reflects the way the Scottish market had developed. The Monopolies Commission concluded in 1969 that the tied house system had some disadvantages and in 1977 the European Court ruled that such exclusive purchasing arrangements were against the Treaty of Rome. In 1983 an EEC directive on the subject was in its fifth draft. The brewers were not happy, but some commentators felt that introduction of the directive would not bring significant changes, because existing arrangements could be largely preserved in other ways.

Table 3.15 *Managed/tenanted shares of major brewers' tied estates*

	Managed	Tenanted
Bass	32	68
Allied	33	67
Whitbread	23	77
Watney	NA	
S & N	67	33
Courage	30	70
Greenall	30	70
Greene King	17	83
Vaux	16	84

Table 3.16 *Major brewers' split of business by type of outlet*

	Free	Loan	Tied estate	Take home[*]
Bass	26	13	50	11
Allied	20	17	51	12
Whitbread	21	12	53	14
Watney	13	9	60	12
S & N	21	32	20	27
Courage	18	12	60	9

Note: [*] Off-licences, supermarkets.

Although tied estates were important there was, in theory, a substantial 'free trade' where premises had no formal tie to a brewer. In reality, however, many free outlets operated under 'loan ties' where the owner of the outlet had received low interest loans in return for guaranteed sales of a brewer's products, often to the exclusion of other suppliers. In 1981 brewers' loans to the free trade were estimated at £350 million. The proportion of major brewers' business derived from these different sources, including the take-home trade, is given in Table 3.16.

The importance which brewers attached to investment in their tied estates and in the loan trade was reflected in the substantial increases in investments planned for retailing in the future. Mr Charles Tidbury, Chairman of the Brewers Society, referred to a 'dramatic switch' when commenting on brewers' investment plans in April 1983. About 75% of the planned investment of £1.58

billion for 1983—85 would be spent on retailing compared to 66% in 1980—82 and 46% in 1977—79. This switch in investment reflected overcapacity in the industry. Some observers estimated that the industry had a capacity of 55 million bulk barrels. However, it was not clear that any of the larger production units would be closed.

Taxation and licensing

Two different taxes were levied on beer: excise duty and VAT. Excise duty was levied on the strength of beer prior to fermentation, while VAT was levied on the final selling price. In mid-1983 tax amounted to 23p on a pint of beer costing 60p. In the fiscal year ending 31 March 1983 it was estimated that tax and VAT on beer would amount to £2,460 million, or approximately 2.8% of the government's total tax receipts. In addition to its concern over tax receipts, the government was also anxious to reduce the problem of alcohol abuse (the number of UK adults with a drink problem had increased by 40% over the last ten years to 470,000). However, in a booklet published in 1981, the government did not accept recommendations that were made for the systematic use of tax rates as a means of regulating consumption. Nevertheless, health and social implications clearly entered the government's calculations and some curbs on advertising were to be considered for the future.

The brewing industry hoped that the government would eventually implement the recommendations of the Erroll Committee (1972) that: '...a personal licensee be permitted to sell intoxicating liquor, by retail, for on-consumption at any time between 10.00 a.m. and 12.00 p.m. midnight.' The brewing industry felt that the public house was at a competitive disadvantage to clubs (opening hours, amusement machines, access for children) and to supermarkets (opening hours). Pubs could only have amusements-with-prices (AWP) machines on their premises, while clubs could have jackpot machines capable of giving much bigger prizes and capable of earning sufficient money to subsidize the bar prices.

Technology

Two aspects of new technology were of importance to the brewing industry, namely microcomputers and microelectronics. Microcomputers were likely to have an effect on the number of staff employed in general office work. The impact of microelectronics would be in production. However, modern breweries were already highly automated so that the impact on employment levels would be minimal. Indeed, in June 1983, figures from the Department of Employment showed that employment in brewing and malting was only 59,000. This compared with 248,000 employed in public houses, including 57% part-time.

3.2 INITIAL READING

3.2.1 Skimming

The first step is to skim-read the case. This means that you do not stop to re-read things you may not have understood or to highlight things you think important. Your objective is to try to grasp what is in the case. After this first reading you should be able to describe in your own words what the case is about. If at all possible, read the case for the first time at a time when you know you won't be able to do much more than read it through. This allows the material to 'mature' in your head until the time for the real work arrives. It is quite incredible how much you will have retained and how much of the initial work of comprehension will already have been done unconsciously. This procedure also prevents a feeling of frustration. In the early stages of analysis, you will find yourself reading and re-reading sections of the case. It is easy to create an information overload which then leads to boredom, making the analysis that much more difficult. Spreading the process out makes the whole thing more enjoyable.

Read the case in the first instance like an exciting novel. Don't try to evaluate. Don't begin to decide what the problems might be. Suspend your judgement until a later stage. If you look for problems before you have begun to understand the case there will be a temptation to perceive information selectively so that your view of what the problems are will be reinforced and you may miss other problems. However, if you confine yourself to the actual description then the temptation is reduced. You will still have to select since you cannot follow up every possible aspect of the case. But the basis of selection will be broader and this will encourage you to explore the case with a more open mind. For the same reasons try to give equal attention to every bit of information. Those boring-looking appendices may contain information crucial to your understanding of the case.

3.2.1 Highlighting

Students are often urged to go through a case 'highlighting the key pieces of information'. The availability of yellow highlight markers has done much to encourage this practice. But what is a key piece of information? Simply picking out what strikes you as interesting or important is an unsystematic way of tackling a case. On its own it is both wasteful and dangerous. Highlighting is wasteful because you find that you finish up underlining every other sentence or figure.

Reviewing what you have done, you may feel that you do not understand the situation much better than when you started.

Highlighting is dangerous because it encourages premature judgement. An early judgement may lead you to select only that information which fits your preconceived view. This is a major problem for students new to the case method. They wish to get on with the analysis and grab at the first idea that comes along. Highlighting only encourages this process which, needless to say, is not a good habit to acquire. Highlighting is best used in conjunction with the processes of restructuring, extending, relating and summarizing which are described later in the chapter. It provides a way of classifying information which you are then going to work on. For example, you could go through a case underlining all the information relating to profit and profitability. These data could then be worked on as required. In this situation you know before you start what you are looking for and why it is being highlighted. This not only makes your task easier but it also forms part of a systematic technique which you know is building towards a better understanding of the case situation.

3.3 ORGANIZING THE INFORMATION

3.3.1 Objectives

Your objectives in organizing the information in the case are to help you to understand the situation described. The process of organizing, i.e. working with the information, also helps you to memorize or at least know what exists and where in the case. The end product of this organization process should be a compact picture or model of the case situation, in your head and on paper. Again, it should be emphasized that what you are aiming for is a description and an understanding of the case. Don't begin to look for problems or solutions.

There are a number of ways in which you can organize the information. Five are set out in the following sections, which you may find useful. The process involved can be likened to that of building a model. You assemble and unpack the materials and then begin to use various techniques to construct a representation of reality; in this instance the reality underlying the case data. Your 'model' represents both more and less than the data from which it is derived. More because it should describe the underlying structure and processes; less because it is a summary stripped of detail.

3.3.2 Indexing

In long cases it frequently helps to compile an index to the case material. This serves to highlight the easy-to-forget areas like appendices and illustrations. An index for the Wolverhampton and Dudley Breweries case might look like this:

- The failed takeover bid
- Early history
- Brewing activities
- Product range
- Retailing
- Other activities
- Davenport's bid
- Trading performance
- Future prospects
- Financial statements (Tables 3.1–3.3)
- Production investments 1977–83
- Public houses: new outlets and refurbishment
- Hotel locations
- UK beer demand (Table 3.7)
- U.K. wine and spirits demand (Table 3.8)
- Economic factors affecting demand (income, price, unemployment)
- Imports and exports
- Changing drinking habits (what and where)
- Packaging trends
- Competition
- Regional and small breweries
- Pubs – tied and free trade
- Taxation and licensing
- Technology

This case is essentially made up of two parts. In addition the order of topics is not always what you might consider logical. Indexing thus begins to make you think about organizing the data in a way which you find helpful. Notice also that the headings in the case are not necessarily those used in the index. You should use whatever terms best describe the content from your point of view. You are the one who will need to use it.

Indexing may immediately suggest whole areas of information that are missing. You should note what these might be. In this instance there is, for example, little in the way of information about the management of the company. What to do about missing information is discussed in section 4.1.3. Indexing can be taken a stage further by the use of cross-references. Any section in the case may deal with several topics. For a particularly complex case it is sometimes useful to cross-reference the sequence or contents list against another index. For example, in the Wolverhampton and Dudley Breweries case the section on product range also describes the characteristics of the local market, price levels and taxation. Information on any of these topics might be required in the later stages of analysis so that it would be useful to know where it is. This suggests another way of developing the information in the case.

3.3.3 Restructuring

Cases are normally written so that they are easy to read. This often means that they are structured in ways which are not necessarily the most useful for analytic purposes. For example, a historical write-up may discuss the personality of the managing director in several different time periods. It would help to understand the situation better if all of these pieces of information were grouped together. For example, here is some of the information relating to Wolverhampton and Dudley's mild beer:

- Mild Beer
- 'Traditional draught beers conditioned in the cask'
- Brand names 'Banks's' and 'Hanson's'
- Taste depending on ingredients and local water
- 'Accounts for half of brewery production'
- 'Nationally mild accounted for a declining share of about 10% of beer sales'
- 'Seen as a low-quality low-priced beer in much of UK'
- 'WDB's mild has a good reputation'
- It has won prizes
- High specific gravity
- Price 'at a level 3–5p below competitors' for historic reasons now difficult to change.

Restructuring may be carried out in two ways. First, the nature of the case may suggest what categories you would use for restructuring. In the Wolverhampton and Dudley Breweries case it would seem sensible to collect together information on the takeover bid, the national market for beer, the local market for beer, local beer retailing, trends in alcohol consumption and the production process. These are all topics suggested by the information in the case.

An alternative method of restructuring is to bring to the case an analytical framework: either a general one or one specific to the discipline you are studying. An example of a general framework is that originated by Kenneth Schnelle which relates mainly to organizational case studies. It has three broad categories into which the information in a case can be placed as follows:

1. The organization: to do with the organization's position with

respect to other organizations, its structure and its goals and objectives.

2. Operations: to do with how the organization currently operates; this category is subdivided into the main functional areas – planning, control, etc.

3. History: to do with past actions, decisions and policies and their results which have led up to the current situation.

If you were studying personnel, marketing, production or strategy, the frameworks set out in Table 3.17 would be appropriate.

Accountants, design engineers, architects and educational technologists all have similar frameworks. They may be as simple as a list of variables that theorists have discovered to be useful in describing the phenomena they habitually study; they may be as complex as a well-articulated theory, e.g. Porter's model of competitive forces in an industry. At this point in the analysis you are simply using these frameworks to help you organize the data. You are not yet beginning to test or articulate them: that will come later. In each case you have to decide whether a particular framework is a useful way of organizing the information. The key criterion is whether it results in better understanding. For the Wolverhampton and Dudley Breweries case the strategy framework has proved helpful but it is not the only possible choice. A useful by-product of restructuring the information is that it quickly reveals what is missing. For example in the Wolverhampton and Dudley case there is little on organizational structure, production technology, distribution or consumer motivation. These may or may not be vital to a complete understanding of the situation. However, the use of a discipline-based framework as a check-list at least ensures that you are made more aware of areas of ignorance.

3.3.4 Extending

Extending may be regarded as the stage beyond restructuring. Extending means to combine information in ways that create new information and hence improve understanding. One of the ways of extending the information in the Wolverhampton and Dudley Breweries case would be to make a chronology chart (see Table 3.18). The order in which events occur and the intervals between events are often crucial in understanding a case. Here we get the impression of a rather staid and stable company beginning to become more proactive in the 1970s and even more so in the early 1980s. In section 3.3.6 (on 'relating') the cause of this change will be investigated.

Table 3.17 Analytical frameworks

Personnel	Marketing	Production	Strategy
Industrial relations	Marketing organization	Management systems	Goals, aims and objectives
Manpower planning, recruitment and selection	Consumer behaviour	Facilities planning	Economic and social environment
Employment	Market characteristics	Production scheduling	Competitive environment
Training	Market segments	Inventory control	Markets environment
Management development	Price	Quality control	Organization capabilities
Performance appraisal	Product	Work performance	Generic strategies
Pay	Distribution channels	Human engineering	
Health and safety	Advertising and promotion		

Table 3.18 *Chronology of the Wolverhampton and Dudley Breweries case*

1890	Founded by amalgamation of three local breweries
1909–17	Further acquisitions
1928	Takeover of Hanson's
1960	Takeover of Shifnal's
1977–82	Heavy production investment
1983	Failed bid for Davenport's

Tabulation is the process of collecting information from different sources and displaying it together in the belief that greater understanding will be the end result. In the Wolverhampton and Dudley Breweries case most of the important information has already been tabulated in a reasonable form, but a further example of the process is given in Table 3.19. From this table it is possible to argue that there seems to be a relationship between owning hotels and turnover. The exceptions are Whitbread, which has far fewer hotels than average, and Wolverhampton and Dudley Breweries, which has rather more. This does no more than suggest that the latter is already a more diversified and balanced company than would appear from a superficial analysis of the case which concentrates on brewing rather than on other activities. It also qualifies the statement that 'WDB had not expanded in hotel or off-licence and wines and spirits activities in recent years'. The company already owned these hotels largely as a result of the takeover of Shifnal.

The interpretation of the table requires a certain amount of caution, since it provides an example of what might be called restrictive form analysis. The sales figures for the large breweries are taken from consolidated accounts and include sales for activities unrelated to brewing. Thus WDB's sales figures in Table 3.2 are larger than they should be if reasonable comparisons are to be made. The difference between Wolverhampton and Dudley Breweries and the other brewers may be less than it appears. One should then argue that the differences represented in the table are maximal rather than actual.

Tabulations can often only be expressed in restricted form. Sales must be at least ..., or costs must be greater than .... Information in a restricted form – for example, the figure lies between X and Y – is obviously not as instructive as we would like it to be. Nevertheless it is still useful information. Students often baulk at making the rather cumbersome calculations involved; they do not realize that they can reduce the uncertainty in the data quite considerably by

Table 3.19 *Sales and number of hotels by brewery*

UK brewers	Sales (£000)	Number of hotels
Bass	1,713	104
Whitbread	842	6
Allied	644	42
Courage	644	35
S & N	588	40
WDB	73	13

using this technique. And any method by which more pieces of the jigsaw can be slotted into place should not be ignored.

Graphic extensions of the information available in the case can provide useful insights. Bar charts are useful ways of displaying time periods and sequences. The organization chart is a useful way of outlining the structure of an organization. Tree diagrams provide a visual digest of complex relationships, as in Figure 3.1.

Maps may be used to sketch out geographical information such as factory locations, distribution networks and sales force territories.

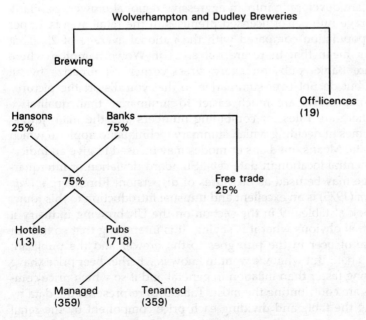

Figure 3.1 Wolverhampton and Dudley Breweries' activities

This can lead to surprising results. Few people are accurate judges of geographical distance or areas. Diagrams or sketches can provide insights about the layout of a factory floor or the form and function of a product. In each case you would be abstracting information from the case and rearranging it in order to create new and additional information.

3.3.5 Summarizing

Summarizing is almost the reverse of extending. There are an enormous number of data, qualitative and quantitative, in a case. Summarizing is a process which you will be doing continually throughout your case analysis. In familiarizing yourself with the case you will need to begin this process.

But first let me sound a note of warning. Summarizing means throwing away information. An average is an excellent summarizing device for many forms of quantitative data but it hides any variation there may be between individual figures. At this early stage you cannot be sure that the information hidden in a summary is not vital to your analysis. For example, you might summarize Wolverhampton and Dudley Breweries as being 'a rather sleepy and staid company'. But recent evidence suggests that they have woken up and are developing into an aggressive regional brewer. Similarly the average number of licensed premises in the retail area is 17 per 10,000 population compared with the national average of 25. That does not mean that there are not areas in Wolverhampton where there are Banks pubs on every street corner. Summarize by all means, but do not over-summarize so that you distort the picture.

Quantitative data are much easier to summarize than qualitative data. There are rules for combining numbers and the main judgement comes in deciding which summary technique to apply to which set of data. Means, medians or modes may be used to give an indication of central location in data sets. Standard deviation or interquartile range may be used as measures of dispersion. Ehrenberg's *Data Reduction* (1975) is an excellent and unusual introduction to this topic. If we look at table 3.9 in the section on the UK brewing industry it is not at all obvious what it is saying. It is interesting that so little of the price of beer in the pub goes to the brewer and the publican: around a half. But what we want to know is whether beer prices have been rising faster than inflation in general and if so which price components are contributing the most. Table 3.20 re-presents the data by inverting the table and dividing each price component by the retail price index and rounding to two significant figures.

Table 3.20 *Increases in components of beer price at constant prices*

	Excise	VAT	Government	Brewer/retailer	Total
1979	3.5	1.1	4.5	10.1	19.2
1980	3.5	2.0	5.5	9.8	20.8
1981	4.3	2.1	6.4	10.1	22.9
1982	4.4	2.2	6.6	10.1	23.4

What is now clear is that the price of beer has been rising faster than inflation: the deflated value would have remained constant if it had not. But more interestingly, the price is being driven up by increases in excise duty and government taxes rather than by the brewers and retailers. Through the process of data reduction it is possible to summarize all the data in the table into one sentence. In addition, the simplified table allows us to see this summary for ourselves, yet at the same time all the data are represented and more detailed analyses, for example year by year, are possible.

This by no means exhausts the possibilities, particularly if the analyst is prepared to make a few more assumptions. The point is that you should not mechanically apply the quantitative techniques that you have been taught. Your should always bear two questions in the forefront of your mind: What do these quantitative data tell me about the situation I am analyzing? How can these data be summarized so that I can clearly and unambiguously communicate them to someone else?

Qualitative data are less easy to summarize. Students frequently tend to leap to conclusions and make broad generalizations based on very little information. That is why summaries of qualitative data should be carefully worded and qualified where necessary. For example, Wolverhampton and Dudley Breweries might be portrayed as brewers of mild, cask-conditioned beers. However, they not only brew a significant proportion of bitter but have also recently introduced Lion brand keg beers. In addition, with 750 licensed outlets, there is an argument for calling them publicans who also brew beer. In other words, you always have to be careful that in your process of summarization you don't prune too much of the data.

Deciding what to keep and what to throw away in case analysis is one of the skills that must be learned. One important point is that the data are always retrievable. Having used some form of data summary in your solution you can always test it to see whether it would be changed if the data upon which it was based were summarized at a lower level of aggregation. Does it matter that Wolverhampton and Dudley Breweries also make and sell keg bitter and package lager? It might if you decided to recommend that they advertise themselves as the brewers of 'natural beer brewed with natural ingredients'.

Summarizing the data in a case is a necessity. You cannot keep all the data in your head, retrieving it only when it is required. In addition, summarizing provides insights that are not necessarily obvious when you are immersed in detail. It allows you to see the wood for the trees.

At a somewhat more theoretical level one can argue that summarization is, in part, the development of concepts. A concept is simply an abstract way of thinking about a situation. It is a summary of some phenomenon that you have data on. Sometimes you will be able to use existing concepts to help you describe the situation. For example, in the Wolverhampton and Dudley Breweries case the Intermediate Technology Group suggests that there are four sources of economies of scale in brewing. The concept of economies of scale comes from economics and neatly summarizes some aspects of the relationship between the costs and size of a brewer.

In addition you will need to create your own concepts. For example, you might label Davenport's a 'community brewer'. This phrase captures many of the characteristics of the firm and helps explain why the bids were consistently rejected. Not all the concepts you employ will be so striking or obvious. To think, you must employ concepts. Some will be so commonplace that you will not recognize them as such. But all will be summaries or abstracts of the reality as portrayed in the case information. They represent the building blocks of the models of the situation you are attempting to build.

3.3.6 Relating

Relating is the process by which relationships between variables or concepts are uncovered. It is the last stage in the building of your model. Isolated facts or summaries, even groups of related facts, are useful building blocks. However relationships are the mortar that binds these blocks together to make a coherent and valid structure. For example it may be useful to note that productivity in a factory has increased not steadily but in a series of sharp steps. It is even more useful to discover that these steps coincide with bonus payments rather than with the conclusion of productivity agreements. A relationship has been identified. When a number of such relationships have been identified, or even assumed or hypothesized, and further related to one another, then a holistic picture or model of the situation begins to emerge. In the familiarization stage of case analysis that is all that is required. You will need this vision to help you to decide what to do or recommend in the later stages of your analysis. Think of the process of establishing relationships as one of prefabricating parts for use in subsequent building operations.

Qualitative relationships (involving qualitative data) are more difficult to establish than relationships among quantified variables. Nevertheless it is possible to identify possible relationships. For example, it is likely that the decline in beer sales in the UK as a whole was being repeated in the West Midlands, that sales volume for Wolverhampton and Dudley Breweries was static or falling and that only price increases were keeping sterling sales value on the increase. It is also likely that the bid for Davenport's resulted from the desire by the board to continue to grow, but by external rather than internal means.

All that can be said at the moment is that a set of possible relationships exists. The fact that variables are not always quantified obviously makes the teasing out of relationships difficult. Another source of difficulty is that few relationships are confined to just two variables. This means that multivariable analysis is required. Frequently the data in the case are not capable of supporting analysis of this kind. For example, you may wish to discover which variables correlate with total sales volume. Two of the variables you choose are quantified, but one is quantified for a much shorter period than the other. Another two variables are only available as qualitative data. Finally the three remaining variables have not been measured at all or, if they have, the data are not contained in the case.

In this sort of situation you have to be content with squeezing what you can out of what is available. You must not expect too much of two or even three variable analyses. Other, unmeasured, variables will often get in the way and camouflage the relationship. However, at least in the first instance, you must treat the data as they are and not as you would like them to be.

There are three ways in which you can 'test' the relationships you have identified. First of all you can think carefully through the relationships to check whether your thinking is logical. In particular it is helpful to try to discover other hypotheses which would also 'explain' the data. For example, in the example cited above the bid could also be explained by a belief that Whitbread was about to make a bid of its own. You would need to weigh the evidence for both explanations.

Second, you can look for evidence elsewhere in the case that might support your explanation. For example, the increasing emphasis on the free trade suggests that Wolverhampton and Dudley Breweries were facing problems in their tied trade and so would be keen to look outside their existing area.

Finally, you can look for evidence outside the case. In this instance you will be less concerned with specific pieces of data which are highly relevant to the case, e.g. the organization chart for Wolverhampton and Dudley Breweries. Rather, it would be helpful to have a piece of research which identifies the factors which lead firms successfully to oppose bids. All of these tasks are highly complex, but they provide practice at skills which are vital in complex problem-solving situations. You are being asked to behave as a scientist or detective collecting and weighing evidence in order to come to an understanding of what has been going on.

In terms of examining *quantitative relationships* you will, as in the qualitative case, have to be content in most case studies with correlation rather than causation. In other words, you will be looking to see how two or more variables co-vary, that is, increase or decrease together. That does not mean that one varying causes the other to vary. But it is probably the best that you can hope for in the absence of long runs of immaculately collected times series data or experiments. This is the real (simulated!) world and you must live with believing and assuming rather than knowing. The data in Table 3.21 provide an example of the problems of relationship estimation using typical case study data.

With so little data there is little point in calculating formal statistical measures of correlation such as correlation coefficients. With more data on more variables, very sophisticated multivariate analysis is possible and indeed desirable. Such techniques as multiple regression, discriminant analysis and canonical correlation, as well as non-parametric methods, are readily available through package systems such as the Statistical Package for the Social Sciences. Unfortunately, in practice it is rare for a case, unless specifically written with such applications in mind, to contain enough good quality quantitative data for this type of analysis to be possible. What you will have to do is work with what you have and combine judgement and qualitative data to get sensible results as in the situation described below. What we see in Table 3.21 is what we might expect: the demand for beer is inversely correlated with price. But it would be premature to jump to conclusions. There are only three data points, so the sample is very small. In addition, it is more likely to be relative price increase which impacts upon sales rather than absolute price levels. In practice, we know that beer prices were

Table 3.21 *Beer volume related to price increase*

	Volume (in barrels)	Price (p)
1979	41.7	41.4
1980	40.0	54.6
1981	38.1	67.5
1982	37.0	75.3

rising faster than other prices so the result is not affected by deflating price levels with the Retail Price Index. However, it is also known from other data in the case, unfortunately on a different time basis, that other more expensive types of alcohol consumption have been increasing faster than beer consumption. Thus it is likely that part of the volume decrease is caused by substitution not based upon price differentials. Nevertheless it can probably be concluded that price rises haven't helped beer sales, but it is difficult to estimate how important they are in this process.

A very different kind of analysis – *ratio analysis* – is possible using WDB's profit and loss accounts and balance sheets. The figures for the most recent year, 1983, make interesting reading and give us some measure of the structure of the company. But each figure in isolation tells us relatively little. We need to compare it with other figures in order to see relationships. This technique is known as ratio analysis. By relating various accounting figures to each other it is possible to build up a picture of the configuration of a firm's operations as described by their accounting system.

There are a number of bases for comparison that one might take. The first is on the basis of time. Trends in the absolute values can be seen more clearly if the growth in the absolute figures is calculated as an index, as in Table 3.22. An alternative would be to calculate the percentage growth year on year. In this case it is clear that sales are growing faster than profits. However, there is an important proviso to be made about all such time-based analyses. In most economies inflation is a common problem. Since the figures for WDB are in current value terms it would make sense to deflate them by applying a suitable deflationary index. In this instance there is a reasonable argument for using the Retail Price Index since sales are to final consumers. If the company being analyzed has particular costs or sales which are subject to inflationary factors different from those of the economy as a whole then a more specific deflationary index may need

Table 3.22 *Trends in turnover and net profit before tax*

	Sales	Net profit before tax
1974	107	89
1975	143	110
1976	188	135
1977	225	150
1978	263	185
1979	304	212
1980	342	235
1981	396	266
1982	432	295
1983	466	325

Table 3.23 *Assets and liabilities as a percentage of capital employed*

	Current assets	Current liabilities	Net current assets	Investments	Fixed assets
1978	20	(32)	(12)	8	104
1979	19	(31)	(12)	8	103
1980	18	(31)	(13)	9	103
1981	20	(31)	(11)	6	103
1982	22	(30)	(8)	7	100
1983	21	(32)	(11)	9	101

to be used. Such indices will only be found by reference to industry sources. Similarly, the percentage which each item in the balance sheet represents of the capital employed, or the percentage which each item in the profit and loss account represents of the sales, will reveal changes in the structure of accounts. An analysis of this type for the assets of Wolverhampton and Dudley Breweries is shown in Table 3.23. The short form of profit and loss account does not permit a cost analysis in this case.

Again, such a table must be treated with some caution. The figures are 'stocks' at the year end rather than the flows which are represented in the profit and loss accounts. Nevertheless, one or two interesting points emerge. Net current assets are negative, which would be unusual for a manufacturing operation but is more common in retailing, implying a fast stock turnover. There is also, over time, a small reduction in the fixed asset base matched by a reduction in 'net current liabilities' and an increase in investment, the latter due to the bid for Davenport's.

A more complex set of relationships, which almost amount to a model of the organization in monetary terms, can be very nicely illustrated by means of a pyramid of ratios. The pyramid shows how each facet of the business contributes towards the achievement of a key objective of any profit-making organization: return on capital. It shows that the same return on investment can be achieved in a number of ways by one ratio compensating for another. The relationships between different aspects of the firm's operation are clearly exposed. A pyramid of ratios for Wolverhampton and Dudley Breweries is shown in Figure 3.2.

This is a somewhat simplified version used here only to illustrate the principles involved, and since not all of the data are available it is necessarily incomplete. There are a number of possible ways of calculating profitability for a company: profit gross or net of tax, capital employed based upon total assets or net assets. For a discussion of the pros and cons of each method you are referred to Pendlebury and Groves (1990) as a good example of some of the texts available on the analysis of company accounts. In this instance net profit before tax to average capital employed has been chosen and the figure for Wolverhampton and Dudley Breweries is around 22.5%.

This is further broken down into two key ratios – net profit to sales and sales to capital employed. The important thing to notice here is that these two ratios, when multiplied together, give the original return on capital ratio at the apex of the pyramid. In other words any change in profitability can only be achieved by a change in one or both of these ratios. This type of interrelationship operates throughout the pyramid. A change in any of the variables will result in a change in profitability unless there is an exactly counterbalancing change in another variable somewhere in the pyramid.

The left-hand branches of the pyramid describe the operating results of the firm. They reveal the balance between profit and the many categories of cost that are needed to generate it. These ratios cannot be calculated for Wolverhampton and Dudley Breweries, but now at least you know what you would like to know. In some instances it might be possible to estimate the ratios from other data in the case. The right-hand branches of the pyramid are concerned with the utilization of the capital assets of the company. The net sales to operating capital ratio is inverted at the apex of these right-hand branches. This is simply a mathematical convenience. The components of operating capital can only be separated out if they form the

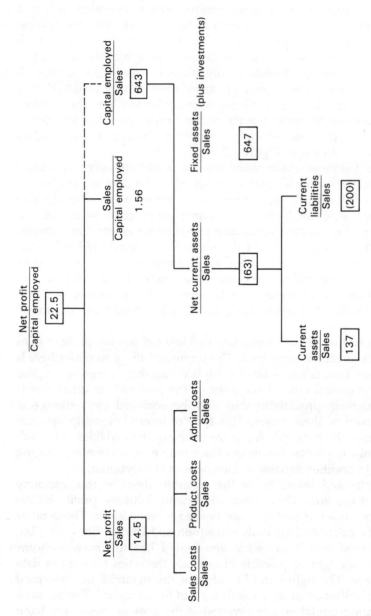

Figure 3.2 A pyramid of ratios for Wolverhampton and Dudley Breweries (1983)

numerator of a ratio. In addition the result is multiplied by 1,000 to give values per £1,000 of net sales. The first components of operating capital to be split off are current and fixed assets (plus investments). The relationship between these two ratios is descriptive of the kind of operation that the firm is running. Note that the two ratios add to give the capital employed to sales ratio. The fact that fixed assets are positive and net current assets are negative (indicated by brackets) immediately suggests that the composition of net current assets should be examined. This is done in the next level of the pyramid. Here we see that current liabilities are larger than current assets, a point commented upon earlier. In practice this means that the assets employed are lower than they might be because the firm is essentially employing assets other than its own. While this is desirable in profitability terms it may be less so when cash flow and exposure to risk are taken into account.

It would be possible to take the analysis further by looking at the composition of both the current assets and current liabilities. In addition, if the fixed assets data had been disaggregated, it would have been interesting to look at its structure in relationship to the sales it was having to support. The basic rules of the pyramid still apply. It is important to note how each of the ratios contributes, possibly via a series of other ratios, to the overall profitability of the firm.

It is possible to take the comparison further by looking at the change in the pyramid of ratios over time. In Table 3.24 data for 1979 to 1983 is presented in tabular rather than pyramid form, but the interpretation remains the same. The striking feature of the time series is how little any of the ratios vary. 1981 provides a good example of the compensation that often occurs in pyramid analysis. Although the return on capital did not change from the previous year the net profit to sales fell by 3%. However, this was exactly compensated by a fall in capital employed to sales of almost 4%. In summary, Wolverhampton and Dudley Breweries have clearly been performing very steadily and have maintained the structure of their operations for a number of years. A range of other analyses could be undertaken. In particular you could look at the liquidity and financial stability of the firm by calculating ratios like the current ratio (current assets to current liabilities). In addition it is possible to examine the efficiency of some of the firm's activities such as stock management (stock turnover) and employee productivity (sales per employee). For a more comprehensive treatment of these other ratios, and of the accounting conventions that might be used to calculate them, you should refer to Pendlebury and Groves (1990).

Table 3.24 Pyramids of ratios for Wolverhampton and Dudley Breweries, 1979–83

	Net profit (%) / Capital employed	Net profit (%) / Sales	Capital employed / Sales (per £1,000 sales)	Net current assets / Sales (per £1,000 sales)	Fixed assets / Sales (per £1,000 sales)
1979	23.4	14.5	620	(73)	640
1980	22.9	14.3	623	(79)	643
1981	22.9	13.9	605	(72)	626
1982	22.7	14.2	623	(56)	633
1983	22.5	14.5	643	(63)	647

Completing a ratio pyramid like this gives a case analyst a very good feeling for the structure of a company's operations. It provides a well-established framework within which to work and pinpoints the relationships that are vital to understanding any commercial organization. It is also a very quick, though somewhat mechanical, method for organizing the accounting data which most cases contain. Finally, it is the first stage in a process designed to uncover problems in a firm's operations. The differences between one firm's ratios and those of other firms operating in the same or similar industries afford clues as to that firm's strengths and weaknesses. When backed up with other evidence they form the basis for defining problem areas. They also offer hints of possible solutions. Problems and solutions are the themes of the next two chapters and ratio analysis will be discussed again in those contexts.

3.4 TAKING STOCK

At the end of this initial process of understanding a given situation you should have a broad picture of what the position is, as well as some rather detailed descriptions of individual parts of it. Remember that you should not yet have begun to identify problems: you are merely describing. For example, in the Wolverhampton and Dudley Breweries case we might conclude that the firm has been in a rather stable position over the last few years as evidenced by the financial data. It has chosen to attempt a takeover and failed and has been left with an investment. The market for its unusually locally concentrated product is apparently changing in a number of different ways which may or may not be affecting the sales of the company. None or all of these statements may contain a problem. None have been expressed as such in this summary. In practice there is no need for such a summary. It is important, however, to know your analyses well so that you can use them in the next stage of the process. Before that you need to examine the quality of the materials you have been dealing with.

Step One: Understanding the Situation (II)

4.1 EVALUATING THE INFORMATION

4.1.1 Objectives

Up to now it has been assumed that all information is the same. This is clearly a dangerous assumption. The information in a case differs quite considerably in a number of ways. Since a case is only comprised of information, it must be assessed and evaluated before and while it is being used. In a way information comprises the building blocks of a case analysis. You need to understand the nature and quality of the materials before you begin to build. Many a brilliant case analysis has fallen down because it was built upon shaky informational foundations. The information in a case may be said to differ in at least three respects – precision, validity and relevance. Each is discussed below but it will be argued that only the first two have practical application at this stage of case analysis.

4.1.2 Precision

Precision refers to the degree of uncertainty implicit in a particular figure or statement. Precision is really a continuous variable but for purposes of illustration a four-category system seems appropriate, as illustrated in Table 4.1. Missing information is included in this classification because it could be said to represent the ultimate in imprecision. It is a very important category and will be discussed in some detail later in this chapter. On the whole it is preferable to have more, rather than less, precise information. For example, you might build a strategy on the 'fact' that 'The company placed considerable emphasis on the quality of its beers ...' but what does 'considerable' mean in this context? It might mean that it is totally dedicated to quality or it might mean that it puts rather more emphasis on quality

Table 4.1 *Examples of different degrees of precision in Wolverhampton and Dudley Breweries case*

Degree of precision	Case examples
Precise	Date takeover abandoned, company accounts, number of employees.
Imprecise	'...the company placed considerable emphasis on the quality of its beer.' '...the level of beer consumption in the Wolverhampton area was still above average...'
Very imprecise	'It was common practice in the industry...' '...these were not extensively promoted.'
Missing	Costs, company organization and personalities, sales by product and by area.

than on price or delivery. Your view about which applies will make a substantial difference to the policies you might recommend.

The problem is, therefore, to highlight imprecise information; precise information can look after itself. Three procedures can be used to help. The first is to read through the case especially in order to pick out imprecise information. It will be too much trouble to note all the examples. However, you might wish to identify where they occur and be aware of them in subsequent analysis. The second is to carry forward the imprecision into the later stages of analysis. It is too easy, for example, to summarize 'considerable emphasis is placed on quality' to 'they think quality is paramount'. The qualification may make all the difference in the world. It is very easy to forget how the information was originally couched. The usual tendency is for qualifications to be forgotten and precision to increase as the analysis proceeds. This can lead you to draw unwarranted conclusions and should be avoided. In the early stages, when you are looking for the major problems and devising solutions, precision may not be so much of a problem. These are essentially exploratory processes and you may not care, or be able, to dot every i and cross every t. In fact the third method is simply to ignore the problem until later. However, when you come to evaluating and choosing between alternative solutions, precision does become important. The difference between alternatives may hang on the precision of a statement in the case text. At this stage you may wish to look back at the case and check on the precision of the statements or data that form the planks of your case.

The danger with this approach is that you may not be able to check on all the sources of data that you used to come to a particular view.

4.1.3 Improving precision and filling gaps

Cases are never solved solely on the information contained in the case. At a minimum level, case analysts bring to the case information concerning facts but, more importantly, relationships which they believe describe how the world works. That is to say, they make assumptions which they believe are valid in the context of the case. At the other end of the scale, case analysts may collect specific information concerning the case situation and use this to augment what is already there.

In both instances this is a response to imprecise or missing information. From the first stage of case analysis onwards, you will become aware of information gaps, or concerned at the lack of clarity in some of the statements made. Since what is important will change as your analysis progresses, you may find that you may have to repeat the search for supplementary information a number of times. So, although collecting further information is discussed here, it may be relevant to any stage of the case analysis process.

The first thing to check is whether or not your case instructor will allow you to 'go outside the case'. Some will probably encourage you to do so. It allows you to learn the skills of information collection as well as information processing. It also adds a dynamic dimension to the case method. In effect, different students will be analyzing different cases. However, problems can arise. Not all students may have equal access to information sources. It is also possible that students new to the case method will invest too much time searching and not enough in analysis. There is a tendency to believe that the answer is out there somewhere if only it can be found. A case instructor may want to discourage this attitude. He or she may wish to encourage the development of cognitive skills rather than the skills of data collection and so suggest that you confine your attention to the data that are already available.

Why are data missing? Having identified imprecise or missing information which you believe important to your understanding of the case, the next stage is to ask the key question, 'Why is it missing or incomplete?' This must be considered before deciding how, if at all, the information could be obtained. In general, there are three possibilities.

First, it may be that the information is simply unobtainable. In the Wolverhampton and Dudley Breweries case it would have been very useful to have an attitude survey of mild beer drinkers to see how they rated the pubs as against the beer. It is highly unlikely that such a survey existed at the time the case was written and, even if it did, it is unlikely that the firm would have allowed it to be published. Secondly, it is possible that the case writer did not include the information although it was available to him or her. A decision may have been made to exclude or qualify information because it was thought that a better case would result. In the Wolverhampton and Dudley Breweries case details of production processes and distribution are missing because the authors wished to concentrate on the marketing and strategy aspects of the situation. It may be that the case writer would have liked to include information but failed to do so. Sometimes casewriters are denied access to key pieces of information when writing cases – information which would have been readily available to decision makers. It is clear that in the Wolverhampton and Dudley Breweries circumstances the case writer wrote the case based upon external sources. That is almost certainly the reason why the details of internal company operations are largely absent. At other times case writers become so enmeshed in the process that they fail to realize that they have not collected vital information. Too often students think that because the information is not there it must be irrelevant. This is a very unwise assumption.

Although internal information of this kind may be available, you should not attempt to collect it. It cannot be stressed too firmly that students should not approach the organization described in the case. The organization has already been inconvenienced by allowing the case writer access to people and data. It cannot be expected to be very happy about doing the same for every group of students who are assigned the case to analyze. For similar reasons, students should not attempt to uncover the identity of anonymous organizations described in a case.

Thirdly, there is information which is not included in the case most probably because the case writer wished to keep the case short. This is likely to be mostly environmental information. For example, it might have been possible to discover the composition of the board of Baron Davenport's Charity Trust during the takeover bid. This information may be obtained from reliable secondary sources. It is relatively easily available and cheap to collect. It does not directly involve the organization in the case. Whether it proves valuable or not will depend on the analytical skills of the case analyst.

One final point needs to be made and this is concerned with hindsight. In some instances it is possible to discover what actually happened to the organization or the industry after the point in time

61

when the case is set. One situation may be that you know what decision was taken and what resulted from it. If this is so, then you have more useful information than is normal in case analysis. You do not however have the solution. What would have happened, for example, if they had made a different decision? You can still analyze the case in the normal way. You are simply better informed than you would normally be. Hindsight helps in this instance, but it should not determine the outcome.

A different situation occurs when major and unpredictable change in the environment has happened since the time when the case was set. Prime examples of this are the Gulf War, high rates of inflation (which make the figures in the case look absurd) and technological breakthroughs in areas like microtechnology and telecommunications. In principle, case instructors should not set cases when both they and their students know that the future environment will not behave in a way that was predictable at the time. However, there are arguments for doing so occasionally. Students have to immerse themselves in a case. It is therefore useful practice to see how they would have coped in the situation in question knowing that the future held a revolutionary change they could not know about. A belief in parallel universes helps! Another argument is that it reminds students that case studies are simulations and not reality. Thus they should seek actively to learn and experiment rather than simply react or behave.

4.1.4 Validity

The validity of a piece of information may be defined in terms of whether it is an accurate representation of the situation it purports to describe. This definition implies a particular philosophical view of the world although it may not seem so to the reader. It assumes that there is an objective reality 'out there' which may be more or less accurately measured and described. It also implies that the only problems are concerned with our ability to make the necessary measurements. There is another view which will be described later in the chapter. For the moment, however, the definition given at the beginning of this section will be used.

There is no necessary relationship between precision and validity. A lie can be stated in very precise terms. Indeed, this is a well-known technique for making a lie believable. It is obviously helpful to try to establish the validity of the information in the case. Analyses or recommendations based upon what might be regarded as invalid, or even partially valid, information will not be very useful. Establishing, or at least questioning, the validity of information should be carried out at the earliest possible stage. Leaving it until later may mean wasting time and effort.

Establishing validity can be thought of as a two-stage process. In the first stage you can simply follow the clues supplied by the case writer. The most obvious clue is whether the information is stated as fact or opinion. The following facts and opinions are fairly easy to distinguish:

Facts
- 'Wolverhampton and Dudley Breweries was formed on 14 May 1890.'
- 'The company operated two breweries.'
- 'The big six brewers controlled 76% of the 48,958 tied pubs.'
- 'WDB's mild beers had a relatively higher gravity.'
Opinions
- 'The declining sales of beer through pubs were linked to a change in the role of the pub.'
- 'Wastage levels were reputed to be among the lowest in the industry.'
- 'There are serious doubts about the future of beer drinking.'

Opinions differ from facts in several ways. They are seen through someone else's eyes and will therefore be partial. They often concern events or situations about which it would be very difficult to produce evidence that would convince someone that they represented facts. In the Wolverhampton and Dudley Breweries case it would be difficult to prove that 'The price differential was (thought to be) important to customers'. In the first place it is not clear how importance could be measured since there are a variety of alternative possibilities. In the second place these measures all have problems of accuracy and validity in their own right. In particular, if you attempted to measure behaviour by altering the price the result would be confounded with other events occurring at the same time. On the other hand, if you attempted to measure attitudes, you could not be sure that they would be consistent with behaviour. Opinions are frequently concerned with relationships as well as facts. A whole variety of reasons are put forward in the case to explain the decline in draught beer sales. Which, if any, are responsible and in what measure, would be very difficult to decide. However, opinions about relationships can be useful in providing us with hints about how things work, but they are only hints. You will clearly have to regard all opinions with a degree of scepticism. It may be that you have no alternative but to treat them as valid in the absence of evidence to the contrary. However, before doing so it will be worthwhile going through a second stage of validation.

This second stage procedure should be applied to both facts and opinions. It consists of asking about each piece of information: 'How was that obtained or measured?' Like anyone in intelligence work you should be capable of evaluating the source of your information. Let's look at some examples: (a) 'In 1983, sales reached £86.4m with a 10% increase in profit to £12.5m.' These data clearly came from the company accounts and can be regarded as valid in the sense that they represent an output from the firm's accounting system. However, it should be remembered that accounting systems are based upon conventions and assumptions that may be accurate without being entirely valid in the sense that the word has been used here. (b) 'Labour relations were good, with few disputes.' This information may have come from a source in the company, or an industry expert, or even a competitor. In any event it is unlikely that it is based upon a quantitative study of industrial disputes in the brewing industry.

This raises a general point about case writing. In order to compress and clarify the case, case writers may write statements which appear as facts when they are, in reality, opinions. They may be the opinions of people they have interviewed or they may be the case writer's own. A case writer may write, 'The widget is a good, well-made product.' This reads better than either: 'Mr Smith believes the product to be well made', or, 'Industry opinion is that the widget is a well-made product'. However, the original statement gives you no basis for assessing its validity because it does not reveal its source. You should always beware of bold statements like this. Try to imagine where the information could have come from. Then you will be in a better position to decide how valid it is likely to be.

In deciding whether an opinion statement is accurate you will probably want to examine two things. First, the general credibility of the source: is the person concerned in a position where he or she can assess and report on situations accurately? For example, you would probably believe Wolverhampton and Dudley Breweries' finance director when he is quoted as saying, 'We are not planning any other acquisitions'. He is in a very good position to know. On the other hand, you would place less weight on the *Investors Chronicle* view that the best buys in the smaller breweries are likely to be among those diversifying. As external analysts they are less likely to understand the nature of the industry.

Secondly, this examination should include not only the people quoted in the case but also the case writer. You should be aware of what sources he or she may have used and how they have been drawn upon. You will soon get a feel for how a case is put together. This may allow you, in some instances, to question the validity of statements of 'fact' made in the case. You may be able to argue that the case writer could not have known, with any certainty, what he or she is claiming to know. This may happen rarely but is something you should be very much aware of.

Some of my colleagues have argued that questioning the validity of the information in a case is not something that students should be encouraged to do. It may leave them paralyzed and unable to do anything because of their fear that the data are all suspect and therefore useless as the basis for analysis. It is also suggested that it will undermine their opinion of the case experience, the case writer and even the case leader who has chosen the case. I would argue that case analysts should, from the beginning, be taught to be sceptical of the data that they encounter. When they are involved in actual decision making on a regular basis they won't have a case writer to filter and sort out the information for them. They will have to develop the skills of evaluating information for themselves or risk working with substandard materials as they build their models of the world.

It was earlier suggested that there is another way of thinking about the validity of data. This alternative approach argues that there is no such thing as objective reality. All our worlds are socially constructed; we each choose to place our own interpretations on the sense data to which we are exposed. Thus a case study is simply one person's view of the world, and testing for validity is a waste of time. Each view is as valid as the next. There is no way of choosing between them.

Accepting this vision does not, in my opinion, invalidate the use of case studies but it does change one's approach to them. How does someone holding this view survive in the world? People do so by creating their own views of the world and testing them. But they do not judge them by how close they are to a reality that they don't believe in. Instead they use other measures such as relevance, efficiency, comfort, effectiveness, practicality and even, perhaps, beauty. There is no reason why they should not learn the skills of model building and evaluation using case studies. But they will be less concerned about the validity of the case writer's view of the world and more interested in developing their own interpretation of it and how they might act within it. In practice it is apparent that case analysts tend to behave in this way anyway. They choose those interpretations of events that meet their own agendas or world views. It is not wrong to do so; but it is mistaken to do so without realizing what you are doing.

4.1.5 Extrapolating from the information

Extrapolation is a common activity in case analysis. Since you may not realize the importance of this process, it will be worthwhile to examine it fairly fully now. It is quite useful to look at a schema for describing degrees of extrapolation. It distinguishes four categories:

- Facts
- Inference
- Speculation
- Assumption

In inference you are mostly rearranging existing facts in a logical way and adding very little to them. Here are some inferences that could be made concerning the Wolverhampton and Dudley Breweries case:

1. Wolverhampton and Dudley Breweries was annoyed by its inability to take over Davenport's.
2. Customers of Banks's and Hanson's beers are highly loyal.
3. The management see themselves primarily as brewers.

Nowhere are these statements made. However, simply by collecting information together from different parts of the case you can come to these conclusions, without feeling you are making a leap in the dark. Speculations are a mixture of facts from the case, facts imported from other sources and assumptions about how the world works. Here are some speculative statements about Wolverhampton and Dudley Breweries:

1. Wolverhampton and Dudley Breweries decided on the takeover as a way of counteracting the expected decline in sales of beer in its sales area.
2. National brewery companies would never attack Wolverhampton and Dudley Breweries because of their unwillingness to produce good quality mild draught beer.
3. The main reason for the decline in mild and bitter sales is demographic change.

Clearly, the line between inference and speculation is a narrow one. The difference lies in the fact that speculation requires the importation of facts and assumptions into the case situation. The first statement (1) is simply a pulling together of a number of facts from the case and assumes that firms wish to survive and grow. The second statement (2) is an interpretation of an economic theory of competition. The third statement (3) is based upon a judgement that you can extrapolate relationships from one market to another. These examples illustrate the fact that when you speculate you weave together facts, generalizations and assumptions. It is important to remember how the mixture was created. It is all too easy for speculation to become inference and inference to become fact as you progress with your analysis.

An *assumption* is not based upon the facts in the case. It is made because without it you cannot complete the picture or maintain a logical argument. Examples of assumptions you might make in this case are:

1. The accounts are reasonably accurate.
2. Wolverhampton and Dudley Breweries has acted and will continue to act cautiously and sensibly
3. The trends in the market will continue.
4. There will be small regional brewers coming up for sale which would rather merge with another regional brewer than with a national brewer.
5. There will be no move to de-license alcohol sales.

Some assumptions, like (1) and (3), may be so general as to apply to every case. They only become interesting in the odd situation where they don't apply. Other assumptions, for example assumption (5) are fairly specific but so unlikely to be contradicted that they merely safeguard you against the outside chance. Assumptions (4) and (2) are key assumptions. There is no real evidence to support assumption (4). However, there is no real evidence against it either and it opens up an interesting line of enquiry. You may finish up simply suggesting that it should be investigated, but at least it is a creative possibility. It also requires assumption (2) which creates the matched motivation on the part of the company. Any more entrepreneurial, and it might go for more risky schemes. Any less, and it is not likely to risk a repeat of the Davenport situation.

Assumptions should be visible, plausible and rare. Visible because it is easy to let assumptions creep disguised into your analysis. In particular, it is important to know and state your assumptions when discussing or writing up your analysis. Your instructor may not be happy with your assumptions, but at least he or she will have to credit you with the (hopefully) elegant superstructure you have built upon them. If you do not make your assumptions clear, or worse, fail to realize that you are making assumptions, your analysis will be difficult to understand and assess.

Assumptions should be plausible because otherwise it is easy to solve a problem by assuming it away. You could assume that Davenport's changes its mind or that the chairman dies and is replaced by a dynamic MBA who revitalizes the firm. Since you can't rely on these sorts of things happening in the real world, you shouldn't rely on them in a case analysis.

Assumptions should be rare because you can repeat the mistake described above. The more assumptions you introduce, the easier it is to create a different case from the one you have been given to work on and the simpler it is to avoid the issues.

4.2 GUIDE TO USE

Clearly, all case analysts should heed the advice given in section 3.2 on initial reading. For the beginner, organizing the information will probably pay greater dividends than attempting to evaluate it in great detail. Since all of the organizing procedures help to familiarize you with the material in the case, it would be no great waste of effort to experiment with them all. In time you will need to develop your own style when trying to understand the case situation. Trying out these alternatives should help you to find procedures you are comfortable with.

Using systematic methods of evaluating the precision and validity of the information is probably best left to a later stage of skill development. However, you should at least read the sections dealing with these topics and be aware of the problems they create. It should be noted that information evaluations are very useful for refuting someone else's recommendations. They are also likely to impress case instructors. Filling the gaps and extrapolating from the information given are things you will have to do anyway in any case situation. Reading the sections relating to these topics should help you to do them more effectively.

Step Two: Diagnosing the Problems (I)

Step two is concerned with identifying problems, analyzing their nature and structure, and deciding which to tackle first.

5.1 PROBLEMS, OPPORTUNITIES AND THREATS

Before beginning to try to identify problems, it would obviously be worthwhile to attempt to define what a problem is. The most useful definition for our purposes is 'a difference between a current (or expected future) situation and some desired situation'. Problem identification is the search for these differences. In the first step of the case analysis process, the existing situation has been examined and, hopefully, understood. In the second step you will need to compare this with the situation you might expect the organization, or individual, described in the case to prefer. This comparison is dealt with in some detail in section 5.3. First, however, a number of general points concerning problems may usefully be made. Although the word 'problem' is used here, 'problem area' might be more appropriate. It is naive to consider that there is only one problem facing an organization at any point in time – there are usually many. It is also unlikely that these problems will be totally unrelated. They usually occur in related clusters. These clusters might more accurately be described as basic problems together with the symptoms that they generate. The complex structures of problems will be examined more closely in section 6.1. Problems may also differ in respect of being current or future and whether they are 'good' or 'bad'. This gives a two-way classification which is illustrated in Figure 5.1.

Many authors like to differentiate between problems, opportunities and threats. In fact, the differences are not really all that great. The distinction between 'good' and 'bad' problems is necessary to separate opportunities from threats. This distinction has little meaning in the present. Presumably a 'good' problem would be one in which the current situation is rather better than desired. It is

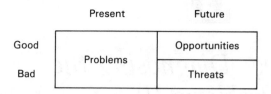

Figure 5.1 Problems, opportunities and threats

difficult to imagine anyone viewing that as a problem. However, in the future an opportunity is clearly a 'good' problem, just as a threat is a 'bad' one. An opportunity provides an organization with the possibility of improving its performance. A threat, if it occurs, will almost certainly cause its performance to deteriorate. But both can be treated as potential problems. When an organization recognizes an opportunity, it sees a gap between what probably will occur and what could occur if it seized the opportunity. In other words, the organization now has a potential problem – how to take advantage of the opportunity. In a similar fashion the organization sees the potential difference between what will happen if the threat comes to pass and if it does not. The problem is how to prevent the threat from occurring or how to minimize its effect if it does occur. Threats and opportunities, it may also be argued, are different because they concern the future. But problems of any kind also concern the future. Obviously, if a problem is only likely to be a problem now and not in the future, it ceases to be a problem. Problems derive their impact from the fact that it is believed that they will continue. In any case, you can only solve problems in the future, not in the past. All of these arguments lead to the following conclusion: opportunities and threats are really just special kinds of problems. You will need to be aware of their special characteristics, but in what follows the term 'problems' will be used in its broadest sense to include both threats and opportunities.

5.2 LISTING PROBLEMS

The first stage in diagnosing problem areas is to list all the problems that you can identify in the case. The list for the Wolverhampton and Dudley Breweries case is given in section 5.3. As stated previously, problems result from the differences between 'what is' and 'what should be'. From your previous analysis you should have a good idea of 'what is'. 'What should be' has now to be determined. In other words you need a set of standards or criteria to judge the current, or expected situation. These standards can come from outside the case situation or they can be the standards that the case characters themselves would employ. Thus there are two basic approaches to the development of problem lists although they can, and should, be combined.

5.2.1 External standards

The most obvious external standards are those of the case instructor. It may be that your instructor will define the problem for you. He or she may say 'concentrate on productivity' or 'the main problem is the attitude of the managing director'. While it is probably unwise to ignore this instruction, it is also unwise to take it too literally. Problems rarely exist in splendid isolation. They are usually related to other problems; they may even be caused by other more fundamental problems. By restricting yourself to just one problem you will usually miss the opportunity of seeing some very creative solutions. It is unlikely that your instructor will penalize you for producing better work even though you ignore the letter of his or her instructions.

In a similar way, the case may contain questions to be answered or a rather explicit statement of a problem. However, you should beware of taking either of these kinds of directions for granted. In the Wolverhampton and Dudley Breweries case the problem is not explicitly identified but it is broadly hinted at. The last paragraph states: 'Against this background observers of WDB were beginning to wonder whether the trading formula which had served the company so well was still appropriate for the 1980s.' The concept of a trading formula is rather quaint but also rather vague so you are left to decide, in rather general terms, whether the company should change what it has been doing. This is not a particularly clearly specified problem nor, in my opinion, should it be. Problems in real life don't come ready labelled and neatly packaged. You need to get used to the idea of using your own judgement to decide what problems there are in a case. In doing so you will be acquiring a very valuable skill.

When you visit a doctor he will, of course, pay some attention to the symptoms you describe. However, he will then go on to make other measurements of your health. He is essentially employing a medical framework of analysis in an attempt to understand the illness you have. He is doing this in two stages. First, he measures the variables that have been demonstrated to be helpful in the diagnosis of illness (temperature, blood pressure, pulse, etc.). Second, he notes which of these values are different from the measurements one would normally expect from a healthy patient. In a similar way you will have to use the frameworks of the disciplines you are learning to help you uncover organizational illness. In Chapter 3 it was suggested that you use the frameworks of the disciplines you are studying to restructure the information in the case. The first step of this diagnosis should therefore be complete. You should have measures, albeit qualitative and imprecise, of some, if not most, of the variables that can be used to describe the dynamics of the organization. You should know what the profitability of the company is, how much it knows about its customers and how it hires people. The next stage is to compare these 'values' with those one would normally expect from a healthy organization. In effect you will be deciding whether this organization complies with generally accepted norms of performance. This immediately raises an enormous problem. You must be aware that the applied social sciences are not exact. There are relatively few general principles which most practitioners and theorists would agree on. There are none if you take the extreme view that principles should admit no exceptions. Some organizations can defy all the current principles of effective organizational behaviour and still succeed. Where does this leave us? At this point in the process you are simply listing possible problems with the purpose of examining them in more detail later. It may be that what is seen as a problem at this stage will not prove to be so later in your analysis. However, it is better to include all the possible problems and then eliminate the doubtful ones later. An inclusive rather than exclusive approach may take rather more time, but the resulting analysis will have fewer gaps and omissions.

The following list of problems was generated for the Wolverhampton and Dudley Breweries case using marketing, strategy and accounting frames of analysis:

Marketing
1. High quality and low price are inconsistent.
2. Apparently no marketing research being done.
3. No market segmentation by pub.
4. Problem of two brand names and possible cannibalization.
5. Confusion as to whether beer or drinking is the product.
6. Low marketing and promotion budget.
7. Local market in decline.

Strategy
1. Vulnerability because of public failure of takeover.

2. Concentration of sales in one product and one area.

3. Much larger competitors.

4. High expectations of investors.

5. Lager dependent on outside suppliers.

6. Risk-averse management.

Accounting

1. High but constant return on investment.

2. Current and acid ratios very low.

3. Undervalued freeholds.

4. High R.O.I due to low investment?

5. Slow-down in rates of profit and sales growth.

In the case of the accounting problems the ratios would need to be compared with those of other regional brewers to discover whether they were too high or too low. This process is described in more detail in a later section. The question mark at the end of problem (4) reminds us that the standards being applied are by no means cut and dried and that this initial listing is both tentative and incomplete.

5.2.2 Internal standards

So far problems have been attributed to organizations: Wolverhampton and Dudley Breweries has this problem or it faces that threat. But organizations are not machines; they are comprised of people and they operate through people. In a sense organizations don't have problems: people do. People perceive problems, are motivated to seek solutions and then are needed to implement them. In some cases people are the problem. People are the link between you, acting as the case analyst, the problems and the solutions. It is impossible to ignore the fact that you have to work with and through people. You have to do this in real life and you cannot afford to ignore it in your case analyses.

There are two main tasks you need to carry out in order to make sure that you specify problems sensibly taking people into account. The first is to clarify the role you will play as the case analyst. The second is to try to determine what the people in the case perceive their problems to be.

Role clarification

Clarifying the role that a student is to take in a case analysis is an area that instructors frequently fall down on. They fail to make it clear to the student who he or she is meant to be. Clarity is of major importance here. If the student doesn't have a role the tendency is to offer vague and general recommendations that are distant from the situation that the people in the case are facing. They are usually not tailored enough to the specific problem and in real life would probably be rejected as impractical. For example, what you recommend would obviously change depending on whether you are the managing director or his young graduate assistant. It is frequently difficult to get down to the nitty-gritty in early case analysis. Being more precise about the role that you are taking greatly helps to prevent operating at too general a level of analysis.

If the instructor fails to make it clear which role you are to take, you should clarify the situation yourself. You may do this directly with the instructor or, if that fails, make your own choice. To help you in this, the two main possibilities are discussed below.

Firstly, you may be asked, or decide, to take the role of one of the characters described in the case. In the Wolverhampton and Dudley Breweries case the obvious choice would be Mr E. J. Thompson, the company chairman. The case is written in such a way as to make the choice fairly obvious. There is certainly one advantage in taking the role of E. J. Thompson: hardly anything is known about him except his comments on the takeover and his family connections with the company. You can make certain assumptions, within reason, about his experience, skills, attitudes and personality. However, it is unlikely that you could 'play yourself' in this role. Few of us have had the experience of being chairman of a major company. The more the character in the case differs from you and the more details there are in the case describing the character, the more difficult it will become for you to play that role convincingly.

In practice there is really only one answer. You need 'to put yourself in the place of' rather than 'take the role of'. You should act as if you had replaced the character concerned rather than attempting to act out his personality. You should still feel constrained by the formal work role and relationship of the position you adopt. A consultant, a chairman or a sales director all have rules that they must adhere to. What is suggested is that you free yourself from the restricting and very difficult task of 'acting in character'. A second and more usual situation is to be asked to act as a consultant to the organization. 'What would you advise the organization to do under these circumstances?' Here you will be looking for more rather than less, clarification. Who could a consultant sensibly be working for in this situation? You can readily make your own decisions on this issue if your instructions are not clear. If the case is given without any guidance as to your role, it is usually best to assume the consultant position. However, make sure that your assumption is explicit; this saves later misunderstandings.

Having clarified your role for yourself, you can now begin to examine your relationships with the other people in the organization. In doing so you may discover even more problems. On the other hand you may solve some of them or realize that in your role they are insoluble and hence better left alone.

Role relationships

Individuals working for an organization will usually have a core of objectives that they hold in common. However, they may not agree on the relative importance of any single objective. In addition, there will be fringe objectives about which they may fundamentally disagree. Since problems are the difference between what is being achieved and an objective or standard, it follows that individuals may not agree on what constitutes a problem. One man's problem may be another man's perfectly satisfactory situation. This is an important point. Problems motivate people to action. The gap between what is and what should be drives people to take measures designed to close that gap. If no problem is perceived, no action results. Alternatively, if a problem is seen where none exists (at least according to you as the analyst), unnecessary actions will result. In both cases this leads to problems resulting from the perception that the people described in the case have of the situation in which they find themselves. Thus, in seeking out problems you need to work out which problems would be crucial for the role you have chosen and at the same time take into account those problems that others are likely to be aware of. There are three sources of standards which people use to measure their current situation and you would do well to check each one to make sure you unearth all the problems you can.

Historic standards

The first source of standards is history. The past is perhaps the most potent source for comparison. If things aren't as good as they used to be, clearly a problem has arisen. The problem may arise in a relative or absolute form. In a commercial organization a fall in profits below last year's will usually be seen as a major problem. For a theatre company a steady decline in audience would be a major cause for concern. In both cases there has been a change in a basic measure of performance. However, relative changes may also be important. In some organizations, used to fast growth, a slowing of that rate might be very worrying although sales, profits and other measures of performance continue to rise. It is a question of what the organization has become used to: history conditions our expectations. Conversely, in some public enterprises management might feel happy to have limited the rate of increase of deficit year on year. The main underlying principle is to judge the current situation in the context of past performance. Any sharp change, either good or bad, is usually a sign that a problem exists. For Wolverhampton and Dudley Breweries profits had been growing, but slower than sales, and real volume had been on the decline. By historic standards their growth performance was beginning to falter. It is tempting to conclude that the bid for Davenport's was a result of this perception of the current situation.

Environmental standards

The second source of standards comes from the environment in which the organization operates. Most frequently a comparison will be made with competing organizations. Are we as profitable as our competitors? Are we as efficient? Are we as socially responsive and responsible? The choice of peer organizations is largely a socio-political one. It may be that an organization would be quite content to simply out-perform other divisions or subsidiaries in the same group. Or it may use the whole industry or market in which it operates as a basis for comparison. A very large multinational organization may only compare itself with organizations that operate on a similar world-wide basis. The peer organizations need not necessarily be in the same business or carry out comparable activities. The standard for comparison may be quite remote. An organization might strive for a 'Rolls-Royce' reputation, 'Marks and Spencer' quality or the team spirit of Liverpool Football Club. In each situation the standard becomes real and important if it drives the organization to do things to meet that standard.

This is an area where external information can usefully be collected. If you know that the case is based on a real situation and the accounts have not been disguised, then it will be well worthwhile attempting to develop your own inter-firm comparison pyramid of ratios. For most types of organizations operating statistics are published and available. Indeed, this type of analysis is very important to accountants. Inter-firm comparison of accounting ratios is a very powerful and frequently employed tool. There are a series of publications and data bases which provide comparative data by firm size or, more importantly, industry group. There exist, however, a number of dangers that it is wise to be aware of in this type of analysis. Clearly, the choice of comparable firms is rather important. It would not be helpful to compare Wolverhampton and Dudley Breweries with one of the major brewers. In addition, even regional brewers of the same size may be rather diversified and hence not comparable. In an industry where every firm is badly run, the standard against which you judge the organization may not be high enough. The reverse argument applies for a very well-managed industry. Comparisons are being made with what is rather than what should be. Also, you may discover that in some major areas an organization performs far worse than any competing organization. However, the organization may not regard this as important: it may not see them as relevant bases for comparison.

Wolverhampton and Dudley Breweries probably compares itself with other regional brewers such as Vaux, Brown Matthew and Greenall Whitley. The management of the company must be aware that its return on capital is high for this group, and indeed for the industry as a whole. However, it must also be aware that it is the largest of the regional brewers not diversifying into other related lines of business. In this respect it is closer in profile to the very small brewers. It might view this difference positively or negatively. At any rate, it will be aware of it and it will guide and constrain the company's actions.

Control standards

A third basis for comparison stems from use of formal planning and control systems within an organization. Typically, this means that an organization decides what it will achieve in a given time period, sets performance standards and compares actual performance with these standards. By definition, a problem arises when a gap (or variance) develops. In this case the standards are set by the organization. These should not, however, be taken at face value. Organizations can create problems by setting very optimistic targets. These may be used as a way of motivating employees. In this case, it is not expected that targets will be met. Conversely, if a pessimistic target is set it must not be assumed that because it is met there is no problem. In both cases it is worth evaluating the targets independently. In the case of Wolverhampton and Dudley Breweries there are no past control figures or future planned or budgeted figures specified.

The closest to objectives or targets is contained in the statement by Mr Thompson: 'However, it resolved a situation which was beginning to inhibit our expansion plans'. Thus it is clear that plans of some kind exist and that they presuppose expansion. Wolverhampton and Dudley Breweries would therefore regard anything which prevented them from expanding as a problem. They have set a standard for the future and if it is not met they will be motivated to do something about it.

5.2.3 Future problems

Problems are only worth considering if they are going to remain problems. It is always a useful exercise therefore to examine the list of problems you have already produced to forecast what might happen to them in the future. Did the problem result from a unique combination of circumstances which is unlikely to occur again? Is the problem likely to continue at its current level? Is it likely to get worse, or to get better?

One of the most obvious problems for Wolverhampton and Dudley Breweries is the decline in draught beer sales. A crucial question for them is whether the phenomenon is purely temporary or permanent, so that the product will eventually disappear. There is no way of telling without relating this trend to other trends which you believe may be causing it. This in itself may not give you an answer. If the trends are, for example, demographic, then it is often possible to forecast their future values. If beer will only be drunk by the over-45-year-olds, then you can estimate the future size of that group with some accuracy and judge whether the problem is going to get better or worse. However, if the trend is more social in nature, such as a move to lighter-tasting drinks, then there is no way of knowing whether it is likely to continue. You will have to come to a judgement based upon a model of society and what drives its behaviour. Threats and opportunities are potential future problems. They can be identified in the present, but have not yet occurred and, of course, may not do so. In some case studies a threat or opportunity may be the central problem. For Wolverhampton and Dudley Breweries a major threat is that of a competitor attacking its home market. There are reasons why this has not happened in the past and these will be discussed in more detail in the next chapter. However, conditions are changing and it could be argued that the threat is now more likely than it has been in the past. In addition, while the shares are obviously closely held, there is a possibility that Wolverhampton and Dudley Breweries itself could become a victim of a hostile takeover bid. Another threat comes from changing technology. It is possible that ways of packaging draught beers will emerge which will allow drinkers to have a draught pint at their firesides. These are just some of the many possibilities.

There are a number of opportunities of which Wolverhampton and Dudley Breweries could avail itself. The most obvious of these is the increasing importance of traditionally brewed beers. While overall sales are in decline, sales of many traditional beers are not, and indeed new breweries designed to meet these tastes are appearing. It is also likely that a number of the regional brewers who have moved away from traditional brewing will find themselves in financial trouble and may come up for sale. It is often difficult when identifying opportunities not to stray into putting forward solutions to existing problems. For example, an opportunity might exist to franchise Wolverhampton and Dudley Breweries' brand names. In a sense this is halfway between an opportunity and a solution. Wolverhampton and Dudley Breweries would be creating an opportunity rather than taking advantage of one. There is a fine dividing line. However the most important point is to ensure that the issue is considered at some stage in the analysis rather than worrying about what category it falls into.

5.3 PROBLEM LISTING FOR WOLVERHAMPTON AND DUDLEY BREWERIES

Attacking the Wolverhampton and Dudley Breweries case from a number of different directions has generated the unordered list of some of the problems it may be facing set out below. Notice that threats and opportunities are also included. You should aim to produce a similar list as the first stage of diagnosing the problem in any case that you tackle.

(a) Bid failure

(b) Expansion plans confounded

(c) Concentrated in one area

(d) Expectations of City and stockholders

(e) Continuing decline in beer sales

(f) Restricted management expertise and risk-averse behaviour

(g) Two brand names

(h) Highly concentrated in brewing

(i) Reliance on outside suppliers for lager, spirits, etc.

(j) Confusion between brewing and retailing

(k) Low perception of mild quality outside local area

(l) Low price/high quality expectations by local market

(m) Low promotion and marketing budget

(n) High proportion of managed pubs

(o) Increasing competition within area, especially in the free trade

(p) 'Other' activities marginalized

(q) Threat from competitors, especially Whitbread

(r) Unemployment in local area

(s) Changing tastes

(t) Changing patterns of leisure

(u) Increasing importance of traditional beer segment

(v) Possibility that small brewers may come up for acquisition

(w) Slow-down in rates of profit and sales growth

(x) Investment in Davenport's

(y) No marketing research being done

(z) Confusion about whether the product is the pub or the beer

The list is terminated because there are no letters of the alphabet left! What is being demonstrated is that any case will contain a large number of problems. You will now have to decide how they are related, which are the most important, and whether there are any you have missed.

Step Two: Diagnosing the Problems (II)

6.1 UNDERSTANDING PROBLEM AREAS

You now have a list of 'raw' problems. Some will be important; some will not. Some will be clear and explicit, others will be diffuse and difficult to describe. Perhaps most important of all, many of the problems will be related. It will be your task in the next stage to explore and clarify those relationships. They are important for two reasons. First, if you attempt to solve a problem without reference to other problems the organization is facing, you may get into difficulties. It may be that the problem you are concerned with can only be tackled after another related problem has been solved. For example, in the Wolverhampton and Dudley Breweries case, it would not be very sensible to tackle the problem of expansion without knowing how that is likely to affect sales in the home territory. It could happen that solving one problem may make another problem worse. Increasing price would probably accelerate the decline in beer sales. These two problems cannot really be tackled if they are isolated. There is a second, and more positive, reason for clarifying the relationships between problems. Certain problems occur as the symptoms of more basic problems. If you can identify these key problems, you may be able to solve a whole array of problems 'at a stroke'. This is not always going to be the case. However, it will at least give you an idea of which problems are more fundamental and should therefore be given priority and time.

The process of building towards a comprehensive understanding of the totality of problems facing an organization is probably best tackled in three phases. The first stage involves setting up your initial working hypotheses or models. You can do this by organizing your 'raw' list of problems into a number of different problem areas. A problem area is defined as a group of related problems. For each problem area you will then tentatively need to specify the relationships that you believe exist between individual problems. The result will be a number of 'skeletons' which map out the problem areas you have identified.

The second stage is to put flesh on these 'skeletons'. To do this you will have to theorize, collect evidence, check out your theories and continue to refine and review until you are happy that you have a good understanding of each problem area.

The third stage is to prepare problem statements for each problem area. This is important not only to clarify and summarize your own thoughts, but also to allow you to communicate them later when you are presenting your findings.

6.1.1 Structuring problem areas

Your task under this heading will be to group problems into problem areas and try to link them. To do this you will need to understand three concepts which deal with causal relationships, i.e. relationships which describe cause and effect. The three concepts are symptoms, multicausality and mutual causality.

Symptoms

Not all problems are created equal – some are more fundamental than others. Some problems cause other problems to occur. A flu virus might give rise to a headache, sore throat and aching joints. These are symptoms of the basic problem: the action of a virus. In a similar way it will be useful in organizing problem areas to distinguish between problems and symptoms. One such 'vertical' relationship from the Wolverhampton and Dudley Breweries case is tentatively mapped out in Figure 6.1. The arrows indicate a causal relationship. In this case decline in beer sales in the Wolverhampton and Dudley Breweries area is thought to lead to increased likelihood of entry into the local market by one of the major brewers, a slow-

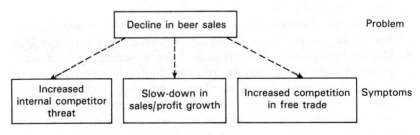

Figure 6.1 Problem/sympton relationship

down in sales/profits growth for the firm and an increase in competition in the free trade in the area.

One way of testing a problem/symptom relationship is to ask whether the symptoms would disappear if the problem were solved. In the situation modelled in Figure 6.1, it is likely (but not certain) that resumption in growth (in real terms) of beer sales would lead to an increase in the rate of growth of sales and profits and a reduction in external competition: the problem/symptom relationship is reversible. However, there may be situations where this is not the case. A problem may result in the creation of another problem which is irreversible. That is to say, removal of the problem will not result in disappearance of the symptom. For example, Wolverhampton and Dudley Breweries' competitors may discover that they are highly competitive in the free trade and remain there even though beer sales increase. There is an important principle at stake here. You will usually concentrate your attention on the more fundamental problems facing an organization. You must be careful not to assume that in solving these basic problems all other problems will disappear. To remind you, it is probably good practice when drawing problem diagrams to indicate reversible relationships with a dotted line and arrow and irreversible relationships with a solid line and arrow.

Symptoms can also be important in their own right. Once they are brought into existence, by more fundamental problems, they can create further sets of symptoms. In other words, they in turn become problems in relation to another set of symptoms. The slow-down in profits may reduce share prices and make it difficult for Wolverhampton and Dudley Breweries to carry through its expansion plans, especially if they involve takeover or merger activity. A whole hierarchy of problems and their associated symptoms and, in turn, the symptoms created by those symptoms, can occur. The symptoms/problem distinction is only useful in reminding you of their relationship one to another. In terms of improving the situation, the removal of both problems and symptoms is highly desirable.

Multicausality

A second major concept to be aware of is that of multicausality. This simply recognizes the fact that many symptoms are caused by more than one problem. This may once again be illustrated by means of a simple problem diagram (see Figure 6.2). The symptoms are presented in a short-hand form in the diagram. What this diagram means is that there are probably a variety of reasons, not all shown here, for the decline in beer sales in the Wolverhampton and Dudley

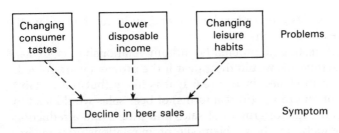

Figure 6.2 Multicausality: local market changes problem area

Breweries' area. Not all of the problems would have an equal impact upon the symptom. But it would be difficult to estimate the relative impact of each. Judgement rather than mathematics is the only way to resolve this issue.

Multicausality introduces horizontal relationships into the structuring of problems. It forces you to face the complexity of problem areas as they appear in case descriptions. Multicausality has another unfortunate side effect. If two problems help to produce the one symptom, then removal of one of the problems may not lead to the disappearance of that symptom. In the illustration above this is exactly the problem that has to be faced. It might be possible, for example, to alter the habits of pub-going locally by spending money creatively on pub decor. However, if this is a minor cause of the decline in beer sales, then the symptom will not disappear. On the other hand, it is possible to find situations where it is the combination of two problems that creates the symptom. When one disappears then the other has no effect: a necessary but not sufficient condition for the symptom to occur. For example, it could be argued that Wolverhampton and Dudley Breweries' desire for expansion is caused by a combination of City expectations and lowered growth rate. If either are removed, the need for expansion is no longer there. The complex relationship between problems and symptoms that multicausality leads to means that you cannot always expect to solve one problem and then watch everything else drop into place. On the other hand, it does mean that you are unlikely to offer simplistic and naive single-cause solutions to complex organizational problems.

Mutual causality

Causality may sometimes work both ways. In other words, problem A may cause problem B which may, in turn, cause problem A. If these are problems, this may be described as a vicious circle. If they are opportunities, they might be said to comprise a virtuous circle. For example, it is arguable that the decline in beer sales could lead to changes in leisure habits as breweries close old pubs or convert them into other kinds of leisure establishments, which in turn help to change leisure habits. Such relationships are always tricky to model since it is possible that the cycle will break at some point and go into reverse. Nostalgia for the old days may create new types of pubs which in turn reinvigorate the sales of draught beers. Nevertheless, you cannot afford to ignore the point that some problems and their symptoms have this mutual characteristic. In the diagrams used here mutual causality is indicated by double-headed arrows.

Problem diagrams

Having understood the concepts of symptoms, multicausality and mutual causality you are now ready to work on your list of raw problems. Your objective is to draw up problem diagrams which are your preliminary ideas or hypotheses of the problem areas and their structures. The type of system diagram used in the figures in this section is well suited to the structuring of problem areas. Verbal descriptions usually lack clarity and are difficult to manipulate. Mathematical descriptions of problems are rarely possible in case studies. Systems diagrams represent a useful middle ground.

You may begin by simply grouping together those problems which seem to you to be related. An alternative approach is to pick out what you believe the fundamental problems to be and then to fit the other problems/symptoms around them. You should attempt to fit in all your problems somewhere. Figure 6.3 is a problem diagram which incorporates most of Wolverhampton and Dudley Breweries' problems as listed in section 5.3. These problems have been grouped into a number of major problem areas, identified by the use of dotted lines.

Some problems were excluded in order to keep the diagram relatively simple. For example, the problem of having two brand names is part of the marketing problem of Wolverhampton and Dudley Breweries in the local area. Others were considered isolated and less important. For example, the investment in Davenport's has other implications but these were thought to be less crucial than the problems included. Isolated problems usually tend to be either relatively trivial or else problems about which there is very little information.

Note that the major problem areas are almost all linked together. In some cases the linkage is so close that the separation appears

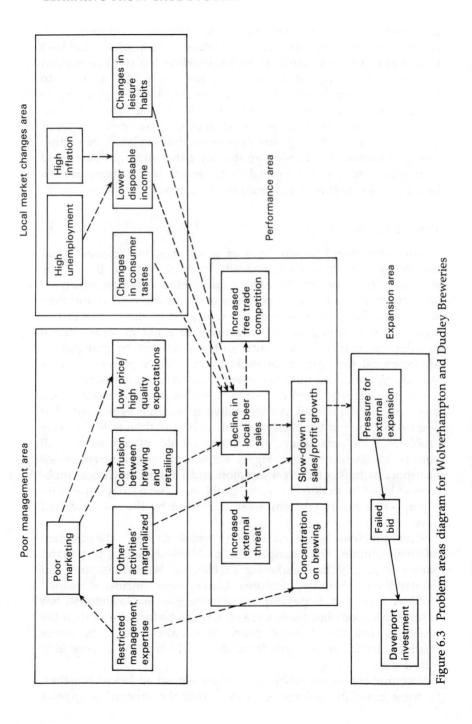

Figure 6.3 Problem areas diagram for Wolverhampton and Dudley Breweries

somewhat arbitrary. This is not very important. The boundaries can always be redrawn in the next stage when the relationships are examined in more detail. Where the links are relatively remote the problems can be treated separately.

It must be emphasized that this is a preliminary sketch. Many of the links are tentative. In some cases it may be felt that other factors may influence a problem but that these have not been identified yet. This is indicated by a question mark and an arrow or an empty box. Nevertheless, diagrams like this form a basis from which to work: a series of hypotheses to check out. In the next section ways in which you can develop and refine this model – putting flesh on the bare bones – will be discussed.

6.1.2 Developing problem areas

The problem area diagrams are essentially frameworks which attempt to capture the problems facing an organization. The next step is to develop those structures; to test and refine the hypotheses you have proposed. The output of this stage of your analysis will be to define, as best as you can, the problems as you see them. This will form the basis of your subsequent analysis and therefore require careful thought and a lot of work.

Developing your problem model is best viewed as a cyclical process comprising three different activities – testing, restructuring and elaborating. Testing means checking the structure you have proposed for each problem area to see if it is consistent with the available evidence. If either a problem or a relationship between symptoms/problems looks suspect, then you might decide to restructure. Finally, when you are happy that the overall structure works, you will want to look at certain key problems and relationships in order to map them out in more detail: to elaborate them. At any stage you may decide to go back or forward to another stage in the process. Looking at a problem in detail may suggest a new structure which then needs testing. Testing a relationship might reveal some interesting ways in which it could be made more detailed. Each activity depends on and is related to the others. The important point is to keep your eye on the goal: detailed, logically structured, well-researched definitions of the problems. All three activities require you to do further research and collect more information. The information can come from a number of different sources. These have already been identified in Chapter 3. It may be worthwhile to remind yourself what these sources are and their main characteristics. Using information in this context is, however, somewhat different from the way in which you will have used it earlier in your analysis. Now you are concerned with specific relationships. You should therefore be in a position to define fairly precisely what information you require. This in turn will make it easier to find.

Testing, restructuring and elaborating are closely linked activities and will be discussed together using the decline in beer sales, changes in tastes, leisure habits and disposable income relationships as illustrated in the problem diagram, Figure 6.3. There are two aspects of any relationship which you will be interested in testing – strength and direction. At one extreme the strength of a relationship may be zero, i.e. there is no relationship between the two problems. At the other extreme one problem may be the single, unequivocal cause of a particular symptom. Some relationships exist by definition. For example, if there is no growth in either the beer or 'other' activities markets, then there is no growth overall. When a problem, like decline in the beer market in the West Midlands, has a number of possible causes, then it is obviously of great importance to estimate the relative strength of each. Only in this way can you concentrate your efforts on solving the key, rather than subsidiary, problems: in this given situation, which is the most important factor? The direction of the relationship may also be important. It has already been pointed out that, because a problem has created a symptom, this does not mean that when the problem has been solved the symptom will also disappear. In this case it is by no means clear that an increase in disposable income, or in people returning to pubs, will increase beer sales. They may spend their money on other things. However, if people choose beer rather than lager, this will affect beer sales, though modified by the other two factors. Every relationship should be examined to see whether it is reversible or not.

As has already been described, causality need not run in just one direction. In some cases it may be impossible to discover in which direction it flows. For example, the relationship between decline in beer sales and changes in leisure habits can operate in either or both directions. Fewer people drinking beer in pubs but more consuming alternative drinks may lead some regulars to decide not to go to the pub any more. Restructuring is the process of looking at the variables you already have and deciding whether the relationships you originally specified are sensible or whether some other structure of relationships might not be better. You may decide to change the direction of causality. You may cut out old links or add new ones.

Elaboration is the next stage in the process. It is unlikely that you will capture the complexity of the situation in your first effort. More likely you will decide that one problem is actually several problems cunningly combined. You will then wish to unpack these problems and explore the relationships among them in more detail. Obviously this is an entirely sensible process. You will feel that you are getting closer to the 'truth'. However, there are limits. Clearly you could continue this process almost indefinitely. At some point there are diminishing returns on your comprehension. There is always a tendency to over-elaborate. In the end it comes down to judgement. One important criterion is the importance of the problem area you are tackling. If it is the key area as far as you are concerned, then it deserves more attention. If it is not, leave it unelaborated.

Let us look at an example to see how the various relationships might be tested, restructured and elaborated. Remember you are not looking for evidence that a problem exists. You have already satisfied yourself earlier that it does. In testing you are concerned with the relationships between problems. Does problem A have an effect on problem B, and if so how strong is that effect? Our example is the problem area that is concerned with changes in the local market. Looking first at the change in consumer tastes, what evidence is there to suggest that people's tastes are moving away from draught bitter and mild? There is substantial evidence in the case that the consumption of other kinds of drinks, particularly lager, is increasing rapidly, so there appears to be a substitution effect. In addition the same trends are occurring in other countries. Furthermore, we know that there is a general trend in society for people to prefer food and drink that is 'lighter' and more bland. Such evidence is brought from outside the case, but there is no reason to doubt its validity providing it is used to support and not to confirm. On the other hand, beer sales as a whole were increasing until 1978 so we should not be too hasty to assume that this is a long-term trend.

As has already been suggested above, the link between declining beer sales and changing tastes may involve mutual causality. Declining beer sales may reinforce changes in tastes and lead to a declining spiral. Thus the diagram could be restructured by adding another arrow to the link between the two variables.

Another problem in working through this relationship has to do with age cohorts. Is it likely that seasoned beer drinkers are giving up beer drinking and switching over to Martini? Surely it is partly due to the fact that younger people are no longer beginning their drinking careers with heavy beers but are starting on lager and short drinks. This is stated as a fact in the case, but it would be interesting to check it out with external data. Nevertheless, it tallies with experience so we would be wise to accept it for the time being. Thus we need to elaborate by splitting the changing tastes box into one concerned with the tastes of new, and one with the tastes of existing, drinkers. To know how important these differences might be we could also add a box which is concerned with the demographic changes predicted for these two groups. In this situation, however, the demographic factor is judged to be not so significant that it deserves a separate box. But this is not likely to be the end of the story. Some middle-aged drinkers are likely to be switching from beer to lighter drinks, so we need to remind ourselves of that possibility and to wonder how much of the decline is due to this factor.

The next step is to bring in the change in leisure habits and explore how that is likely to interact with the change in tastes. People are drinking at home and in clubs more often and therefore fewer people are drinking in pubs. In addition, drinking in pubs is undergoing a change too. Young people and families are more likely to use pubs as social centres. All of these factors are likely to lead to fewer pints of beer being consumed. We might think of restructuring the original relationships by adding an arrow between changes in tastes and changes in leisure habits to show that these two factors are related. If pubs are more like social centres, people are less likely to drink a lot of beer.

Lower disposable income has also been proposed as a factor which is affecting beer sales. This in turn is believed to be caused by both high unemployment and high inflation. It could be argued that lower disposable income will slow the trend to changes in taste since most alternatives to beer are rather more expensive. However, it is also known that reductions in income do not necessarily affect fundamental changes in consumer attitudes and behaviour. I am assuming that relationship holds in this instance. In other words, I am choosing a particular view of the situation which is not taken from case data but is an assumption about how the world works. It is frequently essential to import assumptions and, as pointed out earlier, you cannot do case analysis without it. Thus, lower disposable income is not related to changes in tastes or in leisure habits but is seen to be an independent factor affecting beer sales. Another major assumption is that the factors which affect beer sales in the West Midlands are the same as those in the rest of the country. It could be argued that there are special local factors, to do with local tastes and the concentration of pubs, so that beer sales are less affected by forces operating at a national level. However, beer sales are falling in volume terms though it may not be as much as elsewhere. It does, however, seem to be enough to spark Wolverhampton and Dudley

Breweries into action, so the structure of the model (see Figure 6.4) seems to describe the situation reasonably well.

The process of detailing and elaboration must be carried out with judgement. It obviously will not pay to examine each problem or relationship in the same detail. Here the problem diagram is a great help. It enables you to see the overall structure of a problem area and hence to concentrate your attention on the crucial areas. The output from this stage of the diagnosis will be a fairly elaborate systems diagram of the major problem areas. The next stage is to codify this knowledge by means of succinct problem statements.

6.1.3 Stating the problems

You have reached the end of a long and somewhat complex process at this point. It is now time to take stock and summarize your position. This serves two purposes. First, it will help you to clear up any inconsistencies and errors that may have crept into your analysis of the problem areas you have uncovered. By stating the problems in another way, you will have a chance to review and improve on your understanding. The whole of the rest of the analysis you do will be based upon the problem areas as you have described them. It is hardly an exaggeration to say that completing the definition of the problem takes you more than halfway through the total analytical process. It pays to make sure that the problems are defined as accurately as possible. Students frequently make the mistake of rushing on and attempting to solve problems they have inadequately understood. It then becomes very easy for a case instructor, or fellow student, to knock out the shaky foundations and reduce the elaborate recommendations and plans to rubble.

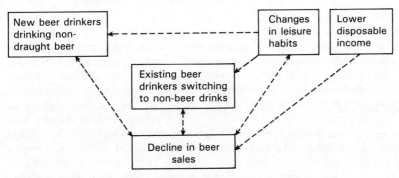

Figure 6.4 Local market changes: problem area diagram elaborated

The second reason for summarizing your understanding of the problem areas is because at some point you will have to communicate and justify your viewpoint. Your current views will largely be in the form of systems diagrams and notes. At some time these will have to be converted back into a form which can be communicated orally or in writing. It is better to do this when the material is fresh in your mind. It may become unintelligible if you leave transcribing it to a later date! Case instructors usually recognize the importance of the problem diagnosis phase and will reward students who tackle this task well, even though the solutions proposed may not be particularly creative or well chosen. It will therefore pay you to spend time polishing problem statements. Discussions of problem areas also occur early in case sessions. The student who can briefly and cogently outline the key problem areas, and the evidence which supports these views, will stand out. Later in the session discussion usually becomes more ragged and it is more difficult to get over a closely argued and complicated viewpoint.

Problem area statements will usually be verbal. This is the form of communication which works best in a case discussion or an oral presentation. For a written presentation, systems diagrams or even mathematical equations can be used, but these are better used sparingly. Problem area statements should be as concise as possible – they should point out the gaps that have created the problems and symptoms. They should also broadly indicate the relationships among problems within a problem area. Problem statements should, as far as possible, avoid giving the appearance of a solution. Sometimes this will be impossible. In general, though, you will want to leave room for a number of alternative solutions to be considered. Below is a problem statement for the 'decline in beer sales' problem area in the Wolverhampton and Dudley Breweries case.

Wolverhampton and Dudley Breweries: 'Local market changes' problem area
Sales of draught mild and bitter draught beers have begun to decline nationally. Because of the strong local tradition of beer drinking associated with heavy industry combined with the quality of the product and its low price, it is likely that the decline is less severe locally than nationally. However, the same factors which are judged to be causing the national decline are presumed to be operating locally. Long term there are fewer people drinking draught beer because young drinkers, who prefer lighter drinks, are replacing older, traditional beer drinkers in the population. In addition, leisure habits are changing so that pubs are becoming more family-oriented. This drives out traditional beer drinkers and encourages a new light-drinking clientele. Even traditional beer drinkers may switch to lager or other light drinks as a result of social pressure. In the short term high unemployment and inflation have led to reduced

consumption of all alcoholic drinks but have probably hit beer sales more than non-beer sales.

In addition to making a problem statement you might wish to list the evidence in support of the statement. This can be in the form of short notes, simply to remind you why you have said what you have said. A problem statement should be completed for all the problem areas you have identified. In the next stage you will need to begin to choose among these problem areas and decide which should have prior attention.

6.2 CHOOSING PROBLEM AREAS

You will usually manage, in most case studies, to identify a relatively large number of problem areas. The next challenge is to choose which problem to solve. You will have limited time and resources and you will obviously wish to use them to the best advantage.

The first point that should be made is that you should tackle only one problem area at a time. In theory this could lead you into difficulties – problem areas are related, and it could be that a piecemeal approach could lead you to solutions which make other problems worse. Nevertheless, it is almost impossible in even the simplest case to keep all the balls in the air at once. Solving all the problem areas simultaneously is just too difficult an intellectual problem. The best compromise is to treat them sequentially and then go through the whole array of solutions making sure that they are consistent. This process will be touched upon later in the evaluation stages of the case analysis process. Given that problem areas are to be tackled one by one it is necessary to have some means of establishing priority among them. Five criteria have been established which should help you in your decision:

1. The first criterion is that of importance to the role player you have chosen to identify with. However, rather than attempt a sophisticated analysis that attempts, at this stage of the analysis, to distinguish between the role player's goals and those of the organization, it is probably best to regard them as synonymous. Any problem area which creates a threat to the organization in its pursuit of organizational goals is clearly going to require early attention. The ultimate threat would of course be extinction. Most cases involve less dramatic situations than this. Nevertheless, it is usually possible to distinguish between problems that are likely to have different effects on an organization's growth, activity, profits

or other measure of organizational achievement. Obviously, the more important the problem area, the higher its priority.

2. A second criterion is that of urgency. A major problem which can only be tackled in the long term might take second place to a problem that requires your attention now. It is important to attempt to judge the time scale of problems. One way to do this is to decide what is the last moment you could leave the problem before it became insoluble, or created an irreversible situation that you would prefer did not occur. The nearer the deadline, the more urgent the problem. Again it is obvious that, other things being equal, urgent problems should be attempted first.

3. The third criterion has less to do with the problem, more to do with the solution. In general it is probably wise to start with the easiest problems: problems which look as though they will be relatively easy to solve. Apart from the obvious psychological boost of working quickly through the easiest problems, there is also a theoretical reason for this principle. Easy problems usually have a number of solutions. If the more difficult problems are tackled later and if there is a conflict or inconsistency between the solutions to the difficult and easy problems, then alternative solutions to the easy problems can be substituted. In the extreme, insoluble problems should be eliminated altogether. These will usually be problems over which the organization, or the case analyst, has little or no control. They should be noted and then ignored.

4. Some problem areas have more leverage than others. The fourth criterion has to do with this quality. It is really a matter of productivity. Problem areas tend to be linked to a greater or lesser extent. If you can solve a problem which casts its shadow over a number of other problem areas, then this is a highly productive move.

5. Finally, there is an educational criterion. The first four criteria ignore the fact that case studies are educational experiences with educational objectives. This must be reflected in your choice of problem area priorities. Case instructors may set cases in order for you to employ particular techniques or concepts, or else to examine a particular aspect of organizational life in some detail. This may lead you to ignore the important, urgent, central problems in favour of problems which allow you to practise particular skills. However, it is also acceptable in my view that you should concentrate your attention on problem areas which allow you to practise the skills you wish to learn rather than those your instructor would prefer you to learn.

The most important, urgent, easiest, central and educationally desirable problem area is the problem to start with. However, as usually happens in these cases, the most important problem may be the most difficult. The most central problem is the least educationally desirable. A compromise is called for; trade-offs must be made. In the Wolverhampton and Dudley Breweries case the choice is to examine the decline in local beer sales as the priority problem area. The first attempt at expansion, in itself a response to this problem, has not been successful. It would seem that the firm might wish to examine the basic problem before trying to find long-term solutions elsewhere. Sales decline in the existing market is probably the most important threat to future survival. In addition it is reasonably urgent, highly central, but not a particularly easy problem to solve.

6.3 GUIDE TO USE

All case analysts, whether experienced or beginners, will probably gain something from reading section 5.2 on understanding the nature of problems, opportunities and threats. A beginner case analyst will probably wish to keep to a simple problem listing (section 5.3) and then choose among these problems using the ideas discussed in section 6.2.

The next stage of development will involve moving from a simple problem listing to problem structuring (6.1.1) and problem area development (6.1.2) before summarizing the analysis done at this stage through problem statements (6.1.3).

Step Three: Creating Alternative Solutions

Step three begins with the creation of alternative solutions to the problems identified in step two. These need to be combined and organized so that choosing among solutions can be carried out efficiently, in a series of stages.

7.1 PROBLEMS AND SOLUTIONS

Developing solutions will be tackled in a similar way to that used for identifying problems. First a bank of possible solutions will be developed and then this will be organized and combined in much the same way that problem areas were created. This method of producing solutions relies on two principles governing creativity. Finding solutions is, after all, the key creative process in the whole of your analysis. Firstly, all other things being equal, the more solutions produced the better the final choice is likely to be. There must of course be limits to this process. Too many solutions make the task of judging them very difficult. Nevertheless, it is probably best to have an embarrassment of riches rather than the reverse. The second principle is that you should postpone judgement of newly created ideas. Creative thought leapfrogs: one idea leads to another. Killing an idea at birth, because it seems at first glance impractical, may close a potentially fruitful line of thought.

All of this suggests that the problem, rather than the problem area, should be used as the basic unit of operation. If you try to develop a consistent set of solutions for a whole problem area, you will inhibit creativity. The need to be consistent will exclude many, perhaps very interesting, solutions to individual problems. What is more, solutions for one problem may suggest other solutions for other problems. The process must be kept freewheeling and free from constraint.

7.1.1 Importance of creativity

The importance of creativity in this step of the case analysis can hardly be over-emphasized. Students of the case method usually perform this task rather badly. It is not that students using the case method are inherently less creative than students using other learning experiences; it is more an attitudinal problem. Case instructors and texts usually stress the logical nature of case work. Cases are said to be about logical problem solving: creating order out of chaos. This is true, but it is only half the story. Problem solving requires creativity too. In many ways the results of creative work tend to be more important than the results of logical thought. Ask a manager which he would rather have, a beautifully described problem with no hint as to how it might be solved or a creative solution to an ill-defined problem. Most would see the value of the former while choosing the latter.

It is quite commonplace to find that case students propose rather pedestrian solutions to the pressing problems facing an organization. However, there is a relatively straightforward way around this. First it has been shown that if people are specifically told to be creative, then their creative productivity increases enormously. It seems that some kind of permission is required before people will allow themselves to indulge in flights of fancy. I am doing more than giving you permission: I am urging you to be creative. I have no doubt you will find it an exhilarating process. You will also find that your case analyses will benefit from a dose of 'blue sky' thinking. A second point is that creativity can be improved by the use of creativity techniques. These techniques will be discussed in some detail in section 7.3.3. Sitting down in front of a blank sheet of paper can be daunting. A few simple but productive hints are all that is required to get over any creative block that you may experience.

7.1.2 Relationship of problems to solutions

Problems and solutions do not necessarily have a one-to-one relationship. In generating solutions you should be aware of this because it should influence the way in which you create and define your solutions. There are three possible relationships between problems and solutions and these are best described in terms of a simple diagram, as illustrated in Figure 7.1.

In situation 1 the solution fits the problem exactly. That does not necessarily mean that it is the best, or even a good, solution. What it means is that the solution is only concerned with that problem.

In the Wolverhampton and Dudley Breweries case, for example, offering price discounts to the unemployed may or may not solve the problem of lower disposable income. It has a one-to-one relationship with the original problem and only a tenuous connection with any other.

The second situation is perhaps more common. A solution may prove to be only a partial solution. In this case it becomes necessary to add another solution to the original in order to fully encompass the problem. You should be aware when you are proposing only partial solutions. It is probably best to form a compound solution immediately; otherwise you may forget that you have left half of the problem hanging in mid-air. Again, Wolverhampton and Dudley Breweries provides an example. Lowering the price may help with the lower disposable income problem, but that may not be sufficient to halt even the temporary decline in sales if some other actions are not taken to counter the effect of changes in tastes and leisure habits.

In the third situation one solution may encompass a number of different problems. Merging with a national brewer is a solution of this kind. It might help declining sales in the local area, offer a route for expansion and profit growth and provide new management expertise. In this case it is wise to include the solution under the headings of all the problems it might help to solve. Broad-ranging solutions may have another characteristic: they may not only offer solutions to several problems but may also reveal new opportunities. In the example given above the size of the combined group would allow Wolverhampton and Dudley Breweries to move into the packaged supermarket trade with its mild, something it was unlikely to be able to do on its own.

7.1.3 General solutions

Problems have been identified and need to be solved. They should therefore be the starting point when looking for solutions. However, they should not constrain you from looking beyond to, perhaps,

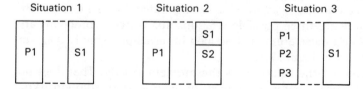

Figure 7.1 Problems and solutions

defining new problems or hopefully new opportunities. What you recommend will be judged on how far forward it pushes the organization, and your chosen role player, towards achieving their goals; this may move far beyond simply solving today's problems.

Thus it is best to keep your solutions fairly general at this stage. For example, one solution to the problem of declining beer sales is to lower the price. This is probably at about the right level of generality as it stands, but you can see that this has within it a whole galaxy of alternatives. How much should it be decreased? 5%? 10%? Should it be confined to the trade or passed on to the public? Should it be in the form of price promotions and if so, long or short term? Restricting solutions to a general nature makes organizing them easier. It both reduces the number to be dealt with and clarifies the main alternatives. Having decided that, at a general level, one alternative is better than another, it then becomes relatively straightforward to decide how that alternative is to be implemented in detail. This top-down approach will be discussed further in section 7.4. For now the advice is not to get involved in detail but to try to see the broad problem–solution picture.

7.2 SOURCES FOR SOLUTIONS

7.2.1 Experience and knowledge

One of the most frequently used sources of inspiration for problem solutions is experience. Having faced similar problems in the past we are often apt to try again the solutions which worked then. This does not imply that you must have extensive organizational experience. We all meet problems in our day-to-day existence with other individuals, groups or institutions. We have a rich background of experience to draw on simply from our knowledge of day-to-day life.

A second source of ideas is knowledge of how other people tackle their problems. Again, we normally have a vast store of secondhand knowledge which can prove to be a treasure trove of possible solutions. In addition, if imagination fails, it is always possible specifically to seek out information about people or organizations facing problems similar to those you are now facing. In your development of solutions, experience and knowledge will be only one source of inspiration. There should be little need to emphasize that experience and other people's solutions may not be a good guide to action. Organizational decision making is frequently hidebound by what has worked in the past. In case study situations you can afford to break free from convention and broaden your problem-solving horizons.

7.2.2 Academic disciplines

As mentioned a number of times earlier, it is unlikely that you will be using case studies in a vacuum. You will normally be using them after, or in parallel with, a course based on an academic discipline such as management, social administration or education. In general it is the applied social sciences that make use of case studies for training purposes. The applied nature of these disciplines means that they have developed a body of normative principles, strategies and tactics which have proved useful or successful in situations which form their focus of study. These principles, strategies and tactics will therefore form a bank of possible solutions from which you may choose. For example, in marketing there are the strategies of market segmentation, market penetration, market development, product development and diversification. In purchasing you might think about vendor-rating schemes, multiple sourcing, materials management and value analysis. As a student of production you would wish to see GANTT charts, critical path analysis, line of balance and linear programming work. You will know what are the relevant principles in your own discipline and will need to search among them for any that are applicable.

In many ways your basic discipline should be your first and most important source of solutions. After all, you should not have to reinvent the wheel each time you face a problem. Other minds have developed powerful tools. It seems inefficient not to consider them. It will also be more appealing to your instructor if you can show that you have at least considered the possibility that what you have been taught has real-life application.

Again, a word of caution. It has already been pointed out that cases have no single analytical solution. The strategy you may decide to include as one possible solution will usually be couched in very general terms. You will have to do a certain amount of bridge building before you can convert it into a specific and usable solution. For example, market segmentation might seem an excellent strategy for Wolverhampton and Dudley Breweries. It would recognize that there are different groups of consumers in the local area who might be more responsive to differentiated offerings that are targeted to their particular needs. Again, it should be emphasized that this is only one source of possible solutions. Too great a concentration on discipline-based solutions may help your understanding of the subject but it will restrict the skills you learn. No applied social science is yet at the stage where case studies become merely exercises in applying principles.

7.2.3 Creativity techniques

Perhaps the most venerable of all creativity techniques is brain-storming. This presents something of a problem to the case analyst since it is essentially a group technique. Of course, it may be that you will be working in a group, in which case brain-storming techniques are particularly appropriate for one session during the preparation of a group presentation.

The basic principles of brain-storming have been encapsulated as 'Postpone judgement, freewheel, hitch-hike, quantity breeds quality'. These can be interpreted in the following practical way. Write every idea down, no matter how stupid or irrelevant it seems. Relax and let ideas come, rather than trying to concentrate on logical progressions of thought. Use your list of ideas to generate new ideas. Keep on, even though your list is long and productivity seems to be flagging. This is the first stage of the brain-storming technique. The second stage involves evaluating the list of ideas you have generated, one for each problem. Many will be immediately discarded, some will be retained for further examination and some will be identified as possible winners. The latter category solutions can pass directly into the next stage of your analysis – organizing solutions.

Modifications to the basic brain-storming format can provide additional stimuli. It often helps to think of a random idea which you then have to link back to the original stimulus. For example, beer is made from hops. Hops suggests athletics: perhaps sponsorship of local sports might be a useful form of promotion. Alternatively, hops suggests leaping over something. Perhaps Wolverhampton and Dudley Breweries should consider linking up with other small brewers in non-adjacent areas, such as Devon or Cornwall. Reverse brain-storming forces you to think of new ideas by reversing key elements in the problem/solution situation. Could the problem conceal an opportunity? Could the solution conceal a problem? What would prevent the solution from being implemented? How might the problem clear up of its own accord? For example, would increasing beer sales reverse the trends in tastes? Lowering price, giving away samples and offering promotions would tend to increase 'sales' which might in turn change tastes.

Morphological analysis is another creativity technique which may prove useful. It requires you to look at the relationships between the dimensions that define a problem. One of the problems for Wolverhampton and Dudley Breweries is the confusion between brewing and retailing. Retailing could be defined to include off-licences, clubs, old-style pubs and new-style pubs. Brewing could be expanded to include beers, spirits, 'light' alcoholic and soft drinks. Combining these two dimensions in a matrix, as in Figure 7.2, allows the exploration of the relationship between them. This in turn may lead to new ideas. For example, what about a non-alcoholic pub? Or draught beer in off-licences? Or packages of products for specific kinds of outlet? By forcing examination of the relationships between the dimensions of a problem, morphological analysis can generate new insights and fresh solutions.

Another powerful set of techniques generates solutions by means of problem redefinition. While this should have been done already in developing problem areas, there still remains scope for radical re-orientations of our view of a problem. Perhaps Wolverhampton and Dudley Breweries should see changing leisure habits as an opportunity as well as a problem and seek ways to profit from it by adapting pubs to non-traditional uses. Declining beer sales is only a problem if Wolverhampton and Dudley Breweries are wedded to brewing. It could be seen as an opportunity to release resources to explore the possibilities of, say, biotechnology.

Looking at the problem at different levels of abstraction is another way of redefining a problem. Declining beer sales is just one aspect of a society rejecting former values. What is Wolverhampton and Dudley Breweries doing or what could it do to work with, rather than against, this trend?. It has high street sites and skills in distribution. It could become a retailer of products that require specialized distribution such as frozen foods, or a developer of entertainment centres.

Analogies and metaphors can be used to escape the bonds of down-to-earth thinking. The local market could be thought of as a well-defended castle. What form of defence would be most likely to put off attackers: a high wall? (Buy all the new pubs coming on to the market.) Boiling oil? (Attack any venture into the area with high profile local promotions.) A pre-emptive strike? (Go after pubs in the heartland of the attacker.) What exactly are the defences and how are they likely to repel attackers?

Starting from a *fresh perspective* can be highly stimulating. Two techniques which do this are wishful thinking and non-logical stimuli. Wishful thinking allows you to remove constraints which prevent you from solving the problem and then asking what you would do. Suppose that Wolverhampton and Dudley Breweries could buy all the pubs and clubs in the local area. Obviously this is not possible, but it might be possible to increase the percentage of outlets owned by Wolverhampton and Dudley Breweries by opening new ones. It might also be possible to give away overall control in

| | Pubs | | | |
	Old	New	Clubs	Off-licences
Beer				
Spirits				
'Light' alcohol				
Soft drinks				

Brewing

Figure 7.2 Morphological matrix for 'Pubs' and 'Brewing'

some pubs in order to get greater control in a greater number of pubs. The trick here is to move back from the ideal to the practical without losing too much on the way.

Non-logical stimuli probably represent the most desperate form of creativity stimulus. This technique requires you to attempt to work back from stimuli (e.g. words in a dictionary) to the problem. For example, the stimulus might be 'elephant' and the problem increased competition in the free trade market. Elephants never forget good deeds done to them; perhaps the same is true for club committees. One possible idea would be to give, rather than 'rent', facilities in the hope that this altruism would be duly rewarded.

Problems are usually defined in terms of their *boundaries*. Relaxing or at least examining those boundaries may suggest problem solutions. Wolverhampton and Dudley Breweries assumes that its customers are largely interested in quality mild at lower than average prices. Perhaps it should consider the possibility of a premium mild at a higher price; or offering a quality traditional bitter; or a lower quality mild at an even lower price. All of these ideas stretch the boundaries of the original problem. This is a rather sketchy outline of some of the creativity techniques that you might find useful. It is easy to dismiss them when you find that you can easily think up half a dozen solutions to a problem without really trying. However, you may not realize how mundane and unimaginative these are until you deliberately try to produce many more solutions using some of the techniques described here. For those who want a more profound introduction to creativity and its enhancement, I recommend Tudor Rickards' books (1974, 1985).

7.3 SOLUTION LISTING

To illustrate the ideas discussed above, a partial solution listing is given here. Some items are based on experience, some on conventional business strategies and some were generated using creativity techniques. The problems which are listed below are confined to the obvious ones which can be identified in the Wolverhampton and Dudley Breweries case.

New drinkers drinking non-traditional drinks/beers:

(a) Produce a 'light' mild.

(b) Accept run-down in mild sales and invest elsewhere.

(c) Promote modern 'nostalgic' tastes in beer.

(d) Aim sampling promotions at new drinkers.

(e) Create new pubs with traditional beers.

(f) Join with other local firms to promote traditional values.

Existing drinkers switching to light drinks:

(a) Create new 'old fashioned' pubs.

(b) Develop loyalty promotions.

(c) Accept the situation and move into light drinks.

(d) Reduce price.

(e) Create 'Switchers Anonymous'.

Lower disposable income:

(a) Reduce price.

(b) Discount promotions.

(c) Target higher-income groups.

(d) Help reflate local economy.

Change in leisure habits:

(a) Create new-style pubs/social clubs but with beer on draught.

(b) Target traditional old-style customers

(c) Lobby for increased licensing hours.

(d) Target non-traditional groups: women, ethnic minorities.

Low price/high quality expectations:

(a) Increase price.

(b) Lower quality through launch of economy mild.

(c) Reduce strength.

(d) Segment pubs by price/brand.

Decline in beer sales:

(a) Diversify into other drinks.

(b) Concentrate on pubs rather than on beer.

(c) Diversify into other geographical areas.

(d) Diversify into other products and 'other activities'.

(e) Quit.

(f) Join with other brewers to promote beer nationally.

(g) Wait for trend to reverse.

This is an incomplete list but it is probably typical of the kind of thing you will produce initially. Just by examining the list other solutions will logically and creatively suggest themselves. If, as advised, you keep the solutions rather general in nature, you should finish up with an unordered but manageable list of solutions. The next step is to begin to organize them.

7.4 ORGANIZING SOLUTIONS

7.4.1 Evaluation cycles

The solution list you produce will usually consist of tens of items. To evaluate each solution independently and choose amongst them is possible. However, it would be a very time-consuming business. Moreover, the effect of any one solution is normally dependent upon what other solutions are also chosen for implementation. This makes a solution-by-solution evaluation process very inefficient.

There is an alternative. Instead of attempting to choose the best alternatives at one go, the process can be broken down into a number of cycles. These cycles can be called evaluation cycles because at each repeat you will be evaluating the differences between alternatives and as a result making choices between them. This process is illustrated in Figure 7.3.

The solutions are not tackled in a random order. This would defeat the object of the exercise. The most general solutions are evaluated first, moving down towards more detailed and more specific solutions at each turn of the cycle. This means that your solution list must

105

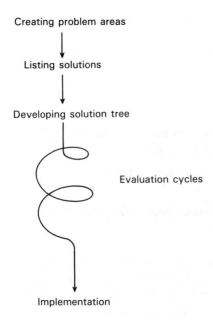

Creating problem areas

Listing solutions

Developing solution tree

Evaluation cycles

Implementation

Figure 7.3   Evaluation cycles

be ordered in terms of how general the different solutions are. You must also recognize the interdependence of solutions and include that in your order process. One way of doing this is to create solution trees.

7.4.2   Solution trees

Solutions exist at different levels of generality. You will discover that some of your solutions are simply describing an alternative way of carrying out a higher level solution. In other words, one solution is encompassed within another. Producing a 'light' mild is simply one way in which Wolverhampton and Dudley Breweries could diversify into other drinks. This is an example of a means–ends relationship. The higher level is the end or ends which it is hoped will be achieved. The lower level is the means by which those ends may possibly be achieved. Each means in turn can become an end for the next lower level. In this way a whole tree of means–ends relationships can be built up. At the lowest level the ends may be so general as to become goals and objectives, e.g. improve return on investment. At the highest level they can become as specific as you like, i.e. on Mondays, starting next Monday, they will offer a 'happy hour' with half-price mild in the pubs in central Wolverhampton. This structure is usually called a means–end chain. However, it will be re-christened a solution tree in this book. The reason for this will become abundantly clear in the next section. A solution tree for one of the problems in the Wolverhampton and Dudley Breweries case, the decline in local beer sales, is given in Figure 7.4.

The most general level of solution is shown at the bottom of the diagram, the most specific at the top. This example is, again, only a partial one. The dotted lines indicate alternative solutions which might have flowed from a particular higher-level solution but which were omitted for convenience and clarity. The solution tree grows

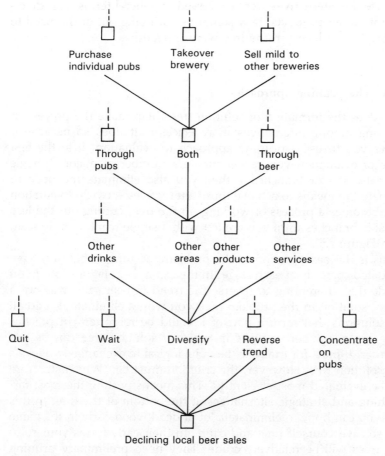

Figure 7.4 A solution tree

out of a single stem and branches out into a series of alternatives. Each point from which an alternative branch grows is called a node. As you move up the tree more and more alternatives (branches) appear and finally they become very specific and detailed (twigs).

The solution tree in Figure 7.4 includes solutions for other problems. This is only to be expected. In developing problem areas you are explicitly recognizing the fact that problems are related. It should therefore not be surprising that the solutions to those problems are also related. For example, the 'reverse trend' alternative would include many of the solutions listed under the change-in-leisure habits problem. The point is to build up the solution set carefully. It is also a useful idea to be alert to new solutions which may suggest themselves when you are 'growing' your solution tree. In this case, because the alternatives were expressed in general terms, e.g. diversify into other products, new solutions springing out of the need to specify higher levels in the tree were created.

7.4.3 The pruning approach

Why does the formation of solution trees help make the process of choosing among alternatives more efficient? It does so because it allows you to use a pruning approach to evaluation. If at the first stage of evaluation you can eliminate a number of major strategic alternatives – or branches – then you also eliminate the need to evaluate the means to achieve those alternatives – twigs. Evaluation then becomes a process of working up the tree, cutting out the less valuable branches until you are left with a single trunk-to-twig stem as in Figure 7.5.

This is the best solution to the problem, assuming that you have evaluated correctly at each stage. In the example in Figure 7.4, if you decide that attempting to reverse the trend in beer sales was not a 'good' solution to the problem then you would eliminate it, and all the solutions that form a part of it could be forgotten. In practice there are a number of ways in which a solution tree can be put together. It may, for example, be quite logical to exchange two levels in a solution tree. However, the criterion must be, 'Which structure can be evaluated most efficiently?' This means putting the most far-reaching and strategic alternatives at the bottom of the tree. In this way you can hope to eliminate a lot of dead wood early in the game and so save yourself time and effort. In their early forms your solution trees will be relatively crude. They need preliminary pruning before they can be subjected to the evaluation process.

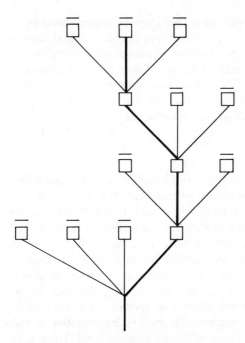

Figure 7.5 A 'pruned' solution tree

7.4.4 Simplifying

The solutions in your solution tree may be more complex than they need be. This is particularly true for solutions near the base of the tree. The more complex the solution, the more difficult it is to evaluate. This situation is rather like having twigs at the base of the tree. They make the whole process of pruning more difficult. They should therefore be removed first. The complexity stems from the fact that solutions differ in the extent to which they are divisible. Take the following examples:

1. Quit.
2. Diversify into other products.
3. Purchase individual pubs.

Non-divisible alternatives

The first alternative cannot really be divided at all. Wolverhampton and Dudley Breweries either quits or it does not. There are really

109

only two branches. In graphic terms this may be represented by a node as shown in Figure 7.6. In practice there may be several alternatives of this type and it may or may not be necessary to include the status quo as one branch. It may have been taken care of elsewhere in the tree. Solutions like this are disparate solutions because they are different in kind, not just degree. Putting it another way, disparate solutions are like nominal or name variables.

Discrete alternatives

The second example is certainly more divisible than the first. How many products should Wolverhampton and Dudley Breweries diversify into? A node for this example might look like the diagram in Figure 7.7. There is a different branch for each discrete addition of one product. This might best be described as a set of discrete solutions. The overall solution can be carried out in a series of discrete alternative steps. All of them conform to the solution, yet adding one and adding ten products must rate as quite radical alternatives. In this instance the identity of the products to diversify into are clearly of equal importance to the number. However, the number is not unimportant because it has clear resource implications. Thus it is important to establish the overall viability of the general solution before looking at the range of alternatives it contains.

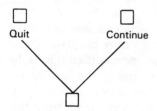

Figure 7.6   Non-divisible alternatives

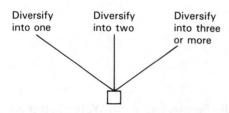

Figure 7.7   Discrete alternatives

Variable alternatives

The final example represents a variable solution set. It can best be described as a fan of alternatives. Any number of pubs from one to several hundred are included. The steps can be as small as one pub and while the set of solutions is not infinitely variable, it might as well be since you would not, nor be able to, evaluate every single number.

Clearly, it would be impossible to evaluate all the solution sets represented by discrete or variable solutions in one go. That is why it becomes necessary to collapse or simplify the solutions you have proposed if they are of this type and if you have suggested more than one solution within the same set. In practice this has already been done for the solution tree in Figure 7.4.

This raises another issue. Frequently, solutions will simply represent one alternative from a solution set. For example, the set of solutions in the Wolverhampton and Dudley Breweries case under the diversification option includes drinks, products, services and areas. In deciding on these alternatives there may be others you have omitted, like countries or businesses. It is therefore necessary to examine the solutions you have generated to see if they can be either simplified or generalized. Don't worry about losing the fine detail of your solutions. That will come at a later stage.

7.4.5 Clarifying

Problem solving would be a very straightforward activity if one could simply try all possible solutions at once. In practice this is simply not possible. Trying one solution usually precludes trying a whole series of other solutions, though not necessarily all possible solutions. In other words, solutions are frequently mutually exclusive. It then becomes necessary to decide which among several mutually exclusive solutions represents the best alternative. The whole process of evaluation is devoted to this decision.

Mutually exclusive solutions

However, before deciding among alternatives, it is first necessary to make sure that they really are mutually exclusive. If you do not, two types of error can result. First, what happens if you treat alternative solutions as mutually exclusive when they are not? Essentially you will be missing an opportunity. Take, for example, the group of solutions illustrated in Figure 7.8. If you regarded these solutions as

111

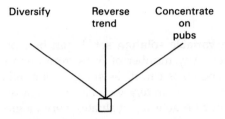

Figure 7.8   Non-mutually exclusive alternatives?

mutually exclusive, and in fact they weren't, then you would be missing the opportunity of employing all three solutions.

Secondly, what happens if you treat mutually exclusive solutions as if they aren't? In this case you can almost be said to be cheating! This is a frequent error by students in case analysis. They throw everything in but the kitchen sink. While this may look impressive, it is not good practice for real life. Often students are not aware of the problem since the constraints which prevent more than one solution from being used are often subtle.

The most obvious constraints are physical and temporal. You cannot both quit and not quit. It is not possible to have a production director and not have a production director at the same time. A product cannot be called both 'Hanson's' and 'Banks's'. Other constraints are basically judgemental. It is a moot point whether it is logically possible to 'diversify' and 'concentrate on pubs' at the same time. In cases like these you will have to make judgements before the evaluation phase. These are necessary to clarify the structure of the alternatives to be assessed. Finally, the most difficult type of constraint is the resource constraint. It is possible to have a set of solutions which can be carried out at the same time, given infinite resources. Since this is never normally the case the limiting of resources restricts the solutions that can be implemented. This in turn renders some subset of the solutions mutually exclusive. The solution set described for the Wolverhampton and Dudley Breweries case in Figure 7.7 probably come under this heading because of resource constraints. The constraints will usually be profitability, cash flow or human, particularly managerial, resources. The judgement, however, need not be a final one in any case. It is always possible to 'add together ' solutions at some later time if it appears that they are not mutually exclusive.

Compound solutions

Where there are a number of non-mutually exclusive solutions, the problem of evaluating them can largely be overcome by the use of the concepts of simple and compound solutions. Simple solutions are those which involve non-divisible actions, e.g. diversifying, and concentrating on pubs. Doing both is a compound solution. Thus a set of non-mutually exclusive solutions, which is, however, limited by a resource constraint, can be made mutually exclusive simply by including a compound solution as another alternative. To Figure 7.7 we simply need to add another solution, 'Some combination of all three'. This can now be evaluated as a mutually exclusive set of alternatives.

The problem of deciding which alternatives are, or at least should be treated as, mutually exclusive cannot be solved during the initial evaluation phase. As alternatives are eliminated more is understood about those that remain. This may in turn lead you to change your mind about which to treat as mutually exclusive alternatives. This is only to be expected: the process of case analysis is essentially an adaptive rather than an optimizing one.

7.5 GUIDE TO USE

Beginners may be happy to come out of step three with a list of possible solutions to evaluate. They should at least understand something about the nature of solutions and so should take in section 7.1. The quality of your solutions will benefit from knowing what sources they derive from and these are discussed in section 7.2. Of particular help would be section 7.2.3, which describes creativity techniques. By learning how to 'grow' solution trees, as described in section 7.4, you will save yourself effort and improve the quality of your analysis. This does however require an investment in time now for returns which only become apparent later in the process.

You may have so simplified your approach to the case that it becomes unnecessary to cycle through the evaluation phase more than once.

Step Four: Predicting Outcomes

Step four requires that the outcomes of each alternative solution should be listed and that some measure of the likelihood of each occurring be estimated.

8.1 INTO THE EVALUATION CYCLE

The next stage in the process of case analysis is to choose between the alternative solutions you have developed. In the last chapter it was pointed out that it is not feasible to do this in one go. It was suggested instead that choices should be made in a series of cycles. These cycles I have called evaluation cycles. Evaluation because you will be 'putting a value on' the alternatives. Cycles because the process has to be repeated for each pruning of the solution tree. This will then enable you to eliminate a number of alternatives. The evaluation cycles begin at a very general, strategic level and move up through the solution tree to the tactical and specific levels.

Evaluation is best divided into two stages. The first requires that the ramifications of a solution be predicted and understood. It is not possible fully to evaluate a thing, event or course of action that is not fully understood. Few people would buy a new car on the basis of a casual glance: we would want to know much more about it even before we began comparing it with other cars on sale. In general, the more data we collect, the better we might expect our evaluation to be. This does not always hold true: sometimes it is possible to become confused by collecting too much data. This is a pitfall to be wary of. Nevertheless, the sheer size of the task of predicting the outcome of particular alternative solutions will usually ensure that too little, rather than too much, data is the problem.

The second stage involves 'placing a value on' the constellation of outcomes that result from implementing a particular alternative solution. This, in many ways, is the heart of the decision process. It is usually the most difficult and complex process. It is also the one that is frequently skated over by case analysts who are afraid to 'open the can of worms'. It will be tackled head-on in the next chapter.

The process of predicting outcomes has also been broken down into two stages. The first requires that all possible or, more realistically, most of the important outcomes stemming from the carrying out of a particular solution should be predicted. Not all of these outcomes will happen. Some are almost certain; others are highly unlikely. It is obviously important to decide how likely each is to occur. It would not be sensible to give a low evaluation to a particular solution because of a possibly disastrous but very unlikely outcome. The outcomes must in some sense be weighted in terms of their likelihood. Only in this way can a realistic picture of an alternative be obtained and used as an input to the evaluation process.

8.2 LISTING POSSIBLE OUTCOMES

Implementing a solution – for example taking over another brewery – is rather like throwing a pebble into a pond. The ripples spread out from the point of impact. They may become less noticeable the further away they are but they are still there and may cause quite important changes. Systems theory is based upon the assumption that a change in one part of the system can affect almost any other part of the system. Unfortunately these changes may be unexpected and unpredictable. It will be your task to predict what they might be.

The outcomes stemming from a solution go far beyond the problem that generated it. The solution may help or hinder the solution of other organizational problems. It may create new problems or new opportunities. It may affect situations which are seen neither as problems nor opportunities. This realization previews a point which will be argued in greater depth in the next chapter. Solutions are primarily generated in response to a particular problem. However, they cannot be judged solely in the light of how well they solve that particular problem. The total organizational impact of different solutions has to be compared. It may even be that a solution which is not judged best for solving a particular problem is chosen because it scores highly in terms of its effects in other areas of organizational performance. It uncovers opportunities which may more than counter-balance its inferior performance in solving the original problem. This, once again, emphasizes the need to do a complete job of predicting the stream of consequences that acting on a solution implies.

Generating outcomes from a particular course of action is, at least

115

in part, a creative process. The creativity techniques discussed in the previous chapter apply equally well here. You will be attempting to make a series of 'if ... then' statements. The next section deals with a number of tips which may be helpful to you in this process.

8.2.1 Key impact areas

Before beginning with any solution, draw up a list of key areas both within and without the organization which may be affected by, or react to, the implementation of a solution. The list might include the following:

1. Problem areas and opportunities already identified.
2. Key individuals or informal groups within the organization.
3. Functional departments and their operations within the organization.
4. External groups or organizations including government, customers, shareholders, unions, media, competitors, etc.
5. Key operating indices such as sales growth, profitability, cost effectiveness and efficiency measures.

There will be other areas which result from your growing understanding of the organization you are studying.

As an example of using such a list, consider the solution: 'take over other regional brewers.' This would certainly increase profit and sales growth but possibly at the expense of return on capital and possibly even control. In addition, if the trends in beer consumption are felt nationwide, the growth would not be organic unless there were useful synergies between the two firms. There could be important economies of scale and a new market for the firm's products could become available. It would do little or nothing for the local market unless the acquisition firm had products that were suitable. Management might on the one hand be able to bring its expertise to bear in the acquisition firm's operations but this might overstretch its capacity. The top management group would be keen on the idea of a non-local merger, but others might be more guarded in their response since the new acquisition might be seen to be competing for resources. There will also be the understandable opposition to large-scale change which any firm, particularly a conservative one like Wolverhampton and Dudley Breweries, has to contend with. The marketing people would probably be more in favour than the production people, since they might expect to have some of their problems solved by gaining access to new markets. The finance department would be delighted to acquire new skills or demonstrate old ones.

The City and the shareholders would probably be delighted, depending on whether it was seen as a strategically defensible move and as long as the price was right. They might be concerned that Wolverhampton and Dudley Breweries was not diversifying. They could be worried about dilution of earnings. The government might be unhappy about increased concentration in the industry and the unions could well be suspicious and sceptical. Existing customers would probably not be aware of the event and even if they were would think of it as a good thing that 'their' brewery was showing others 'how to do it'. They might be apprehensive about possible changes in their pints and pubs. Competitors of all sizes would be concerned and might react rather strongly. On the other hand the larger size of the new 'group' might make them less vulnerable to a takeover.

The long-term effects on the firm would be highly dependent upon the nature of the takeover target. If it mirrored Wolverhampton and Dudley Breweries, then it might be nothing more than the sum of the parts. The extra size and the lack of knowledge of Wolverhampton and Dudley Breweries' management of the new firm might actually reduce profits and turnover in the long run. However, if it complemented Wolverhampton and Dudley Breweries, then there is no reason why quite large gains in all key performance indices should not occur.

8.2.2 Sample outcome listing

As a further example a preliminary outcome listing is given below for three alternative diversification solutions in the Wolverhampton and Dudley Breweries case. These are by no means the only solutions, but they are important. One or two combination solutions also look reasonably attractive. For example, would it be possible to continue to buy pubs in one area while selling mild to breweries in another? However, for the sake of illustration the solutions used will be simple, and not combinations. The viewpoint taken throughout is that of Mr Thompson. Each outcome is expressed as if it were certain. Only later need you consider the probability that it will occur. That probability could be zero but the outcome, if considered important, should be included.

(a) *Attempt to take over another brewery*
   Attempt successful.
   Capital restructuring required.

Cash available reduced.
Joint sales and profits grow.
Scale economies realized.
Management transfers expertise to takeover firm.
Management overstretched.
Internal dissent.
New market opened up.
Synergies realized.
Competitive reaction.
Monopolies Commission referral.
Union opposition.
Opposition within acquisition firm.
Unanticipated problems in acquisition firm.
Increased reliance on brewing industry.
Local markets react adversely.
Shareholders and City happy.

(b) *Buy pubs in other areas*

Little short-term impact on sales and profit growth.
Long-term sales but not profit growth.
No impact on existing market.
Retains concentration in brewing.
Management can handle it well.
Little opposition within the firm.
Limited and selective competitive reaction.
Shareholders and City neutral or impatient.

(c) *Sell mild to other breweries*

Low sales and profits short-term.
High sales and profits long-term.
Neutral or positive reaction in local market.
Marketing people delighted but can't handle it.
Brewers delighted but encounter production difficulties.
Distribution becomes more expensive.
Retains concentration in brewing industry.
Other brewers attempt takeover of Wolverhampton and Dudley Breweries.
Other brewers start to produce mild.
City and shareholders enthusiastic.
Positive reaction inside the firm.
Unions welcome the move.
Supermarkets become interested in canned mild.

Listing outcomes in this way is rather similar to the way that solutions were listed in the last chapter, but the resemblance does not end there. Outcomes, like solutions, must also be clarified, simplified and structured. This not only helps to ensure that all important outcomes are uncovered, it is also a vital step for the second stage of the process of predicting outcomes, i.e. estimating likelihoods.

8.2.3 Clarifying outcomes

The first stage is to clarify outcomes. When an outcome is not certain, then it has at least one alternative. For example, one outcome listed for the takeover option is that sales and profits will grow. But there is also a probability that they will decline or remain the same. These alternatives can be represented by an outcome fan as illustrated in Figure 8.1.

The circle is used to denote the fact that these are alternative outcomes; they are not alternative decisions. Having made the decision to take over another brewer and having succeeded in doing so, the outcomes are then, more or less, beyond the decision maker's power to influence. Whichever outcomes occur will be a result of a combination of variables acting together. In particular they will be a function of other preceding outcomes and the conditions under which the decision is being played out. Under these conditions the best that can be done is prediction, not control. That is why it is important to distinguish between the alternatives emerging from a decision node and the outcomes emerging from what is normally referred to as a chance node. Previewing Chapter 9, the combination of decision and chance nodes is illustrated in Figure 8.2.

This partial diagram suggests that if the decision to take over another brewery is made, then either the takeover succeeds or it fails. Which outcome occurs will be dependent upon the conditions that surround the attempt, e.g. the nature and financial status of the target firm, alternative bidders, City opinion, etc. The outcomes in Figures 8.1 and 8.2 are mutually exclusive alternative outcomes. To

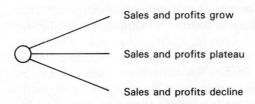

Figure 8.1 Example of an outcome fan

119

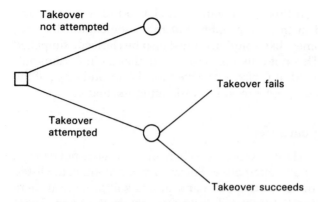

Figure 8.2   A combination of decision and chance nodes

a large extent this clarifies the situation. Identifying one outcome leads to the identification of at least one other and sometimes a whole series of outcomes. This represents a major source of previously un-identified outcomes. Only those outcomes which are more or less certain do not produce outcome fans. In the case of the takeover this would include restructuring the capital and reducing cash available.

Another source of additional outcomes lies in comparing the outcome lists. If an outcome appears on one list it should normally appear on the other lists since the ultimate purpose is to compare outcomes. This is not always strictly necessary. In comparing altern-atives the relative difference between them is more important than the absolute. For example, the outcome, 'Capital restructuring required', is only mentioned for the takeover solution. It would not be necessary in the other two cases so it has been omitted. The topic of baselines for comparisons will be dealt with again in the context of evaluating alternatives in Chapter 9.

8.2.4   Simplifying outcomes

Another important process is that of simplification. It is very difficult to handle large numbers of outcomes that differ only marginally from each other. This problem arose, you may remember, when alternat-ives were being generated in Chapter 7. The solution is the same in both cases: collapse the differences into major groups. For example, in the Wolverhampton and Dudley Breweries case, opposition to the takeover from within the target firm could clearly have been given a whole spectrum of different values rather than just opposition/no opposition. In practice, opposition/no opposition captures the essential differences without going into too much detail. It may be that at a later stage they could be subdivided further. However, this would really only be necessary if the variable in question was a key variable which was paramount in choosing among alternative solutions and if the subdivision was regarded as being feasible. In other words, it makes no sense to identify shades of outcome if you cannot distinguish between them.

In the same way it is not necessarily a good idea to 'unpack' outcomes too much. Clearly profit and sales growth are different variables, but they have been conflated in order to simplify the analysis. The underlying dimension is real corporate growth specified in terms of two key indicators. You will wish to consider more complex outcomes when you are estimating likelihoods and evaluating alternatives, but to give the analysis some shape and order it is best to work at the level of summary variables for the time being.

8.2.5 Restructuring outcomes

The third process is that of restructuring or, more appropriately, sequencing the outcomes. This is necessary because of the ripple nature of implementing a particular solution. It is best captured by the phrase 'one thing leads to another'. It recognizes that outcomes are often, but not always, generated in sequence and are therefore dependent upon one another. An example is given in Figure 8.3.

Again, only part of the sequence is shown. It is a sequence which is concerned with the reaction of the acquisition firm to the takeover. The attempted takeover may succeed or fail. If it succeeds it may lead to opposition in the target firm. If there is opposition, management may or may not be able to cope with it. Beyond the sequence shown, these events are, in turn, likely to affect the profit and sales growth rates which, in turn, would have an impact on City sentiments towards the firm.

At each node all the alternative outcomes have been given, though some may be much less likely than others; for example, history tends to show that it is more probable that little continuing opposition results from takeover bids, especially if they are by firms in the same industry. However, the possibility is there and should be accounted for.

In practice there are other outcomes which would affect this sequence of outcomes. Management failing to cope with the takeover may also be affected by opposition to the takeover in the parent company. This problem can be handled by having alternative sequences of outcomes that come together at the crucial nodes. At such a node

121

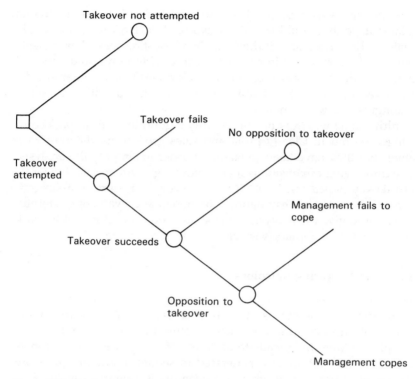

Figure 8.3   A sequence of outcomes

you then know the preconditions for the outcomes and so can estimate the likelihood of the outcomes more accurately. For example,
what is the likelihood of management coping with the takeover firm
if there is a competitive reaction and local markets react adversely?
It is certainly possible to estimate this in cases where the alternatives
and outcomes are few and easily sequenced. However, beyond the
simplest situations the diagrams quickly become unwieldy and I
would recommend them only to the most thorough and persevering
of analysts.

Nevertheless, it does pay to examine all the outcomes, for two
reasons. First, because it helps you to understand the sequence
better. For example, you might ask yourself under what conditions
management being overstretched would lead to a growth in sales
and profits. It could be that its failure to cope results in the firm that
has been taken over being allowed to run its own show with con-
sequent impact upon the bottom line. This is unlikely, but it does
make you question the assumptions you are making. A second

reason is that it makes the estimation of the relative likelihoods much easier and more prone to be accurate. It is important, for example, to realize that a small but finite probability of a disastrous result would often put a decision maker off that particular solution.

Sequences like these illustrate the fact that many of the outcomes in the list you generate may be dependent upon just one or two pivotal outcomes. In the Wolverhampton and Dudley Breweries case the ability of the management to get the best out of the new, enlarged firm is clearly crucial. Sequencing also helps to generate further outcomes. For example, what would happen to profits and sales if management coped but the market continued to decline, or if it didn't cope in the first year or so and did cope thereafter? In effect what you are doing here is building alternative scenarios. The better they are the more likely you are to be able to predict the probable outcomes of the alternative decisions.

Sequencing is vital to the next stage in the process – estimating how likely each outcome is to occur. If outcomes are dependent upon each other, then their likelihood of occurring cannot be estimated independently. The probability of one occurring will affect the probability of another occurring and that relationship must be sorted out before the estimation procedure begins.

One final point about sequencing. It is clear that you could go on for ever creating more and more detailed outcomes. In particular, if you project forward the results of taking a particular course of action, you could continue to plot the consequences far into the future. Not only does this make analysis more complex, it is not really necessary. Case studies are to some extent artificial. They are one-shot situations. In practice, problem solving is a continuous activity. It is therefore reasonable to cut short the time period over which you are attempting to predict outcomes. In real life you would take additional decisions to modify or even reverse the actions you decided were correct at the time. As the situation changes, so you adapt. It is not necessary, as is implied in the case situation, to take irrevocable decisions which will continue to haunt the organization for ever. There are some decisions which are irreversible and thus need special attention in the evaluation process. However, in most cases you should be content to make good decisions for the short term and position the organization well to face the long term. It is unfair to ask anyone to do more than that in a case situation. Even in the short term problems can occur as a result of outcomes not turning out quite as expected. You should be sensitive to such situations and develop contingency plans to meet them. This topic is covered in more depth in Chapter 11.

8.3 ESTIMATING OUTCOME LIKELIHOODS

It is obvious that only one outcome from a set of mutually exclusive outcomes will in fact come to pass. Either profits will increase or they will not. Unfortunately, it is only after a decision has been made that we know the outcome with certainty. Hindsight is not much use before the event. Instead it is necessary to estimate how likely it is that each of the outcomes will actually occur.

These estimates will, in almost all cases, be judgemental. It is possible, in some instances, where there is a long time series of data relating to an event which is more physical than social in nature, that the likelihood of an event can be estimated objectively. This applies, for example, to waste rates on milling machines. It may also happen that the case contains the likelihood estimates of the personalities in the case, for instance: 'Louise estimated that there was only a 50:50 chance of a strike if the new machine was installed'. However, in the majority of cases you will have to make your own judgements.

8.3.1 Likelihood scaling

Two methods of estimating likelihoods will be discussed here. The first is rather a rough-and-ready scaling method; the second involves the estimation of numerical subjective probabilities. Using the first method, outcomes are classified into four likelihood groups – very likely, likely, unlikely and very unlikely. This method is illustrated in Table 8.1.

The list of outcomes presented in Table 8.1 represents only half of the picture. As pointed out earlier, few outcomes are certain. This led to the creation of outcome fans where the occurrence of an event was matched with its non-occurrence or several other mutually exclusive outcomes. In Table 8.1 only one of the outcomes is presented. For example, if capital restructuring is very likely then its alternative, no capital restructuring, will be very unlikely. Likelihoods of estimates for a set of mutually exclusive outcomes must balance. It is not logically possible to have a series of outcomes which are mutually exclusive and which are all very likely to occur. This balancing act becomes very difficult when there are more than two alternative outcomes. Is it possible to have a set of three outcomes judged very likely, unlikely, and very unlikely? Or can a 'likely' be balanced only by two 'very unlikely's? At this point the advantages of a numerical scale become obvious.

Table 8.1 *Likelihood estimates for outcomes: WDB case alternative – take over another brewery*

Very likely
   Capital restructuring required
   Unanticipated problems in takeover firms
   Increased reliance on brewing industry
   Increased takeover protection

Likely
   Cash available reduced
   Joint sales and profit grow
   Competitive reaction
   Shareholders and City happy
   Synergies realized
   New market opens up
   Takeover succeeds

Unlikely
   Management overstretched
   Internal dissent
   Union opposition
   Opposition within takeover firm
   Scale economies realized
   Management expertise transferred

Very unlikely
   Monopolies Commission referral
   Local markets react adversely

8.3.2 Subjective probabilities

One of the most fruitful developments in decision sciences has been the adoption of subjective probabilities judgements. For each outcome the subjective probability of that event occurring, given the implementation of a particular solution, is estimated on a scale ranging from zero to 1.0. A zero probability indicates your judgement that there is no possibility that the event will occur. A probability of 1.0 means that you believe that the event is certain. The scale in between represents any position between those two extremes. Depending on the individual, the area of 'very likely' to occur will usually be estimated at anywhere from 0.7 to 0.9. For 'very unlikely' the range might be from 0.1 to 0.3.

For any mutually exclusive set of outcomes the total of these subjective probabilities must add to 1. In other words, it is certain (probability = 1.0) that at least one of the events will occur. This

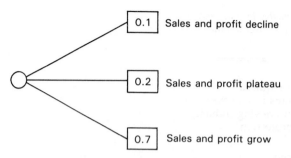

Figure 8.4 Outcome fan with estimated probabilities

makes balancing the estimated probabilities a much easier task. In Figure 8.4 an outcome fan with associated probabilities is shown. Initially the three outcomes are estimated independently. As a result the probabilities may add to more than 1.0 and would therefore need rebalancing to produce the final figures as shown in Figure 8.4.

This is not a mechanical process; it requires careful thinking and not a little judgement. It is also important to think of the other conditions that would be likely to be operating at the same time. For example, management coping with the acquisition firm depends upon a range of variables including the size and culture of the firm, its distance from the West Midlands, the state of the beer market and the economy in general, and so on. Decision theorists call these 'states of nature'. In theory each state of nature that might exist deserves its own chance node. In practice there is a limit to the number of outside variables you can take into account. Formally, we are only examining the relationships between a limited number of outcomes, those identified in Table 8.1. But you should remember that these outcomes will not exist in a vacuum. Whichever one materializes will be determined, in part, by the conditions that surround its birth.

8.3.3 Multiplying probabilities

It is not only the conditions that surround an outcome but also those that are directly linked to it that are important in estimating likelihoods. Consider the interdependent series of outcomes illustrated in Figure 8.5: this is the sequence which was described in Figure 8.3. Only one complete sequence is shown for clarity. The probabilities are those estimated for the situation where Wolverhampton and Dudley Breweries has decided upon a takeover strategy. It is very important to note that these probabilities are conditional probabilities. That is to say, they are the probability of an outcome happening

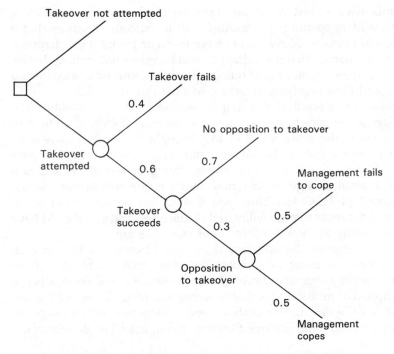

Figure 8.5   Sequence of outcomes with subjective probabilities

under the condition that a number of other outcomes have already occurred or are occurring. For example, what is the probability that management will cope, given that a takeover has been attempted, has succeeded and there has been opposition to the takeover from within the target firm? It is a probability estimated under a very specific set of conditions. However, what is more important is finding a way of estimating how likely this particular sequence of events is to occur. What we are trying to do is link the original decision to adopt a takeover strategy with the outcome that management fails to cope with the resulting situation. This is done simply by multiplying the conditional probabilities throughout the appropriate sequence, i.e. $0.6 \times 0.3 \times 0.5 = 0.09$. In other words, it is estimated that, if Wolverhampton and Dudley Breweries goes on the takeover trail there is about a 1 in 10 chance that its management will not cope. Essentially, what is being done here is to examine, in a quantitative but subjective way, the conditions for a particular set of outcomes to occur. The outcomes at the end of the fan can be assigned probabilities by multiplying the probabilities of the sequence of outcome events which must occur for these terminal outcomes to have a chance of happening. For example, if an outcome requires that a whole series of unlikely events have to occur before it can happen, then the chances that it will happen will be very small indeed. In this way the interdependence of outcomes can be captured in a quantified way and the underlying structure worked through.

However, a word of warning is necessary. The probabilities you assign to outcomes are obviously subjective, therefore subject to error not in the sense that they may be right or wrong – there is no way in which that can be judged – but 'subject to error' in the sense that they are sensitive to your current interpretation of the situation and a small change in that may mean major adjustments to the assigned probabilities. Thus you should not be concerned about small differences in probability, only large ones, and you should have some feeling for how sensitive your estimates are.

To summarize: the end results of your labours will be, for each alternative, a listing of possible outcomes that might stem from implementing that alternative. To each outcome will be attached a likelihood or probability of that outcome occurring. These are the raw data upon which the evaluation process depends. It is a long way towards making an informed choice among available alternatives.

8.4 GUIDE TO USE

It is impossible to choose among alternatives without predicting the outcomes that will result from their implementation. However, it is possible that you will as a novice analyst, do no more than simply list each alternative. Section 8.2 gives some advice which is useful in this respect.

The processes of clarifying, simplifying and structuring these outcomes obviously improves the quality of outcome statements and these are discussed later in the same section.

Outcomes have different likelihoods of occurring. Section 8.3 describes different formal methods of dealing with this problem. Clearly, you must recognize this basic fact about the nature of outcomes. However, you may not wish to include a formal treatment in your analysis.

Step Five: Choosing Among Alternatives (I)

Step five involves evaluating alternative solutions and choosing among them. The process of evaluation may vary from the simple and implicit to the complex and explicit.

9.1 EVALUATION

In Chapter 7, the concept of the evaluation cycle was introduced. It was pointed out that the task of choosing among all the alternative solutions that were generated in step three was simply too difficult to achieve in one go. It was suggested that a series of evaluation cycles be carried out eliminating alternatives at successively lower levels at each stage until just one stem of the 'solution tree' remains. Each evaluation cycle was broken into two parts. The first – predicting outcomes – was discussed in Chapter 8. The second – choosing among alternatives – will be dealt with now.

Choosing among alternatives is, in principle, a straightforward process. Each alternative is first evaluated – that is to say, a value is assigned to it. This value may be quantitative (profit in pounds) or qualitative (achievement of personal satisfaction). However, each alternative, if implemented, would create a stream of outcomes. The values of all of these outcomes must somehow be totalled to get a value for each alternative. This problem is illustrated in Figure 9.1.

This model implies a two-stage evaluation process: firstly, assigning values to outcomes; secondly, totalling these values to provide an overall index of value for each alternative. When each alternative has been evaluated, the choice falls upon the alternative with the highest value.

9.1.1 Suspending judgement

Two important points need to be made about this simple view of evaluation. The first has to do with the number of winners. It may

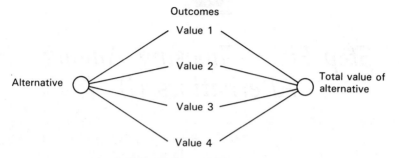

Figure 9.1 Evaluation of an alternative

turn out that one alternative is far, far ahead of any of the others. The next evaluation cycle would then simply concentrate on evaluating which is the best way to implement, at a more tactical level, the preferred alternative. However, it will not usually be so straightforward. There will usually be two or even more alternatives which are quite difficult to choose among. In this case, it may be a better strategy to put off a decision until the end of the next evaluation cycle. If the alternatives really are close, then the differences between them at a more detailed level can be used to decide between them. This procedure is equivalent to suspending judgement temporarily; but it isn't cost free. It means extra work in the next evaluation cycle. It is up to you to weigh the certain costs of that extra effort against the possible benefits of a better decision.

9.1.2 Suboptimization

The second point concerns the relationship between the original problem and evaluation. It has already been pointed out that a solution will, in most cases, have repercussions far beyond the problem it is intended to solve. It may help solve or exacerbate other problems, or it may create opportunities. So while it is true that the problem was the 'creator' of the solutions, it cannot be allowed to be the only criterion for choosing between them. The solutions have to be judged in terms of how far they move an organization or its representative towards the achievement of its goals. This implies a much more general framework for evaluation than simply asking the question, 'How well does a solution solve the problem it was designed to solve'? This last approach may lead to a difficulty which is common in problem solving, that is, suboptimization. Suboptimization occurs when problem solving is confined to one part of a system and attempts are made to find solutions only within the boundaries arbitrarily drawn by the analyst. Classical examples of suboptimization occurred in early attempts to optimize inventory levels and physical distribution systems. Analysts attempted to minimize the cost of holding stock or the overall cost of transporting goods. They ignored the interactions of both these systems with the production and marketing processes. Costs may have fallen in the subsystems studied, but this often meant passing on problems to other subsystems with a resulting decrease in overall profits for the whole system. Operational researchers have learned from their early mistakes. The same mistakes should not be repeated here.

9.1.3 Judgement

The process of choosing among alternatives has been described above in very simple terms. In practice, of course, it is much more complicated. As the chapter proceeds, refinements to the basic process will be introduced. As stated previously, you alone decide how far to go along this road, but first you should be aware of what you may be losing by stopping too early. The simpler methods of choosing rely extensively on implicit, internal judgements. You may be performing rather complex mental operations to come to your choice. It is these rather complicated processes that are brought out into the open and discussed explicitly in the later sections of this chapter. By using the techniques described there, you should accomplish two goals. The first is to be able to defend your conclusions, logically and in detail, rather than with the lame excuse, 'It just seems the best thing to do'. The second is to enable you to improve your judgemental skills and be able to demonstrate to your case instructor that you have done so.

What, then, are the complexities that make it difficult to decide which alternative is best? The first derives from the basic nature of values and the sources from which they can come. You will usually have some choice in this matter and this will be discussed in section 9.2. Values can be positive or negative. In other words, any particular outcome may be for or against the organization's interests. In section 9.3 a simple 'pros and cons' list is described as a way of comparing alternatives and choosing among them. The fact that different outcomes have different probabilities of occurring has already been extensively discussed in Chapter 8. In section 9.4, the 'pros and cons' technique is modified to take this very important factor into account. In section 9.5, for the first time, the differing values of different outcomes will be explicitly recognized and examined. This will be done by the use of importance ratings, i.e. how important is this outcome, good or bad, to the organization?

Importance is clearly a rather vague concept. In section 9.6, explicit single criteria such as survival, cost-effectiveness and profitability are introduced to be used to choose among alternatives. But it is rare that an organization, or the individuals who control it, have a single criterion of success. In section 10.1, the problem of judging among alternatives when there are several criteria, e.g. growth, survival, and social responsibility, is examined. Finally, in section 10.2, a number of methods of choosing among alternatives when the choice involves several criteria are described. Again, it should be emphasized that though these techniques may seem complex they are doing no more than what you do when you make a complex judgement. However, doing it out in the open means that you are less likely to make errors or cut corners.

9.2 SOURCES OF VALUES

Evaluation is the process of putting a value on something. But where does that value come from? It is common in case analysis for this issue to remain unaddressed. Students make decisions based upon some vague notion of what seems like a good thing to do and frequently case instructors do not separate or attempt to draw out the value assumptions which are embedded in a particular choice. In practice I find that it is frequently on the value issues that students disagree rather than on a view of what might happen under specific conditions.

There are three possible sources and you will have to make a choice between them. The first source is the textbook. In any social discipline there are any number of writers who have stated what the objectives of individuals, groups, or organizations should be. For a business organization, the objectives might be profit and sales growth together with a minimum level of employee satisfaction. For an educational system, it might be the attainment of certain levels of educational achievement, measured both quantitatively and qualitatively, within predetermined cost criteria. For an architectural project, it might be simultaneously meeting environmental, aesthetic and client criteria for a given budget. In other words, there have been proposed theoretical goals and objectives that organizations might, in general, pursue. The existence of such systems has both philosophical and theoretical underpinnings. For example, a free market economist would argue for a profit-based system because he or she would value the allocation of resources that such an objective would achieve if all firms adopted it. A Marxist economist would offer an alternative set of goals. Neither is right or wrong: they simply espouse different values.

This approach may be a useful one when the educational objective is for students to understand what goals and objectives an organization could have. It may also be necessary to use prescriptions like these where there is so little information about the organization and the people directing it that it is difficult to predict what goals they may be seeking.

The second source is you: your values, aspirations and dreams. In this case, you simply assume that you have the power to do whatever you want. Deciding between alternatives then becomes a matter of what directions you would like to see the organization take. This is essentially a method for exploring your own values in decision situations; it is a relatively limited exercise which should only be carried out occasionally, as it is simply not realistic enough. Nevertheless, it is sometimes a good idea to make some very limiting assumptions – for example, that everything you decide on will be done – in order to concentrate on just one aspect of case analysis. In this situation, the goal would be for you to confront your own values: the initiative is with you. You will find the comparison of your values with those of your fellow students an illuminating experience. But one word of warning: don't go off and do this without clearing it with your case instructor first. You don't want unnecessary misunderstandings to occur.

The third source is the organization itself as described in the case study. What goals and objectives does it seem to be pursuing? How would it react to this or that change in direction? In practical terms, of course, it is not very realistic to talk of the goals and objectives of an organization. Organizations don't really have goals and objectives. However, the individuals who comprise organizations do. Thus an organization's goals and objectives can be seen as the sum total of the goals and objectives of the individuals it comprises. Summing may not be a very accurate picture of how an individual's views affect the total corporate view – some individuals are more powerful than others. This power may stem from their position in the organization or from their acknowledged experience or expertise. The weight given to a particular view will depend on the situation. An engineer, for example, would have little credibility contributing to a debate on changing the basis of accounting for inventory. Power may also stem from strength of numbers. A department will frequently have a departmental view of a situation because the people working within it are working in the same environment and see problems in the same way. Power blocks or cliques may cross departmental lines. There is, for example, in some organizations a split between loosely structured groups which might be called the 'progressives' and the 'conservatives'.

9.2.1 Understanding organizational values

All of these points are meant to illustrate the difficulty of judging what goals and objectives the organization is actually pursuing. It is important to put effort into understanding the complex value system of the organization you are studying for two reasons. Firstly, because it will determine the value of a particular alternative based upon how well it helps the organization achieve what you think it wants to achieve. This may not be the same value you would place on it. For example, you might recommend the continuation of a legal but deceptive accounting practice although it conflicts with your view of the moral standards businessmen should employ. Nevertheless if, from your reading of the case, you believe that the employees of the organization would see nothing wrong with this conduct then you should recommend it to continue. Effectively, you are acting here merely in the role of an interpreter of corporate values. The second reason for understanding the nature of corporate values is in terms of acceptance of recommendations. It will be difficult, if not impossible, to sell the organization a course of action which runs counter to its basic philosophy. It would be a waste of time trying. If, however, you incorporate the organization's values in the criteria you use to judge alternatives, then the match will be much closer and the implementation of your recommendations that much easier. This point will be covered again in more detail in Chapter 11.

9.2.2 Key individuals' values

In order to map out the values of the organization you will need to make use of many of the analyses you have already carried out. In addition, you might wish to draw pen portraits of key individuals, groups, or departments and attempt to assess what they are likely to be striving for. The following example is from Wolverhampton and Dudley Breweries.

Mr E. J. Thompson: grandson of founder, steeped in the business and a brewer by predisposition. However, prepared to invest and take some chances. Probably prefers incremental to revolutionary change. Runs a tight ship, ambitious, fairly aggressive and wedded to quality.

This view of Mr Thompson is drawn from reading between the lines of the case and assuming that he is the key decision maker in the organization.

In Chapter 5 it was suggested that you take a role in analyzing the case study. In the context of evaluation this means that you should use the values of the person whose role you are taking to choose between alternative solutions. The role you decide to adopt, decision maker or consultant, will strongly interact with the source of values you choose to use. This interaction can best be explained by reference to Figure 9.2. Consultants trying to impose their own or textbook objectives on an organization may be clear about what they want but will find implementation difficult. On the other hand, a decision-making role will make the acceptance of implied organizational goals easy, though for the analyst it will not always be clear what those are. Thus, from the top left to the bottom right in Figure 9.2, clarity of objectives decreases as acceptance increases.

9.2.3 Mapping organizational values

Whichever role you assume and whatever source of values you espouse it is still important that you have a good idea of what the organization's objectives might be. You cannot suggest changes which do not take into account organizational preferences. In some cases this will be necessary because you will have to modify or circumvent them. In others because you wish to work within them. Again it is important to remember that organizational goals and objectives are summations of the goals and aspirations of individuals. However, for an organization to continue to operate, a certain core of missions and directions must be held in common. You should try, from your reading of the case, to establish what these might be. They will affect, at the very least, the likelihood that the organization will

Analyst's role

		Consultant	Decision maker
	Textbook		
Source of values	Analyst		
	Organization		

Figure 9.2 Sources of values and the analyst's role

accept your recommendations. Such a summary has been made for Wolverhampton and Dudley Breweries and it is given below:

Wolverhampton and Dudley Breweries is a mildly ambitious firm that is prepared to take some risks of a marginal nature but is not what might be called truly entrepreneurial. It values quality, independence and stability and would feel uncomfortable outside its traditional spheres of operations. It has its own way of doing things. It rewards loyalty and competence.

Again, this description was compiled by reading between the lines of the case study but it begins to sketch out what values the firm might hold and helps to define the things it would and would not be prepared to undertake.

9.3 PROS AND CONS LISTING

The first, and apparently most straightforward, task in putting a value on an outcome is to decide whether it is, in general, good or bad for the organization. This means taking the list of outcomes you have already generated and deciding whether each one, on balance, helps or hinders the organization in the achievement of its organizational goals. The process is easily described and the output is very simple. However, the actual task is obviously not so straightforward. It relies on the analyst judging the outcome in the light of all the factors affecting the organization and its performance. Since this activity is internal, it is not easy to examine. Bringing this activity into the light of day will be something that the next few sections will seek to achieve. A tentative pros and cons listing is given in Table 9.1 for one of the alternatives facing Wolverhampton and Dudley Breweries.

9.3.1 Balanced outcomes

Most outcomes are not too difficult to allocate. They are obviously either pro or con. There are, however, exceptions. The outcome, 'increased reliance on the brewing industry' is regarded as a 'con' in the list above. In general it is believed to be important not to put all your eggs in one basket. However, there are considerable returns to specialization in any set of human activities so that this outcome has its good side too. In cases like this it is often best to split the 'good' and 'bad' components of a particular outcome. In this case the 'con' would be vulnerability to changes in the beer market and the 'pro' would be realization of economies of specialization.

Table 9.1 *Pros and cons listing for the alternative: 'Attempt to take over another brewery'*

Pros	Cons
Joint sales and profit grow	Capital restructuring required
Shareholders and City happy	Cash available reduced
Scale economies realized	Management overstretched
Synergies realized	Internal dissent
New market opens up	Competitive reaction
Management expertise transferred	Monopolies Commission referral
Increased takeover protection	Union opposition
	Opposition within takeover firm
	Unanticipated problems in takeover firm
	Increased reliance on brewing industry
	Local markets adversely affected

9.3.2 Neutral outcomes

An outcome of the type described above might be described as a balanced outcome: the 'plus' aspects tend to balance the 'minus' aspects. However, you may find that some of the outcomes you generate are not of this type but are still difficult to assign under pro or con headings. These may be called neutral outcomes. They neither support nor hinder the organization in the pursuit of its goals. It may be that this results from an inability to predict what that outcome will lead to in the future: for Wolverhampton and Dudley Breweries the outcome 'stimulates the government to investigate the brewing industry'. This is essentially a neutral outcome: neither good nor bad. It is impossible to know whether this would lead to the bigger brewers being disadvantaged in some way or whether Wolverhampton and Dudley Breweries would now be considered one of the bigger brewers.

Taking the argument a stage further, if an outcome is neutral it cannot be used to help you decide amongst alternatives. Perhaps, then, a better definition of this kind of outcome is 'irrelevant' rather than neutral. It is best ignored since it simply complicates the issue.

The process of assigning outcomes to pros and cons columns provides a useful check on the completeness of your original outcomes listing. Balanced outcomes may need to be divided. An outcome mentioned for one alternative may not have been mentioned for another alternative although it applies equally well. Outcomes may

137

have to be combined or deleted if they are judged to have minimal impact on the organization and its progress.

9.3.3 'T' accounts

If you wish to go no further than this in your evaluation then the time has now come to choose among the alternatives. Two simple methods of doing this are suggested here, although there are obviously others. The first method is to balance your 'T' accounts. This can be done by comparing the pros and cons for an alternative and coming up with a 'net' valuation. This might be on an ordinal (very poor to very good) or a continuous (0 to 10) scale. The alternative with the best rating or score is chosen.

9.3.4 Key differences

Another way of carrying out the comparison is to attempt to concentrate on the key differences between alternatives. The less important and common outcomes are eliminated. The alternatives are then polarized in terms of their attributes. For example: Alternative – attempt to take over another brewer. There may not be one available, therefore it takes a long time and is risky. The rewards may be great and it provides expansion and protection. However, there are also risks with implementation and it is a high profile option. May be outside capability of existing management. It is the high risk/high return route. Another alternative – buy pubs in other areas. This is an incremental and low-risk option, at least in the short term. It is low profile and not likely to attract attention from competitors or the City. May not lead to large-scale returns in the long term but it would always be possible to sell the pubs again. Easily within current management capabilities. Leaves the firm vulnerable to competition. The safe road.

In this way, the essential differences are highlighted and a decision can be more readily made since fewer dimensions need to be considered at the same time.

9.4 OUTCOMES MODIFIED BY LIKELIHOOD DIFFERENCES

It has already been pointed out at some length that outcomes differ in terms of their likelihood of occurrence. This should be regarded as an important way of classifying or modifying the outcomes that are being used to judge the worth of an alternative. Clearly, if an altern-

Table 9.2 *Pros and cons listing with likelihood classification*

	Pros	Cons
Likely	Increased takeover protection Joint sales and profit grow Shareholders and City happy Synergies realized New market opens up Takeover succeeds	Capital restructuring required Unanticipated problems in takeover firm Increased reliance on brewing industry Cash available reduced Competitive reaction
Less likely	Management expertise transferred Scales economies realized	Management overstretched Internal dissent Union opposition Opposition from within takeover firm Monopolies Commission reference Local markets affected adversely

ative has a number of important and useful outcomes, but these have a low probability of occurring, then they should be discounted by a factor reflecting this. Such a modification can be carried out qualitatively or quantitatively.

The qualitative method would simply class outcomes as being of high or low likelihood. This classification can then be incorporated into a pros and cons listing as in Table 9.2. The likelihood levels in this table will normally come from the previous stage of analysis: predicting outcome likelihoods (e.g. Table 8.1). Remember that these likelihoods are not independent. The likelihoods of minor outcomes are likely to depend upon the occurrence of major outcomes. The likelihood structure resulting from the implementation of an alternative can get rather complex. That is why it is prudent to get it sorted out before the evaluation process begins. It is all too easy to allow the value of an outcome to influence your likelihood of its occurrence. In this way, analysts mould the evaluation process towards the alternative they have intuitively preferred from the beginning!

This method focuses attention on the highly likely alternatives. It makes the evaluation much more straightforward because it reduces the number of dimensions that the analyst has to use in his or her judgement. A more detailed approach involves the assignment of probability values as described in section 8.2 and illustrated in figure 8.5.

9.5 OUTCOMES MODIFIED BY IMPORTANCE RATINGS

Outcomes differ not only in terms of their likelihood but also in terms of how much they are likely to affect, for good or bad, the achievement of organizational goals. Again it must be stressed that the importance you assign to an outcome must reflect the particular values you have decided to use to judge between alternatives. The way in which you judge the importance of an outcome will be internal and judgemental. Nevertheless, it is another step along the road towards making more explicit the processes by which you favour one alternative over another.

9.5.1 Importance and likelihood

Importance can be treated in a similar way to likelihood. The simplest classification would use 'important' and 'unimportant' as the labels. Since likelihood levels have already been estimated, both factors can now be used to modify the basic pros and cons listing. This gives a two-way classification as shown in Figure 9.3.

This classification can now be applied to the pros and cons listing for 'Attempt to take over a brewer' as illustrated in Table 9.3. This gives quite a clear picture of where the attention should be directed. Category A outcomes, pro and con, are highly likely and highly important ones. They will therefore be the major grounds for evaluating this alternative, balancing pros against cons. This alternative has the high returns but expected problems with the management of the takeover which may mean that they are difficult to realize.

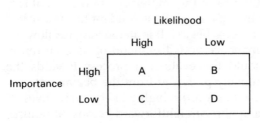

Figure 9.3 Two-way classification of importance and likelihood

Table 9.3 *Pros and cons listing using importance and likelihood ratings*

	Pros	Cons
A	Joint sales and profits grow Shareholders and City happy Takeover succeeds	Unanticipated problems in takeover firm Opposition from within takeover firm Local markets affected adversely
B	Management expertise transferred New markets opened up	Management overstretched Union opposition
C	Scale economies realized Synergies realized	Capital restructuring required Competitive reaction Internal dissent
D	Increased takeover protection	Cash available reduced Increased reliance on beer market Monopolies Commision reference

9.5.2 Importance rating

Importance can be estimated on a somewhat finer scale than important/unimportant. A continuous importance rating can be used. This might, for example, span a scale from 0 to 1, like probability. Combining the two measures could be achieved simply by multiplying likelihood and importance ratings together. This has been done in Table 9.4 where higher numbers indicate the more important and more probable outcomes. A certain (probability = 1.0) and very important outcome (importance = 1.0) would rate 1.0 on the importance/likelihood index.

There is a gap between the group of outcomes above and below 0.3. This suggests that quite a reasonable decision could be made by concentrating on balancing the pros and cons of the 'top' six outcomes. In addition it is interesting that many of the cons have very low likelihood/importance indices.

It is important to be clear about what is and what is not being achieved by these methods. They are simply ways of highlighting the key differences between different alternatives. This helps by allowing you to concentrate your efforts. However, you still have to weigh the pros and cons of each alternative against all the others. Your decision concerning which alternative is best still rests on an internal judgement process.

Table 9.4 *Expanded version of Table 9.3*

Importance/likelihood index	Pros	Importance/likelihood index	Cons
0.63	Joint sales and profit grow	0.60	Unanticipated problems in takeover firm
0.56	Shareholders and City happy	0.49	Opposition from within takeover firm
0.56	Takeover succeeds	0.30	Capital restructuring required
0.30	New markets open up	0.18	Competitive reaction
0.24	Management expertise transferred	0.15	Management overstretched
0.21	Scale economies realized	0.12	Local markets affected adversely
0.14	Increased takeover protection	0.12	Union opposition
		0.08	Increased reliance on beer
		0.06	Internal dissent
		0.05	Cash available reduced
		0.01	Monopolies Commission referral

9.6 A SINGLE CHOICE CRITERION

In the previous section the idea of the importance of an outcome was introduced without really discussing how it might be judged. Importance in this context was simply used as a flag. It allowed you to pick out, and concentrate your attention on, those outcomes which you believed would have most impact on the organization. The next stage is to move beyond saying, 'This is important' to say, 'This is why it's important'.

An outcome, and therefore an alternative, has to be judged in terms of how much it helps or hinders an organization in achieving its goals. In the situation where you are taking a role the organizational goals are seen through the eyes of the role player. In the first instance the set of goals will be narrowed further to just one overriding organizational goal. The consideration of multiple goals complicates the issue. Multiple goals will be discussed in section 10.1 when some of the problems of coping with a single goal have already been dealt with.

If a single overriding organizational goal can be decided upon, then this automatically becomes the criterion for choosing among the alternative solutions you have proposed. The process then splits into two parts – choosing the criterion and measuring each alternative's performance against that criterion. But first of all, what is a criterion?

9.6.1 Choice criterion

A criterion is simply a measurement by which a decision or choice is made. In an examination it may be the number of marks obtained. For a manager, it might be the amount of profit his or her division makes in a year. For a government department it may be the level of spending. In simple situations with a single, well-defined and easily measured criterion, the choice process is straightforward, at least in theory. Simply choose the alternative which scores the most, or least, on the single criterion – the student with the most marks, the manager with the greatest profit, the government department that spends least. For a case study, it might be the contribution of an alternative solution towards the achievement of one measure of organizational success, e.g. sales growth, profitability, cost effectiveness, employee morale or organizational survival. Before looking at how this can be done in practice, there are some problems of measurement to discuss.

143

9.6.2 Measurement problems

Whenever a measurement is involved there are usually three forms that it can take. The first form is possession or nonpossession of an attribute. People are either men or women, an organization either gets a major contract or it doesn't, implementation of a particular solution either leads to an organization's survival or its extinction. These are on–off variables – there is no half-way house. Criteria in the form of attributes are quite useful because they are so clear cut. This point will be made again when 'hurdles and ditches' are discussed in the next section.

The second form of measurement refers to situations where it is known that different things have different amounts of an attribute, but it is not known precisely how different. For example, 'very good employee morale' clearly has more of the variable 'good employee morale' than 'fairly good employee morale', but it is difficult to say how much more. Could it be 50% more, 100% more, or even infinitely more? In this case the problem lies in not having an exact measuring instrument for employee morale. Simply because it is difficult to measure something does not mean that it should be discarded as a criterion. Many, if not most, of the outcomes of the alternative solutions that you generate in your case analyses will be of this type. Can you afford to ignore the differences between a 'low' profit and a 'high' profit simply because you feel you cannot exactly quantify the difference? You will have to accept the fact that in complex situations where the future is being predicted, you will have to work with imprecise and woolly data. This is, however, one of the most important skills a problem solver can acquire.

The third form of measurement is where the scale used is metric, or else may be considered to be metric. Examples include sales, profits and costs measured in pounds, number of employees or percentage of warranty claims on a new product. This is the most powerful type of measurement to work with. The numbers that result from measuring in this way can be added, subtracted, divided, multiplied or operated on by a variety of mathematical techniques. If all criteria could be measured as metric variables, some of the problems of choosing among alternatives would disappear. In the next section it will be shown that often the only way explicitly to choose among alternatives is to convert non-metric to metric variables using judgement as the basis for the conversion.

9.6.3 Choosing a criterion

The choice of a single criterion for judging among alternatives is not usually an easy task. Consider again the sources from which it might come (see section 9.2) – textbooks, you, or the organization you are studying. For a commercial organization, the criterion might be chosen from among this set: survival, long-term return on investment, profit growth, sales growth, cost reduction, personal income or wealth, job satisfaction or career growth. This is not a judgement that should be made lightly or implicitly. Take your time deciding what criterion you should use and state what it is in your class discussion or reports. You can then always defend your choice of alternatives by referring back to the criterion.

Returning to the Wolverhampton and Dudley Breweries case, a defensible single criterion might be real profit growth. The firm seems to have undertaken its takeover bid for Davenport's because it wished to expand. The chairman said as much in his comments on the failure of the bid. The slow-down in profit growth appeared to be a spur for its actions. Thus it would seem reasonable to use it as the single most important criterion.

9.6.4 Qualitative criteria

In some case studies it will be possible to make quantitative estimates of each alternative's expected performance and to choose the best on the basis of a simple comparison. However, this is unlikely to be a common occurrence. If the criterion is, however, less easily measurable, another method is required. The first step is to assess how each outcome for each alternative is likely to contribute towards the achievement of the criterion. This must, of course, take into consideration how likely that outcome is to occur. An outcome can hardly contribute much to real profit growth if it is itself rather unlikely to occur. This means starting from Table 9.3 or something similar.

Examine each of the outcomes and ask yourself, 'How is this likely to contribute to real profit growth?' In particular, think through the implications of each outcome. Look for the links between the outcome and the criterion. Try to estimate the impact of this outcome acting in concert with the other outcomes that implementation of a particular solution would bring. For example, economies of scale reduce costs quite significantly and might be expected to impact upon profits in real terms. Of course, you would have to be as specific as you could about what kind of economies would result and estimate the order of cost savings that they might be expected to provide.

The power of using a single criterion now becomes evident. It becomes clear what to look for. Some outcomes can be seen to be important; others are immediately judged to be irrelevant. Increasing the protection from takeover will not affect profit growth. If the firm is taken over the criterion is invalid in any case. This particular outcome is irrelevant to real profit growth and can be ignored.

9.6.5 Choosing an alternative

In many cases, using the razor's edge of a single criterion, the choice will be fairly evident. Some alternatives will disqualify themselves because they score low measured against the criterion. In other cases the differences between alternatives will be so large as to make the choice inevitable. When differences are small, it may be necessary carefully to rank the alternatives on your judgement of their expected performance against the criterion. In extreme cases you might decide to scale alternatives using numerical values. In essence, what you would be doing would be to ask yourself the question: 'How would I rate, on a scale from 1 to 10, the contribution that this alternative would make towards improvement in the chances of long-term survival?' This procedure would help you to concentrate your attention on what you believe are the most important differences between alternatives in terms of their effect on the single criterion of success.

10

Step Five: Choosing Among Alternatives (II)

10.1 MULTIPLE CHOICE CRITERIA

If you followed section 9.6 carefully you may have begun to suspect that using a single choice criterion is not so straightforward as it looks. There are two reasons why using more than one criterion makes for better decisions. The first is that organizations and individuals rarely pursue single goals. The second is that it is often difficult to link the outcomes stemming from an alternative with their effect on a particular goal. Sometimes it is necessary to substitute several intermediate goals for one ultimate goal. Both of these reasons for moving beyond single to multiple criteria will now be examined in detail.

In practice people use multiple criteria in judging between alternative solutions without realizing it. Imagine a company with the problem of a factory making an unsuccessful product. One of the alternatives would be to burn it down and collect the insurance money. The problem would be solved: the company would no longer have a factory selling an unsuccessful product. But that solution is antisocial, immoral and illegal. In ruling out this alternative you would be implicitly using criteria beyond the simple 'solves the problem as described in the case'. As a less extreme example, consider the alternatives evaluated in section 9.6. The single criterion used was that of real profit growth. Suppose an alternative had been proposed which ensured real profit growth but which involved producing poor quality, weak mild beer. On a single criterion it would win hands down, but it would clearly not meet the implicit objective of brewing high-quality products.

10.1.1 Goals and constraints

Both of these examples are meant to demonstrate that we use multiple criteria in all our decision making. Individuals and organizations want to achieve a mixture of different goals. One goal may predominate at any one time but other goals cannot be ignored. A course of action which supports the pursuit of one goal to the exclusion of others will not, in general, be chosen. Goals may be both positive and negative. We are usually clear about what we want more of. We are usually even clearer about what we want less of, or indeed none of. Goals of this kind are usually called constraints. These are directions in which we do not want to go; areas in which we would not want solutions to take us.

10.1.2 Conflicting objectives

Another point is that very often organizations and people have conflicting objectives. Individuals wish themselves health, wealth and happiness; not just one, but all three! We wish for friendship, but do not wish to have our personal liberty curtailed. We want to be rich, but not at the expense of our leisure time. We wish to help others, but there is a limit to the amount of tax we would agree to have deducted from our salaries.

The problems of handling conflicting objectives are made much more difficult because the decision usually concerns not just one person but many. In discussing cases, the unit of analysis is usually the organization. It is true that for some small organizations this essentially means one person – the owner. However, these cases are rather rare. Even in the Wolverhampton and Dudley Breweries situation there are several people to consider. When there are a number of people who may be involved in the decision, they will all bring their own particular values into the decision process. Very frequently these values will differ. One person may value stability, another may value growth, while a third may value excitement.

10.1.3 Educational objectives

Even where there is one very clear-cut single criterion, it can be argued that a second should always be added to it. This second criterion is that of educational value. To include this we must take a step back. Why are you doing this case study? Obviously in order to improve your analytical and creative skills. However, alternatives may differ in the extent to which they allow you to do this. For example, two alternatives that often appear in case presentations are (a) to appoint somebody to sort the problem out and (b) to collect more information. Of course, these are often legitimate and important alternatives in real life. However, they both score rather badly on the criterion of educational value. If someone is appointed to sort out the problem, this absolves the analyst from doing so. If more information is required, then it is easier to suggest how this might be done rather than making, and defending, a decision based upon the information actually available. If a case analyst wishes to get experience in solving organizational problems he or she may reject alternatives like this on educational grounds. In effect you will be saying, 'I realize that other alternatives were probably as good but I chose to pursue this one, because in developing it I thought I would get more mileage out of the case'. A case instructor will usually support a student doing this provided that it is done explicitly and with advance warning.

10.1.4 Uncertainty

The second reason for multiple criteria is uncertainty. This uncertainty can come from two sources. Firstly, it will usually be difficult to get a precise measure of a particular organizational goal. Secondly, it may not be easy to predict how much a particular alternative contributes to the achievement of a particular organizational goal. Both of these uncertainties can be resolved by splitting a single goal into multiple subgoals.

Suppose one goal of an organization is stability. How can this be measured? Employee turnover rates? Constant profit growth? Continuing to operate within existing technology? In practice it is unlikely that just one variable can capture the flavour of the goal as originally laid down. Several measures will usually be needed. All of these may be insufficient in themselves, but together encompass the original goal and provide a reasonable measure of it. Figure 10.1 illustrates this idea in relation to the corporate goal of stability. These subgoals in effect are substitutes or proxies for the original goal. Not unnaturally they are therefore called proxy goals. They 'stand in' for the important goal because it cannot be measured directly.

The second source of uncertainty is similar to the first. The difference is that the goal is easy to measure, but the ways in which it might be achieved are not. Take, for example, the goals of sales growth or profitability. Both are easy to measure; what is difficult is predicting how a particular alternative course of action will affect these variables. Again, the answer is to break down the main goal into a series of subgoals as in Figure 10.2 for the goal sales growth. Thus, you would expect sales growth if prices rise, if new customers are obtained and if existing customers buy more. The effect of any one alternative on these proxy goals is easier to measure than the

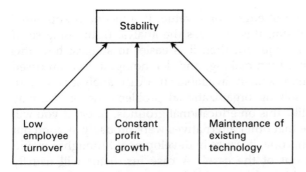

Figure 10.1 Proxy variables for the organizational goal: stability

effect on the ultimate goal. Of course, it is always possible that good performance on one subgoal would be more than offset by poor performance on another. For example, increasing price might, and usually will, reduce both the number of new customers and the usage of existing customers. You will need to watch for these effects when judging between alternatives. Nevertheless, the process of creating proxy variables will alert you to the different routes by which a particular course of action can affect a particular organizational goal. In the case of the alternative − 'attempt to take over a brewer' − for Wolverhampton and Dudley Breweries, it is clear that the main contribution to sales growth will be through new customers for its existing products. Figure 10.2 makes clear how crucial this factor will be in judging the success of this strategy.

10.1.5 Generating multiple criteria

Now that the reasons for multiple criteria are understood, a practical method for generating them is required. The place to start is with a general list of the goals of an organization taken from a textbook, from your understanding of the organization and the people in it, or from what you would want an organization to achieve if you were in charge. Refer back to section 9.3 for a detailed discussion of these three sources of organizational goals.

For Wolverhampton and Dudley Breweries, the following shortlist might have been generated by Mr Thompson if he had been asked:

1. Long-term growth in sales
2. Long-term growth in profits.
3. Maintenance of control.
4. Quality products.

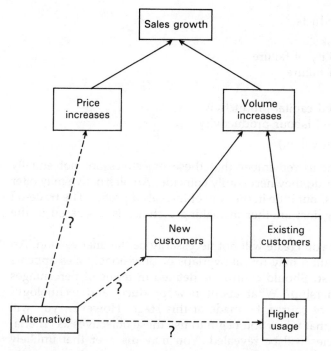

Figure 10.2 Proxy variables for the organizational goal: sales growth

5. Medium risk.
6. Efficiency.
7. (Educational value.)

This list could have been longer, but it encompasses the major elements of the values ascribed to Wolverhampton and Dudley Breweries as summarized at the end of section 9.2.

The next step is to examine each of these objectives – soon to be criteria – to see whether they need to be replaced by proxies. The original Wolverhampton and Dudley Breweries list has been expanded to the one given below:

1. Long-term growth in sales:
   (i) new customers
   (ii) higher usage.
2. Long-term growth in profits:
   (i) higher sales
   (ii) lower costs
3. Maintenance of control.

4. Quality products.
5. Medium risk:
   (i) probability of failure
   (ii) costs of failure
6. Efficiency:
   (i) increased capital productivity
   (ii) improved labour productivity
7. (educational value.)

It is important to remember that these objectives are not equally important, nor do they necessarily coincide. An alternative may offer increased sales, but little in the way of increased profits. The trade-off of one goal against another in making a choice is discussed in the next section.

The first list you create will not necessarily be the final version. An initial examination may reveal overlaps or omissions. Sales appears twice in the list. Should control be defined in terms of percentages of share ownership? What about new products and technology? Changes can, of course, be made at this stage. However, you will normally find that when you begin to use these objectives as criteria, their deficiencies will be revealed. You may discover that unlikely alternatives will score better than the ones you thought the most suitable. This will usually be because you have omitted a key criterion which only occurs to you when a decision has to be made. Alternatively you may find that some criteria have no discriminating power at all and can be omitted. The choice process should be seen as adaptive. It should not degenerate into simply a mechanical procedure.

10.2 METHODS OF CHOOSING USING MULTIPLE CRITERIA

10.2.1 The choice problem

The problem you have to face is essentially the following: to choose among a small number of alternatives each with a number of predicted outcomes, by judging how they help in the achievement of a number of alternative goals. This can probably be illustrated best by means of a matrix, as shown in Figure 10.3. The alternatives, e.g. 'attempt to take over a brewery', are A1 to A5. The criteria against which they are to be judged, e.g. 'efficiency' are shown as C1 to C5. The performance of an alternative (A1) on any criterion (C3) is shown as p13: for example, how the takeover by Wolverhampton and

Criteria

	C1	C2	C3	C4	C5
A1	p11	p12	p13	p14	p15
A2	p21	p22	p23	p24	p25
A3	p31	p32	p33	p34	p35
A4	p41	p42	p43	p44	p45
A5	p51	p52	p53	p54	p55

Alternatives

Figure 10.3 Multiple criteria choice process

Dudley Breweries of another firm might lead to increased overall efficiency for both firms.

The choice process described here is in two parts. The first part attempts to eliminate certain alternatives before any comparisons are made. In some situations, all but one alternative can be thrown out and therefore the choice has been made by a process of elimination. The second part, if it is necessary, requires a comparison to be made among the surviving alternatives by combining their performances on all the criteria and choosing the alternative with the best overall performance. The term 'combining' is deliberately vague. It does not necessarily imply a simple summing process: it may be more complicated than that. However, the overall position is simple – the best combined performance on all criteria wins. The most appropriate input into these two processes would be the 'T' accounts described in section 9.4, an example of which is given in Table 9.2. This is essentially a summary of the pros and cons of each alternative modified by the likelihood of their occurring. It provides, at a glance, an excellent basis for judging the performance of an alternative on any criterion. In particular, it reminds you that all outcomes are not equally likely. The probability factor must be carried forward into the judgement of performance against criteria. A very favourable performance must, for example, be downgraded if it is unlikely to occur.

10.2.2 Hurdles and ditches

It is common in popular sporting events to limit the entry. This is done so that the contestants have the best conditions under which to be judged. The limitation is achieved by specifying that only applicants who have previously surpassed a certain performance level may enter. A similar principle may be used in evaluating alternative

Table 10.1 *Maximum and minimum values of criteria*

	Minimum	Maximum
New customers	2% p.a.	20% p.a.
Higher usage	0% p.a.	5% p.a.
Higher sales	5% p.a.	25% p.a.
Lower costs	0% p.a.	−10% p.a.
Maintenance of control	51% voting shares	
Quality products	As good as average competitor	
Probability of failure		0.8
Costs of failure	?	?
Increased capital productivity	0%	15%
Improved labour productivity	2%	20%
Educational value	Must permit full analysis	

solutions in a case study. Only the solutions which clear certain hurdles or ditches will be allowed to continue on to the full comparison procedure.

Hurdles and ditches can operate in one of two ways. In the first type, an alternative must exceed a certain value measured against the criterion. For example, using the education criterion, an alternative must allow a student practice at developing a complete action programme. An alternative described as 'sell up' would not meet this criterion and would be eliminated. The second type of hurdle or ditch eliminates certain alternatives if they do exceed a certain value measured against a criterion. Any high-risk option, e.g. 'move into biotechnology', would automatically be eliminated from consideration in the Wolverhampton and Dudley Breweries case. It exceeds even the medium level of risk tolerance that Wolverhampton and Dudley Breweries' management is believed to retain. Hurdles and ditches can be created by examining each criterion and putting a maximum and/or minimum on each. This has been done in Table 10.1 for the Wolverhampton and Dudley Breweries criteria developed in the previous section.

Some criteria cannot be assigned maximum and minimum values. This is no problem since it simply means that you will have less chance to prune out unwanted alternatives early on. Note that the first three items in Table 10.1 have both maxima and minima. This, in a sense, is a reflection of every organization's need for stability. Too much growth could be as unacceptable as too little. Note also that some criteria have a minimum and some have a maximum. This clearly depends on how the criterion is defined. Two are expressed in rather qualitative terms.

Again, it should be pointed out that these values should be used adaptively. Try to see if they eliminate any alternatives. If they do, are you happy that they have, or do you feel they need to be changed? In practice none of the three alternatives in the Wolverhampton and Dudley Breweries case set out at the top of Figure 7.4 were eliminated by the hurdles or ditches. However, in checking them against the list one or two values that were regarded as unrealistic were changed.

A second form of elimination is possible. This occurs when an alternative clearly performs worst against all criteria. There is no way in which it can, because of the differing importance of different criteria, compensate for bad with good. It is definitely the worst and can be dropped.

The reverse situation is less likely but more interesting. It is possible to find a situation where one alternative outperforms all others on all criteria. In this case it cannot be bettered and the choice is obvious. This rarely happens in practice simply because most alternatives have good and bad points. The weighing of pros and cons in these circumstances is dealt with in the next section. None of the alternatives in the Wolverhampton and Dudley Breweries case currently being evaluated performed best or worst overall.

10.2.3 Weighing overall performances

The alternative with the best overall performance is the one which will be recommended to the organization. How is overall performance to be judged, though? As with many of these procedures the task is twofold. First, the individual performance of each alternative measured against each criterion must be judged, i.e. a value must be assigned to each of the p in the matrix in Figure 10.3. Second, these values must be combined in some way to give a single overall value. The alternative with the highest value is the alternative of choice.

Combining performances is not necessarily a straightforward process. Consider the following hypothetical example concerning two alternatives where the data are more than usually precise. The first alternative is expected to boost return on investment to 15% over a five-year period, the second to 12%. The first alternative requires a short-term cash payment of $500,000, the second does not. Which of these two alternatives should the organization choose? Consider first the performance of the alternatives by the two criteria: return on investment and cash flow. Since neither alternative is superior on both criteria, some way must be found for combining their performances. This is made difficult by the fact that the criteria use different measures. Return on investment is a ratio and cash flow is measured in money terms. They cannot simply be added. Some way must be found of converting both these values to a common basis. The simplest method is to use a common scale for each criterion. This will usually be a 1 to 10 scale with 1 indicating a very poor performance on this criterion and 10 a very good performance. The scores measured against any one criterion are best estimated by examining all the alternatives together. Then you have some measure of the range of the values involved. This in turn makes it easier to allocate particular alternatives to particular points on the scale. For the example used above, the values illustrated in Figure 10.4 may have been decided upon.

These numbers can now be added and the second alternative comes out best. But this leads to another difficulty. The above method of combining the performances of different alternatives on different criteria assumes that all criteria are equally important. This is obviously not the case: some criteria are far more important than others. This can be reflected by weighting each criterion to reflect its importance. Thus in the example given above, if return on investment is regarded as twice as important as cash flow, then it could be given a weight of 2. Alternatively a total weight value of 100 could be allocated among the criteria. This method is shown in Figure 10.5. Alternative one now becomes the choice.

		Criteria		
		Return on investment	Cash flow requirement	Total
Alternatives	One	8	5	13
	Two	5	10	15

Figure 10.4 An example of choosing using unweighted criteria

		Criteria		
		Return on investment	Cash flow requirement	Total
	Weights	67	33	
Alternatives	One	8	5	701
	Two	5	10	665

Figure 10.5 An example of choosing using weighted criteria

This method is not without its drawbacks. It assumes that the choice is best made by a linear additive $(ax + by)$ combination of the performance of the proposed alternatives on different criteria. It is entirely possible that non-linear functions would be a better representation of the way people's values cover the alternative values. It may also be that performance values should be combined in some other way than adding. For example, multiplying the values penalizes the alternative with a good overall performance marred by one or two bad points and this might be just the choice structure you desire. There is a vast variety of choice rules that could be used. In effect, the more sophisticated rules are attempting to give a more accurate representation of how decision makers combine alternatives with different values and come to a single overall judgement.

However, in practical terms, these sophistications require more time and data than are normally available in a case analysis. The simple linear additive method works quite well to spell out the crucial trade-offs that have to be made when coming to a final judgement. It is easy to understand and it is straightforward to experiment with the scales and weights if the results do not seem to accord with our intuitions. Also it can easily be input into a spreadsheet programme which allows adjustments to be made very simply and quickly.

Choice procedure: an example

The procedure, then, is as follows. The list of criteria obtained as described in section 10.1 must first be weighted. As an example, this has been done for the criteria generated by the Wolverhampton and Dudley Breweries case. A shortened list has been used to simplify presentation (see Table 10.2). The first weights assigned will usually require adjusting until a pattern that seems to map the values of the organization emerges.

Each alternative is now rated on a scale from 1 to 10 on each criterion. Again it should be emphasized that the 'T' accounts described in section 9.3 are the best summary of the outcomes expected from each alternative and their likelihood of occurring. Remember that the likelihood must figure prominently in the assessment of the value to be given to an alternative in relation to any criterion. In a sense each outcome is being weighted not only by how much it contributes to a criterion but also by how likely it is to occur. Having weighted the criteria and scaled the alternatives on those criteria, a matrix like that shown in Figure 10.6 can be constructed. The scores for each alternative can then be calculated and the overall best solution determined.

Table 10.2 *Criteria weights for Wolverhampton and Dudley Breweries case*

	Criteria	Weights
C1	New customers	10
C2	Higher sales	20
C3	Lower costs	15
C4	Maintenance of control	25
C5	Probability of failure	15
C6	Increased capital productivity	5
C7	Educational value	10
		100

	Criteria weights							
	C1	C2	C3	C4	C5	C6	C7	Weighted totals
Alternatives	10	20	15	25	15	5	10	
Take over another brewery	8	10	7	5	6	9	8	725
Buy pubs in other areas	10	8	5	9	10	2	6	780
Sell mild to other breweries	10	10	5	8	9	2	8	800

Figure 10.6 Example of an evaluation matrix: Wolverhampton and Dudley Breweries case

If a number of these evaluations are to be carried out, it is useful to create a spreadsheet format.

Perhaps it might be worthwhile commenting in detail on this evaluation matrix. Alternative three, selling mild to other breweries, comes out on top. It represents a low-risk option that does not entail much chance of the firm losing control. In this it contrasts with the takeover option which is high profile and might draw attention to the firm, leading to bids. It also scores higher than alternative two, albeit marginally, because the volume of sales is likely to be higher without risking any further capital. However, the differences are small and would probably disappear if the weights were changed only slightly. In this situation it is best to go into more detail and perhaps experiment with the weights to see how sensitive the outcome is to such changes. In this case, as discussed earlier, it might be sensible to carry two alternatives forward to the next stage of the evaluation cycle.

10.3   GUIDE TO USE

At the very minimum, a student should decide what values he or she will use in choosing among alternatives (section 9.2). Failure to do so very frequently leads to inconclusive case reports and discussions. The next step, of producing 'T' accounts, does not take much extra effort, but very quickly clarifies the differences between alternatives (section 9.3). Modifying these accounts in the light of the different probabilities that different outcomes have of occurring is a useful additional step (section 9.4). Beginners will not wish to go beyond section 9.5 which discusses combining importance ratings with likelihood estimates.

Sections 10.1 and 10.2 represent a practical approach to a very complicated decision process. It involves choosing among alternatives with different outcomes of different likelihoods against not one, but several, different criteria. This is the crux of the process which we call judgement. Students should aim to try out all the techniques discussed in these three sections before they complete a case course. They not only provide practical techniques for decision making, but also provide individuals with personal insights into the process.

Step Six: Rounding Out the Analysis

Step six bridges the gap between the process of analysis and communicating the results of that analysis. It involves detailing and making contingency plans.

11.1 DETAILING

In Chapter 7 the parallel concepts of evaluation cycles and solution trees were introduced. It was suggested that these were necessary simply because evaluating all the alternative solutions was too difficult to achieve in one attempt. To remind yourself how these concepts work refer to Figure 7.5. A solution tree is simply a way of structuring alternative solutions. The most general and strategic solutions are at the bottom or trunk. The most specific and tactical solutions are at the top (twigs). At each level there are a number of mutually exclusive solutions stemming from a node. The purpose of an evaluation cycle, as described in detail in Chapters 7 to 10, is to 'prune' out all but one of these solutions. In the next cycle the pruning is carried out at the next node in the solution tree. In this way a compound solution is built up from trunk to twigs, from ends to means.

Clearly, an important decision is when to stop. It would be possible to go on ad infinitum adding more and more levels to the solution tree and evaluating the options at each level. The question is, 'How much detail is required?' Basically this comes back to the perennial problem of depth versus breadth. With a given amount of time at your disposal you must allocate your effort between these two competing ends.

11.1.1 Breadth and depth

A broad analysis would be one which extensively examines a large number of competing general solutions or strategies and chooses

160

amongst them, but which says little or nothing about how they might be implemented. An analysis in depth would devote less time to choosing among solutions at the general level and more to working out the details of how they might be implemented.

Beginners at case analysis frequently inhabit the extremes. It is not unusual to see statements like, 'The company should do more research', or, 'They should pay more attention to industrial relations'. This is certainly taking the broad view. But most case instructors would not resist the temptation to ask, 'What kind of research?' and, 'What kind of attention to what aspect of industrial relations?' In other words, they are asking for more detail: less breadth and more depth. To be accurate, the kind of student who produces statements like those mentioned above is hardly likely to have much breadth to his or her analysis either but that's a problem for the case instructor.

There is a second type of student who likes to get straight to the heart of the matter. He or she ignores all the major strategic issues and gets down to the detail of writing copy, devising timetables or designing machine modifications. This type of student frequently has considerable industrial experience and is presumably repeating the behaviour which was normal in the work situation. A case instructor in this situation would usually attempt to pull the student back from the problem and get him or her to take the broad view.

In practice there is really only one way to decide what level of detail is appropriate. The decision is primarily an educational one and lies with the case instructors. It is up to them to decide where they want to put the emphasis: which skills they wish students to practise in which situation. It is your job as a case analyst to make sure that you know what level of detail is required. If it is not clear, ask. It is useful to get a specification by example. Does the case instructor want a pro forma cash flow forecast for the new product? Will it be enough to describe a general factory layout rather than to specify exactly where each machine will go? Having got this information in advance you will be able to use it to help determine the 'height' of your solution tree and the number of evaluation cycles you need to do.

Up to this point the major concern has been with the level or quantity of detail, but what about the quality of detail? This is to a large extent determined by the nature of the solution tree which is in turn a function of the creativity of the individual concerned. But there are some general kinds of detail that it is essential that you include in your case solution. Other kinds of detail would be beneficial provided that they are at a level consistent with that required by the case instructor. These types of detail are in very general categories and each will be discussed in turn below.

11.1.2 Implementation

Organizations don't implement solutions, people do. An important point to ask yourself is, 'How will this decision be implemented?' This may seem to require no more than a fairly straightforward allocation of responsibility to existing departments and/or individuals. However, this ignores the politics and sociology of the situation. You will remember that when the outcomes of a particular decision were discussed in Chapter 8 the reactions of individuals and groups in the firm were also taken into account. These 'internal' outcomes can be used in two ways.

The first way is in the evaluation cycle along with other outcomes. Some of these outcomes will be positive, i.e. those which people in the organization prefer and which will reward them in some way. Thus they will impact upon the beneficial outcomes, like productivity increases, and make them more likely to happen. They may even tap directly into evaluation criteria, for example job satisfaction. Others may be negative and may help prevent the achievement of positively rated outcomes. In general, since most people are conservative with respect to change, the more radical the alternative the more likely it is that it will be constrained by the supposed implementors.

The second way is to use these outcomes to develop an implementation plan. In essence this means that you go into more detail in specifying the alternative you have chosen after you have chosen it. For example, in the Wolverhampton and Dudley Breweries case, if the alternative chosen was to sell mild to other breweries you would have to decide how that was actually going to be done and who was going to do it. You would have to consider what their attitude to the proposal would be.

You may discover that your solution implies major reorganization. If this is the case you may have to rework your evaluations since this is an outcome that you missed on the first run through. Making a department responsible for the whole, or even a part, of your solution implementation does not mean that it will be carried out. You may therefore consider how your plan might be presented to its implementors so that its chances of success are enhanced. This may mean no more than careful explanation and consultation. Alternatively it could mean a change in the entire reward system of the organization. The importance of getting the 'people' aspects of the implementation right cannot be stressed too much. There is a great temptation to consider only what might be called the technical and economic dimensions. But organizations are people and there is no point in assuming that if you, or your role player, have decided that this is the best alternative then others will either agree or, having agreed, will do anything to put it into effect.

It is always worthwhile considering the *timing* of the actions that you will be recommending. It may be enough simply to run through the events to see if there is a feasible timetable. Having convinced yourself that there is, you may not even include it in your report. However, you may discover that your pet solution requires reworking in order that a particular sequence of events occurs in a particular order. You may have decided, for example, to use the annual exhibition of furniture manufacturers to launch your new easy chair only to discover that it can't be researched, developed and manufactured in time. Timing is frequently ignored by case analysts but it is of course a very important factor in determining the success or otherwise of a particular solution. Collect extra marks by including a time scale in your presentation.

Although they should have been considered in the evaluation of the solutions, *resources* are a factor which might usefully be examined again at the detailing stage. Students frequently forget that money, people and materials are limited in an organization, at least in the short term. Beginners are frequently embarrassed by questions such as: How is this going to be paid for? How many extra personnel will be needed? How will managers cope with the extra work load? Is there space on the current site for the new development? Are high street sites readily available?

While it is true that you cannot implement your solutions and get *feedback* on their performance, that does not mean that you should ignore feedback entirely. Part of the detailing of your solution might include provision for feedback. This may be no more than a listing of key parameters, e.g. sales, staff turnover, cash flow, profit. Alternatively, you may feel it necessary to specify a continuing research programme which will allow detailed monitoring of the implementation of your solution.

In the evaluation cycles you will have become aware of the advantages of your preferred solution. When sketching in the detail you should keep these factors in mind. In particular, it is important to ameliorate the *disadvantages* as much as possible. For example, if a particular alternative means fewer employees, then a detailed plan for redundancy negotiations and payments, redeployment, early retirement and so on should be worked out. This will never convert a disadvantage into an advantage, but at least it should lessen the impact. All of these types of detail should, in truth, have been picked up in the development of solutions. However, it is too much to expect that this will always happen. To consider them again at the detailing stage is to provide a safety net.

11.2 CONTINGENCY PLANNING

It has been a repeated theme throughout this book that the case method suffers from being a static learning experience. The case situation is a snapshot at one point in time. Case analysts have to make far-reaching, grand slam, one-off decisions which it is hoped will set the organization on the right path far into the future. In practice, decision making is rarely carried out in this fashion. It is more usually a sequential, adaptive process. Managers take a small decision, look at the effects, take another decision, and so on. Rarely do they have to keep all the balls in the air at once. In addition they can usually reverse a decision before its consequences become disastrous.

It seems only fair that case analysts should be allowed some measure of latitude in their decision making to bring them closer to a real-world situation. This can be done by means of contingency planning. It is not without its costs. The whole process of case analysis becomes more complex and the learning experience may not be quite so useful in some ways. Nevertheless it is an option that should be carefully considered. It will be more appropriate for some case studies than others.

11.2.1 Unconditional decision making

The method of solution evaluation described in Chapters 7 to 10 required that unconditional decisions be made. The uncertainty inherent in making decisions about the future was handled by weighting possible outcomes by their subjective probability of occurring. The option of changing one's mind was not allowed. This essentially is what contingency planning is about. It may best be illustrated by a diagram such as in Figure 11.1.

Unconditional planning requires that an unconditional decision be made in 'case time'. This decision takes into account the fact that each decision has a number of possible outcomes each with an estimated probability of occurring. The solution with the highest predicted value is chosen and no conditions are placed on that choice. It is final and irrevocable. The value of taking that decision will only become known when a particular outcome actually comes to pass.

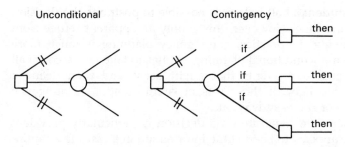

Figure 11.1 Comparison of unconditional and contigency planning

11.2.2 Conditional decision making

By contrast contingency planning allows for conditional decision making. At 'case time' a decision can be made as to which general course of action to take. But when the outcome of taking that decision is known, then a second, unconditional, decision comes into play. This means that the plan responds, albeit in a pre-programmed way, to changes in circumstances. The original conditional decision is couched in 'if... then' terms. If a particular outcome occurs, then the decision is to do this. If a different outcome occurs, then the decision will be to do something else.

In the Wolverhampton and Dudley Breweries case one of the problems with the 'attempt to take over a brewer' alternative is that there may not be a suitable brewer available for sale. The decision may therefore be couched in conditional terms: attempt to take over a brewer for six months and, if this fails, attempt to sell mild to a major brewer; and if this also fails, continue the policy of buying pubs in different areas. This corresponds much more closely to the way that decisions are actually made. However, it differs in one important aspect and this reveals a major weakness in the technique. With contingency planning it is necessary not only to identify the outcomes of a particular course of action in advance, but also to decide what to do in the light of that information. In real life the decision can wait until the outcome actually occurs. Thus contingency planning is much more complex than either real-life decision making or unconditional planning.

11.2.3 Postponing decision making

There is an additional problem to do with the nature of the learning that takes place during case studies. Many students are reluctant to commit themselves to a decision. Contingency planning apparently

165

allows the student a bolt-hole: it is possible to postpone the decision to some future time. However, this is only an apparent refuge from decision making. In practice, contingency planning is much more complex than unconditional planning – it has to take into account all the combinations of events that might occur and then define a decision in the light of those sets of circumstances. Contingency planning is not the easy way out.

This tendency to hang fire on a decision is particularly prevalent where there appears to be too little information in a case. The contingency plan then takes the form, 'Do research and, depending on the results, follow through a particular course of action'. For example, if more than 50% of the workforce, when questioned, oppose a productivity deal, then do not go ahead with it. The problem is that research is rarely as straightforward and unequivocal as that. Suppose, for example, that in the above survey 51% of the workforce opposed the deal. Is 50% really such a clear-cut parameter on which to take two very different courses of action? Again, what about the situation where more than 50% oppose the deal but for relatively trivial reasons? With minor changes in the deal it could gain overwhelming support. Yet the contingency plan states that the deal must be dropped.

In some cases it is quite possible that the only defensible decision is to collect more information. These cases are rarer than they might at first appear, but they do occur. They are relatively rare, not because most cases have a wealth of relevant information, but because in practice decisions are always taken with insufficient knowledge of the situation and the way in which it might develop. When case instructors force students to take decisions in conditions of great uncertainty they are helping to prepare them for real-life decision making. As has already been pointed out, the missing information will probably be different in the case situation and in real life. However, it is the skill of making decisions under certain conditions that is being practised. The accuracy of the decision context is probably not all that important.

11.2.4 Collecting more information

Nevertheless, there are situations when the decision will be made to collect more information. In this case, contingency planning at some level is essential. It is simply unacceptable to call for more information without saying what it will be and how it will be collected. It is impossible to say what will be collected without knowing what decisions will be made based upon the information collected. In other words, it is still necessary to go through all the steps described in the previous chapters up to the point of evaluating alternatives. Alternatives cannot be directly evaluated in this case, so the task becomes one of asking what information will help decide between them, and what values the parameters should take in order to make one decision as opposed to another. As an example, imagine the situation of an organization attempting to decide which of two product ideas to develop. It is possible to identify three major pieces of information that would be helpful in making a choice: anticipated production costs, and customer and retailer reactions to the alternative offerings. In this situation it would be expected that ways of measuring these variables would be put forward by the student. In addition, against a background of knowledge of existing product performance, it would be possible to estimate at what level a product idea must perform in order to be worthy of development: for example, production costs at least 20% less than those of existing products combined with retailer and customer preferences in a ratio of 2:1 in favour of the new product when compared with existing products. These values can be determined in advance by a process similar to that used in the evaluation step described in Chapter 9. The only difference is that the evaluation produces not a choice among alternatives, e.g. product A or product B, but criteria for making that choice. The 'winning' product must be better than the 'losing' product by these margins on these important evaluation variables.

In summary, contingency planning is a powerful but rather complex technique. It should probably only be used when conditions for its use are really favourable. Some of these conditions are listed below:

1. When the outcomes which signal different decisions are clear (e.g. a strike does or does not take place).
2. When the outcomes are all reasonably likely to occur (there is little point in planning for a very unlikely event).
3. When the decisions would be very different depending on the outcomes (e.g. a subsidiary would be expanded or closed down).
4. When there is not enough information in the case on which to base a defensible decision.

11.3 GUIDE TO USE

Case students need to know when to draw the line in their analysis and how much detail to work to. This is the subject matter of section

11.1, and it is probably required reading for all new case students and may even make experienced case analysts think again about this important topic.

By contrast, section 11.2 is much less likely to be immediately useful. It does however explore some of the boundaries of the case method. Without actually using the techniques of contingency planning students may be made more aware of the continuing nature of case situations and adapt their analyses to take this more into account.

Step Seven: Communicating Results (I)

Step seven calls for a broad-based and planned approach to the communication of case analysis results.

12.1 INTRODUCTION

One of the most significant changes that has occurred in case study work in the last ten years has been the improvement in the communication of results, particularly orally. Clearly schools and colleges in the UK at least have spent more time preparing their students for presentations and face-to-face discussions. And that is as it should be. It is hardly any exaggeration to say that at the completion of step six of the case analysis procedure described here you are only halfway to your goal. No matter how logical, creative, exhaustive and detailed your analysis is, it counts for nothing if you fail to get it over to your audience. However, there remains a major misconception: treating the process of communicating results in too narrow a fashion. Typically students view the process as one of 'writing a report', 'making a presentation', or 'sitting a case study examination'. What is needed, for more effective communication, is a broader framework for looking at the communication process. The one that I favour is summarized in the following widely used definition of communication:

Who says what to whom through what channels, how, in what contexts, to what purpose and with what effect.

This definition does not itself describe how to communicate effectively. It simply identifies the factors or variables which should be taken into account when making communication decisions. It can be made more helpful by structuring these factors into a four-step approach to case analysis presentation.

Step 1: decide aims – to what purpose.

169

Step 2: analysis – who and to whom.
Step 3: preparation and execution – what and how.
Step 4: feedback – to what effect.

The first step requires an answer to the question, 'Why communicate?' It is concerned with the overall aims or purposes of the particular communication process you are involved in. Why you are planning to do something clearly affects what you intend to do and how you intend to do it. You might, for example, choose a different content if you were trying to obtain high marks rather than trying out a new-found analytical skill.

The second step is an analysis of the audience and the presenter(s). It is an analysis because, on the whole, you will have little choice in these matters. Yet understanding the audience and your fellow presenters will, or at least should, affect the content, structure and style of your presentation.

The third step, preparation and execution, is the decision-making step. The major decision will be concerned with the what and how of communication. This step is split into two stages, although these will differ in importance depending on the kind of presentation that is involved. In fact the kind of presentation will strongly affect many of the communication decisions that have to be made and this will be considered now.

You may have noticed that the factors 'through what channels' and 'in what contexts' do not appear in the four steps outlined above. This does not mean that they are unimportant. Their impact will be discussed, but in a somewhat different way to that used for the other factors. First of all, it is useful to combine channels and contexts so that they are more specific to case presentation. The channels for case presentation are oral or written. The contexts, in broad terms, range from informal case discussion to the highly formal case examination. Combining these factors gives the four main types of presentation used for case reporting. These are:

1. Case discussions.
2. Oral presentations.
3. Written case analyses.
4. Written case examinations.

From now on the context and channel factors will be replaced by these four types of presentation. Type of presentation is a factor like 'who and to whom'. It is, to a large extent, a variable outside the control of the presenter. However, it does have a very important impact on the 'what and how' decisions. In fact the impact is so great that it really only makes sense to discuss these key decisions for each type of presentation separately. Thus step three, preparation and execution, is divided into four sections, one for each type of case presentation.

Step four involves discovering what effect a particular communication has. This is obviously important since it affects both short- and long-term actions. If everyone in the front row nods off to sleep in your long oral presentation, that may stimulate you to cut it short or liven it up. If your case instructor describes your writing style as too journalistic, you will want, in future written case analyses, to make it rather more formal. Step four is about feedback. In the remainder of this chapter steps one, two and four will be discussed. Step three, which requires a more detailed treatment, will be the subject of Chapter 13. One final point needs to be made in this introduction. There is a conscious break between the previous analytical steps and this, the last one. Communicating results is about the outcome of the analytical processes and not about how they were done. Thus the step-by-step procedure will not, in general, be the best way to structure the communication of your results.

12.2 DECIDING AIMS

The first and most basic question which must be answered is, 'What is this communication designed to achieve?' Few students give this question much thought, yet activity without direction is, by definition, purposeless. There are three types of aims which you might wish to achieve when presenting a case analysis. These are educational, assessment and social. They are not only relevant to the presentation but will also affect every other aspect of case analysis. But it is in the presentation that their influence will be greatest.

12.2.1 Learning goals

In this context the learning goals are those of the person communicating the case results and as such they may be very diverse. They could include acquiring knowledge of all kinds and at all levels, improving skills and, perhaps, even changing attitudes; in short, all the things for which the case method has been traditionally used in education and which were described in Chapter 1. In addition, and to complicate matters, they will also include learning to communicate well.

If learning is your primary goal, this has implications for how you might expect to behave in case situations. An essential element of learning is feedback. You would probably choose to communicate in quantity both to the case instructor and to fellow students. You would not have to worry too much about taking risks, but you might occasionally be made to look foolish for trying out an idea that did not work. The goals of particular pieces of communication would determine their content. You might wish to try out a particular technique – say, financial ratio analysis. You might want to practise oral communication skills. You may wish to explore fellow students' values by concentrating discussion on the effects of redundancy on the workers during a particular case discussion. Your choice is wide though constrained, of course, by the case instructor and your fellow students. All of this requires a certain amount of reflection, not to mention planning. Case studies often generate high levels of emotion and it is sometimes difficult to remember that they are, first and foremost, a learning experience.

12.2.2 Assessment aims

The second group of purposes relates to assessment. This includes both formal assessment – the marks obtained for written case analyses, oral presentations or even participation in class discussions – as well as informal. Informal assessment may be broadly defined as what the case instructor thinks of you as a student. The two forms of assessment are often highly correlated, but cause and effect are often difficult to disentangle.

It should be noted at this point that learning and assessment are not unrelated; however, neither are they synonymous. In the first place your goals may overlap but be different from those of the case instructor. This point will be discussed in greater detail in section 12.2.4. In the second place assessment instruments are notoriously unreliable and lacking in validity. As a result the case instructor may choose the least problematic form of assessment designed to measure the most salient pieces of behaviour. For example, a written analysis of a case, confined to descriptions of the problems facing the organization, will be much more reliable and valid than attempting to assess how an individual student's attitudes have changed by listening to an open case discussion.

Your assessment objective may not necessarily be in terms of achieving maximum marks. You may decide that a satisficing policy of just passing courses may suit you. You may consider marks to be a constraint rather than a goal. Nevertheless this still means a concentration on getting marks, albeit a limited amount of them.

To get good, or even adequate, marks means concentrating attention on the assessor. This, in almost all cases, is likely to be the case instructor. You will need to try to understand how to communicate to him or her. This is not necessarily a cynical strategy. The case instructor, in some senses, adds dynamism to the static case material. In essence, he or she may be thought of as something of a real-world substitute. He or she points out where students have misread or misunderstood information. He or she highlights errors in logic which in the real world would lead to catastrophe ('You haven't enough cash to do that!'). He or she evaluates recommendations by the ultimate criterion of deciding whether, in his or her judgement, they would be successful.

12.2.3 Social aims

Case presentations are social situations. All of the factors which govern social behaviour come into play. In particular you are likely to have social purposes which cover such areas as status, prestige, respect and liking. You may wish to be perceived as an expert, a warm human being, a creative thinker or an excellent communicator.

Pursuing social aims leads to a variety of forms of behaviour. You may choose not to debate a point with a fellow student who you are sure is wrong but whose friendship you value. You may attempt to enhance your status by making frequent contributions which are little more than summaries of what has already been said. You may feel it is your duty to help out fellow students by allowing them to do the easiest part of a presentation. It is even possible, given enough confidence, to hand out rewards. These, and other, examples of social behaviour occur in any group situation. They will rarely be the central concern of someone involved in making a case presentation. Nevertheless, they exist to mould and constrain behaviour, and their impact should be understood and allowed for.

12.2.4 Choosing among aims

In practice, in most situations, you will choose a mixture of learning and assessment purposes modified and constrained by social purposes where appropriate. The balance will vary from student to student and from occasion to occasion. Of particular importance in making a decision is the ratio between learning and assessment objectives. As stated earlier, it is likely that your learning objectives and those of your case instructor will not totally coincide. The case instructor has an agenda of what he or she wants to achieve. On average this might be fine for a whole class, but there will always be some individuals who do not agree any of the time; most of the class may not agree some of the time. Case instructors may criticize 'red herringing'. They blame students for not seeing the point of the case. This may be a symptom of conflicting learning objectives. The instructor wishes to emphasize one area of knowledge or skill, the student or students would prefer to examine another.

The trade-off, then, is clear. If you and your instructor agree for most of the time on what it is you are trying to achieve, then there is no problem. If you disagree, then you must decide on the balance. How much effort should you put into doing what you want to do and how much into what your case instructor wants? It is perhaps a sad reflection of the state of education today that few students even realize that they have a choice.

Clearly the most important source of information governing the choice to be made is within yourself. 'What am I really trying to get out of this experience? How would I feel if I got really low marks?' It is difficult to make decisions in abstract. Sometimes, if you go ahead and try a particular balance between what you want and satisfying the case instructor, the trade-offs can be seen more clearly. You can then continue to adjust as the case course proceeds.

What is important in each of these situations is not the actual mix of objectives or purposes chosen. It is the fact that a conscious choice was made from the available alternatives. You cannot begin to make a sensible communication decision until you have some notion of what it is you are trying to achieve. You may change your mind as the course proceeds: that is to be expected. What is important is that a coherent set of explicit and well-considered purposes, and means of achieving them, should have been worked out.

12.3 ANALYSIS: TO WHOM?

Perhaps the most common piece of advice given in books on report writing is, 'Write for your audience'. This seems obvious, almost trite. After all, communication is not complete until it is received. The audience is obviously the target to be aimed at and must be kept in mind. It is easy to convince presenters that it is an excellent principle to follow. It is less easy to ensure that they follow it. It is all too simple to become so concerned with trying to understand for ourselves what we wish to say that we neglect to consider those to whom we wish to say it.

12.3.1 Audiences and their characteristics

Audiences depend upon the type of presentation. A written case analysis or examination will normally only be seen by the case instructor. An oral presentation or case discussion will involve both the case instructor and fellow students. These two audiences differ in terms of two important characteristics: (a) knowledge/skills and (b) motivation for attending to a communication from a presenter.

Knowledge

There is clearly a major difference in the levels of knowledge and skill between case instructors and the students they teach. At the lowest level this means, for example, that the case instructor knows the facts of the case better. The instructor will also know what problems are likely to emerge in discussion, what solutions may be proposed, and which is likely to emerge as the 'best'. Such knowledge will be even deeper if the case instructor has taught the case many times before. At a higher level, the instructor should be expected to have a wider grasp of the discipline being taught. He or she should also be more skilled in the arts of communication – both receiving and sending. In short, the case instructor is a professional and the students are, as yet, amateurs.

Motivation

The second characteristic of importance is motivation. The case instructor will have a number of objectives in mind when reading a case analysis or listening to a case discussion. He or she will probably be attempting to assess individual students. He or she will need to be attentive, especially in case discussions. He or she will weigh contributions from a number of angles: how logical they are; how they build upon other contributions; how creative they are, and so on. These are very complex judgements. The case instructor will also be looking beyond assessment of the individual student. He or she will be gathering evidence about the quantity and quality of learning going on. He or she may be looking, in a case discussion, to redirecting students' attention. In reading written case analyses he or she may be drawing conclusions about how to run the next session.

One final point about the case instructor is worth making. Having done a case several times, a case instructor may come to know it too well. He or she may, for example, fail to recognize a new and original approach. In a limited sense, a case instructor may be said to have a closed mind.

Fellow students

Students really only form an audience for case communications in class discussion. In this situation they form an audience with rather different characteristics from those of the case instructor. Frequently they have not fully mastered the facts in the case. A particular situation may come as a complete surprise because they failed to see a footnote or interpret a table correctly. Unlike the case instructor, they may have tackled the case in only one way. A different approach might find them completely at sea, particularly if it involves the use of complex, analytical techniques or convoluted arguments. They are not fully familiar with the concepts and techniques of the discipline. This means that a simple statement may be miscommunicated because students are still trying to remember what, for example, a particular Act of Parliament said. The motivations of students also differ from those of the case instructor. Students, as discussed in the last section, will wish to learn and obtain a good assessment. They may or may not believe that they will learn much by listening to their colleagues.

In summary, then, the case instructor can be viewed as an expert and interested listener, but with definite ideas about what the case is all about. Fellow students form an inexpert and diverse audience concerned with their own problems of understanding and making good impressions on the case instructor and each other.

12.3.2 Choice of audience

In fact, at the most general level, there is very little choice to be made. Written analyses are read only for the case instructor. Even in oral presentation or case discussions there would be little point in addressing just one audience to the exclusion of the other. However, because of the heterogeneity of the audience a subsidiary choice must be made. This is the decision concerning 'At what level to pitch the communication'. Pitch it at too high a level and you will lose the less intelligent or ill-prepared student. Pitch it at too low a level and you risk giving the wrong impression to the case instructor.

It is always possible, of course, to adopt a mixed strategy. This means aiming some of the communications at one audience and some at the other. It is not too difficult to do this in a free-form case discussion. Since contributions are likely to be discrete and to some extent unrelated, they can be aimed in different directions without too much worry about inconsistency. However, in a formal case presentation this is more difficult. It implies a simple structure for the least well-equipped students to follow with occasional more detailed and complex asides for the case instructor. A mixed strategy is not an easy form of communication to master, but it may be the only solution in some instances. Ultimately the choice depends upon your selection of objectives. An assessment objective will usually, but not always, mean addressing the case instructor. A learning objective will usually mean addressing both.

12.3.3 Researching audiences

The primary source of information will be classroom behaviour. You will need to analyze not only the content of what goes on in class, but also the process. How does what is said reveal things about the speakers? It may be that the class is short on quantitative expertise and shuns any analysis of this kind. It may value experience and example rather than theory. It may not be doing the reading specified as essential to the case course.

The case instructor may be particularly keen on creative and unusual solutions. He or she may appear to be weak on the accounting side. He or she may never direct questions to students by name. Data like these are useful in building up a picture of the key characteristics of your potential audience. These data will become more numerous as the course proceeds. In theory, therefore, you should have developed quite a reasonable understanding of your audience, which in turn means that you must consider adapting your plans to fit in with the changing picture.

12.3.4 Reaching audiences

Having identified and understood your audiences, the next step is to remember to prepare your communication with these audiences very much in your mind. This principle is often forgotten in practice, particularly in case discussions and presentations when the communication cannot be reviewed and revised before delivery. You will find it only too easy to disappear into a world of your own making. You may finish up talking to yourself and be surprised when your audience does not understand. You will often fail to step back from what you are doing to take a broader view. This piece of advice bears repeating any number of times. Keep the audience constantly in mind. Even more specifically, imagine a particular person (or two or three) in the target audience, hearing or reading what you plan to communicate. What would their reaction be? Would they understand all the terms used? Would they be able to follow the line of argument? Would it run counter to any of their current attitudes or values? Would it be within their range of experience? Questions like these serve to keep feet well and truly on the ground.

12.4 ANALYSIS: WHO?

The characteristic of the person or people delivering a message will obviously have a major impact on the communication process. Two dissimilar presenters making the same presentation will have different effects on an audience. Understanding the influence a 'sender' may have is essential if the message is to be transmitted effectively. The situation becomes even more complex when the presentation is prepared and executed by a group.

12.4.1 Individual presentations

The 'who' effect should not be confused with the 'how or what' effects. The class quantitative methods expert could present an inaccurate and inappropriate piece of statistical analysis but, since the source has credibility, the audience is more likely to question its own understanding rather than the expertise of the presenter. The message is given a particular value because of who is delivering it as well as how it is being delivered and what is being said.

There are a number of different dimensions along which an audience can assess a communicator. These include intellectual abilities and skills, attitudes and personality characteristics, as well as how knowledgeable and experienced an individual is judged to be. Clearly these are all perceptions that an audience may have. They may not necessarily coincide with your own views of yourself. Nevertheless, since the audience's perceptions will affect the way in which a message is received, it is their views which must be understood and taken into account.

Your first task will be to try, as honestly as you can, to judge what your audience thinks about you. It might be worthwhile to write a short pen portrait of yourself as seen through others' eyes. Think back over your past experience in class and ask yourself how you may have appeared to others. It may even be worth discussing it with friends.

The second task is to make sure that you work within the perceptions that others have of you. If you don't, you will simply not be credible. It is futile for an 18-year-old to use phrases like 'In my experience ...' If you failed the accountancy examinations, few of the people who know this are going to take your break-even analysis seriously. A student who has consistently argued that 'money is the only motivator' can hardly be expected to be believed when he or she recommends a 'job enrichment programme' in a case presentation. The key question to ask is, 'Will they believe this coming from me?'

It is important not to exaggerate the source effect in communication. An audience can change its view of a presenter because of the presentation. In many case presentations the audience will know very little about the presenter. On the other hand it is important that the source and the message reinforce rather than contradict one another. Since the source is fixed, the message, or at least how it is presented, must be adapted.

12.4.2 Group presentations

Oral or written group presentations are quite common in case courses. They present a number of additional presentation problems as well as some worthwhile opportunities. What one should look for are ways of exploiting the opportunities while avoiding the most obvious pitfalls.

Group work should be more creative, effective and fun. Greater creativity stems not only from a larger pool of ideas, but also from the fact that one person will 'spark off' another to produce even more brilliant ideas. Increased effectiveness should result from simple division of labour. If each member of a group is given a part of the whole task to perform, then the whole analysis can be completed very much more quickly. Working together, for most people most of the time, is more enjoyable than working apart. When motivation is hard to maintain, the discipline and enjoyment inherent in group work is often crucial.

The major problem of group work is harnessing the resources of the group to achieve specific ends. Creativity is of little use if the results are not used. Division of labour is a waste of time if the tasks do not dovetail together to produce a coherent whole. There is little enjoyment in working in a group which is divided and fractious.

To avoid these problems it is necessary to build and maintain an organization to carry out the necessary tasks. Co-ordination of effort is the main requirement and the traditional methods of co-ordinating involve rules and roles. The trick is to ensure that these guide, but do not constrain, the group's efforts. The first order of business might be simply to decide what rules and roles will apply.

179

Rules and roles

Rules could cover such things as when and where meetings are to be held, how long they will normally be, what members should have done before the meeting, how work is to be allocated, etc. Roles could cover both administrative (chairman, secretary) and specialist (accountant, mathematician) functions. On the whole I favour administrative roles. Their function will be to see that the machinery operates relatively smoothly. They will be concerned with process rather than content. Specialists are less easy to justify. Case analyses require complex tasks to be performed. It is difficult in the first place to cut the whole up into meaningful parts. It is even more difficult to put those parts back together into a coherent and sensible whole. That is not to say that specific and well-defined tasks cannot be delegated, e.g., 'Diane, could you look up the wording of the relevant Act before next time?' But asking Clive to look after marketing, Vera to take care of production and Dennis to watch over accounting simply will not work in most situations. In other words, most people should do most things. This means that the group may be less efficient, but better co-ordinated.

All of this assumes that the group can discuss such issues from the first meeting of the group and with reasonable chances of coming to some amicable and workable solution. In practice it may be that rule and roles will have to emerge rather than be decided upon because there are social problems or because some participants don't see the need, or prefer to work more informally. There is nothing wrong with an emergent strategy as long as a strategy does emerge. Working in a chaotic or divided group is a useful learning experience but one which should not be repeated too often

Co-operation and conflict

Co-operation rather than conflict should be the order of the day. However, this cannot be left to chance. Co-operation is more likely if people like each other. Thus time spent 'horsing around' should not be begrudged. It not only provides rewards for the individual but also helps to build relationships. It is time spent maintaining the machinery. Conflicts will however arise on occasions. These are better dealt with by pre-set rules than by continuing acrimonious debate. For example, it may be agreed that all major differences will be resolved by voting, or that individuals disagreeing with a particular approach may disengage from tasks associated with it.

Groups can also enhance their performance by spending some time discussing how they are working. Again, this should be seen as a legitimate use of the group's time and not as idle navel gazing. However, not everyone is comfortable with process analysis. They can, however, be justified on the grounds of efficiency and learning. 'If we don't sort out how we are working we will never get finished on time'. Practical suggestions, – 'Why don't we split into two groups to discuss the two main issues?' – should be the order of the day.' Character assassination should be avoided at all cost! Much of what has been discussed so far relates to the initial phases of the analysis. But in the final analysis a written report or an oral presentation is required. How should groups handle this final phase of their task?

Written group presentations

For a written presentation the sequence of events might be as follows. An initial meeting would discuss the case in general terms, perhaps using the step-by-step approach described in this book. Gaps in analysis or information might be recognized and individuals would be asked to fill those gaps. A second meeting might move quite close to providing an overall structure, and even some of the detail, for a first draft. This first draft should then be written by a single individual. While this means a lot of work for one individual, the alternative is even less desirable. A number of individuals could write separate sections. This would almost certainly mean having to attempt a major rewrite in committee. It is almost impossible to do this with any efficiency. A single unified draft can, however, be amended within the group especially if there is access to a word processor. A second draft might be necessary, but this could be the work of another individual. The important point is that strategy and minor amendments should be done in the group; writing should be done outside the group.

Oral group presentations

An oral presentation would probably benefit from adopting a similar sequence. However, the final draft in this case is not a report but something approaching a running order. Again, one individual should be responsible for structuring the group's agreed position. In addition to amendments to the structure, the group would also have to be responsible for designing the visual aids to go with the presentation. The group may be able to opt for an individual or

181

group presentation. If an individual is presenting, then the presentation structure is handed over to that individual to flesh out in a way that fits his or her own personal delivery. However, the least the other members of the group can do is to be an audience for the rehearsals and provide useful and constructive feedback.

If more than one member of the group is to present, then some additional decisions have to be made. How will the presentation be split up? Natural breaks will exist within the flow of the presentation and these should be used as points at which to pass over the presentation. It is my experience that the simplest and least risky format is for each presenter to have one section of the presentation each. However, with experienced groups, prepared to work hard in rehearsal, a more free-form presentation, with each presenter speaking several times, is extremely effective.

Links must be prepared so that handover is as smooth as possible and the structure can be described in personal as well as content terms. ('I'm starting off with a look at some of the major problems the organization has. I'll then hand over to David who will... and finally Wendy will pull it all together at the end and summarize what we have all said.') Within each section each presenter should be allowed to use his or her own presentation style as long as it fits within the agreed structure. Different presentation styles offer variety and interest. The message should, however, remain clear beneath the different treatments. Finally the whole presentation must be well rehearsed. The handovers must be done quickly and smoothly if they are not to be disruptive. Visual aids must be carefully planned so that delays are not created as each new presenter arranges his or her material. Rehearsal breeds confidence, which is very necessary when the complexities of a group presentation are being attempted. Doing case analyses in group settings provides opportunities as well as posing problems. A theme which has run throughout the book deserves repetition here: you should be aware of what alternatives are available to you and make conscious, clearly thought-out decisions rather than be driven by events.

12.5 FEEDBACK: TO WHAT EFFECT?

Although feedback is the last step in the four-step sequence of communication, its placement here can be justified because it can occur before, during and after communication. It also requires some thought and planning before the event if it is to be captured and used to improve your performance. Understanding the timing, level, sources and kinds of feedback helps in this planning process.

12.5.1 Timing and level of feedback

Feedback can occur at several junctures in case presentations. In particular, it is possible to rehearse an oral presentation in front of a sympathetic audience, watch for response during the actual presentation, and ask for the case instructor's reaction afterwards. In principle, the earlier and greater the feedback the better your performance is likely to be. For example, you may arrange rehearsals with an invited audience, or get someone else to read through a written analysis, or ask your case instructor to mark 'mock' case examination answers. All of these examples imply that there is one major piece of communication for which you have to prepare. Therefore it is important to get supplementary feedback as much and as soon as possible.

Not all feedback occurs at the same level. To take two extremes: you may note the effect on an audience of slowing an oral presentation or you may ask your case instructor how your case analysis skills are developing. These are at very different levels of generality. The more general the level of feedback, the more information you must expect to collect.

12.5.2 Sources and kinds of feedback

Feedback comes from people: fellow students, the case instructor, friends and, paradoxically, yourself. You can listen to or read your own words, and a salutary experience this can be. Communicators are often so busy thinking about what they are going to say or write that they ignore what they have just said or written. But the shortest, and therefore very powerful, feedback loops are between the lips and the ears, the pen and the eyes. In short, be aware of what and how you are communicating while you are doing it. Where the communication is oral, audio or videotaping your presentation is a salutary and highly effective form of feedback. While many presenters hate to hear or see themselves, it is dangerous to cut yourself off from the most direct form of feedback there is.

In practice, though, you will mostly rely on your audience for feedback. Some of this will be solicited, some unsolicited. Unsolicited feedback comprises all those messages which your audience sends back to you unasked for. For example, someone may ask a question during an oral presentation which indicates that you have not got over your point. Of course, feedback can be non-verbal as well as verbal. Yawns, raised eyebrows or rapt attention can provide you with very good indications of what effect your communication is having.

Unsolicited feedback is direct and open but may not be very revealing. Sometimes it is necessary to go behind the immediate response and ask people how they react to what you have communicated. Case instructors provide this kind of feedback routinely for written case analyses and oral presentations but will not, unless specially asked, comment in any detail on how you have performed in a class discussion or case examination. Fellow students may be prepared to discuss your performances or comment on written work before it is handed in. However, you should be aware of the burden you are placing on them and use this resource sparingly. Friends, acting as audiences for oral or written presentations before the event, may also be asked what the communication problems are and how they might be resolved. Recording classroom presentation provides another and more permanent form of feedback.

12.5.3 What feedback to collect

If you are planning to collect feedback you must decide not only how you are going to collect it but also what you are going to collect. Primarily this should be determined by your communication aims. If you are concerned to improve your oral skills, then feedback concerning your speaking performance is required. If you are not sure that you understand the application of a particular technique you may ask the case instructor to comment on how you applied it in a particular written case analysis. Such an approach means looking ahead to the actual communication situation and deciding what feedback you are going to collect and how you are going to do it.

Often the most valuable bits of feedback occur unexpectedly and are unplanned. You may suddenly realize that you have been spelling a word incorrectly since primary school or that you have misunderstood a basic psychological concept. This means that when you are communicating you should be as receptive as you can to all kinds and forms of feedback, which is easy advice to give but difficult to carry out: it requires an attitude change more than anything else. Remembering that communication is a two-way process is a good start.

You may learn not only from your own actions but also from those of others. Vicarious learning can be a very powerful experience. This is particularly true when someone is doing something wrong rather than right. Watch how others perform and write, and see how the audience, including you, reacts. Educational opportunities abound if only one can take advantage of them.

Step Seven: Communicating Results (II)

13.1 INTRODUCTION

In this chapter the preparation and execution of the communication of case results will be discussed. This will be done separately for each of the four major types of case presentation – case discussions, oral presentations, written case analyses and case examinations. It was argued in the last chapter that these procedures are really so different that they require separate consideration. That is not to suggest that certain principles do not apply to them all. They do, but their application in each context is sufficiently different to make separate treatment easier to understand.

13.2 CASE DISCUSSION

Case discussions are the least structured procedure for communicating the results of case analyses. The amount of structure is largely at the case instructor's discretion. At one end of the spectrum some instructors choose to adopt a minimum interference strategy. At the other end instructors can set particular questions to answer, or structure the discussion by prompting and questioning. Even in this situation, however, a considerable amount of freedom exists.

This freedom often makes case discussion seem confused and chaotic. It is usually difficult to present long and complex arguments orally. Fellow students interrupt to make their own points. Arguments are simplified and this leads to misunderstandings. Contributions cannot be planned in detail, so they are sometimes badly presented and fail to communicate. Because analysis and communication are occurring at the same time, students miss whole chunks of discussion and points have to be repeated. Frequently the discussion cycles, apparently endlessly, around a series of central issues. Occasionally it will switch abruptly to another task. In summary, the content and presentation of contributions are made under difficult conditions and this must be recognized in preparing a case for discussion.

13.2.1 Case discussion: preparation

Most of the preparation for a classroom discussion has to do with content. By the very nature of the situation, 'what you say' and 'how you say it' decisions will be made on the spot, in the classroom. Likewise it is clear that practising presentation of points to be made during a classroom discussion will not be a very effective use of time: prepared speeches rarely find a place in the case debate. However, there are ways in which points can be prepared, in outline, so that they are more likely to be well received.

The major priority in preparing for a case discussion is *organization*. At the lowest level this means organizing and indexing your notes so that you know where everything is. You must be able to find the relevant material in the heat of debate. If there is little structure imposed by the case instructor, then it is important to create a system that allows you quick and easy access to the work you have done. Since the discussion can go in any direction you must be able to flip a few pages and remind yourself of what you decided about a particular piece of information, solution, or outcome. It is particularly important to keep track of analysis you might have thought unimportant or solutions you rejected. Since the discussion can follow any track, they might actually turn out to be rather important. If the case instructor imposes a predictable structure on the discussion, then your material organization should reflect that structure. If, for example, he or she always asks the same lead-off question, you should prepare an answer to it culled from your rough notes. If the sequence of the discussion is always the same, then organize along parallel lines.

The process of organizing the material helps you achieve another important task, that of memorizing the key aspects of the case and your analysis of it. The balance between memory and notes is an individual decision. Most students rely too heavily on memory, rather assuming that they will not be able to use their notes efficiently in class. This is a fallacy and a dangerous one. It often means that the level of discussion stays at a more superficial level than it would have done had the students organized their notes to make them more easily accessible.

At a more detailed level, it is important to summarize and clarify your results by means of *points*. The 'point' is probably the most useful unit of presentation in a classroom discussion. It recognizes the difficulty of sustaining long and complex arguments. A point essentially summarizes a part of your analysis and might look like this:

'There are three major solutions and two minor ones:

1. Close the plant.
2. Reorganize it
   (a) into divisions
   (b) by unions.
3. Expand it.

These points do not stand alone. They will usually be related in what one might call arguments. Here are four points which form part of an argument.

1. The factory has been losing money for the last three years.
2. The cash flow position of the group (analysis of Appendix 3) has recently taken a turn for the worse.
3. The order book (Table 6.4) looks good for the next three months but deteriorates rapidly thereafter.
4. In about six months there will be tremendous financial pressure from the group to close the factory.

It might just be possible to get all these points across at one go, but it is more likely that after one point has been made, other people will make the others and it will be left to you to sum up with the last point. These points are obviously organized within the structure you have chosen to use. They simply represent the best and most succinct summary you can provide, in convenient units, of the analyses you have carried out. They provide a springboard for the oral contributions you wish to make. They should therefore be written in such a way as to make them easy to get across. This does not mean writing out small prepared speeches. It does mean trying to figure out how best you might get over a particular point.

There are a number of ways in which this might be done. A diagram or matrix written on the blackboard might be a very effective way of getting over a complex point. You will obviously have to prepare this beforehand and be prepared to capture the blackboard during the discussion. Lists are useful ('I think there are three reasons why the company should go ahead with this'). If a point comes from an exhibit, it pays to stop the discussion so that everyone has access to it before you start your explanation ('If we can all look at table 5.3 on page 6, production capacity is given here as 1,500 tonnes ...'). Relating the point to a familiar concept or experience also helps ('There seems to be a prime example of cognitive dissonance in this case. When the chief accountant decided ...' or, 'This is exactly the same problem that ICI is facing now. The product line is ...'). You are simply trying to find 'hooks' upon which to hang key points so that they can be more readily understood.

13.2.2 Case discussion: execution

One of the important options that you have in a classroom discussion is what role or roles to assume. Few students realize that they have a choice. There are two main types of role: content roles and process roles. Content roles are those where individuals lay claim to being experts in terms of some parts of the content of a case. Process roles are those roles which affect the structure and the flow of the case discussion almost without regard to the content. The benefits from students taking roles are twofold. It gives the individual a clearer view of what he or she should be doing within the case discussion. It also helps to improve the quality of case discussions by ensuring that certain specialist functions are being carried out. This adds width and shape to the discussion. However, you should not take the concept of role playing too seriously. In particular you will want to switch roles between cases or even within a case.

Content roles all revolve around the concept of an expert. Individuals taking such roles signal by their classroom behaviour their readiness to act as an authority on one aspect of the case ('I've spent a lot of time analyzing the accounting data in this case'). The expertise can be along a number of dimensions. These include techniques (accounting, quantitative, etc.), experience (general or specific to the case), description (marketing, production, psychology), stage of analysis (analytic, creative, evaluative) or even one particular aspect of the case. What the expert says in essence is: 'I have studied the case in one particular way and here are my insights which I expect will be useful.' Experts add breadth to the discussion of a case. There is, however, a chance that they do so at some personal risk. If an expert concentrates on one line of attack, then his own viewpoint will necessarily be rather narrow. It is a mistake, I believe, to let an expert role dominate the way a case is analyzed. The expert role is a communications role and should be assumed after a more general analysis has been completed.

In contrast, *process roles* require little preparation, and switching roles is much more likely to occur. Process roles are those roles which help support and develop the process of discussion. A number of such roles have been identified here, but the list is far from complete. The *librarian's* role is to ensure that no data are overlooked in any discussion. He or she keeps pointing out relevant paragraphs, exhibits and appendices without necessarily progressing the discussion any further. The role is rather limited in scope, but in the early days of a case course it can be a very useful one. The *questioner's* role is to add depth and clarity to the discussion. Clarity is added through questions like, 'Sorry, Helen, I didn't understand that. Could you go through that again?' Depth is obtained through questions like, 'But why do you think management would go for the redundancy rather than the redeployment option?' This is a delicate role to play. Fellow students are apt to believe that asking questions is easier than answering them and that the questioner is taking the easy option. Case instructors may feel that their role is being usurped. It is a role to be taken sparingly and perhaps interspersed with the taking of other roles.

The *integrator's* role is to weave together the strands of the discussion and to make something out of them. An integrator goes beyond what is said ('If George's cost analysis is correct and if we assume that the forecasts in Table 1 are OK, then the product has to be a winner'). An integrator is particularly useful in the first few cases, in very complex cases, or when the general level of preparation is low. These are all situations where more analysis is going on inside the classroom than outside it. An integrator will usually have had to do fairly intensive preparation.

The *controller's* role is perhaps the most demanding role of all. In a sense it is the role that the case instructor would play if he or she wished to adopt an interventionist role. Controlling the discussion means a number of things. It means ensuring that most of the major topics are actually covered. It means ensuring that all topics are covered in depth. It means controlling interruptions and red herrings. It may also mean acting as a referee when the discussion gets rather too heated for comfort. All of these interventions require social skills of a high order. Done well, this role can be enormously rewarding to the individual and the group. Done badly it can prove disastrous.

In addition to specific role behaviour some comments might usefully be made about general case discussion behaviour. One of the most important decisions to be made concerns *level of involvement*. Students raised in some educational traditions tend to be diffident and self-effacing. They are taught not to push themselves forward or offer opinions unless directly asked. Clearly, this is highly limiting in a case discussion. In general, my advice would be to get more involved than you feel comfortable with. However, this level of involvement has to be carefully monitored. It is all too easy for the rest of the class to relax in the certain knowledge that one or two individuals will make the running. It therefore pays to break up the pattern occasionally.

The counterpoint to contributing is *listening*. Few of us are very adept at this essential skill. In a case discussion it is all too easy to let the mind wander. Sometimes shutting out the discussion is necessary in order to think through something; at other times it is all too easy to suffer lapses of concentration. To get the most out of case discussions requires effort. The greatest effort is that of concentrating on what is being said and what it means. One major aid to listening and understanding is to map out the shape of the discussion. You may even want to do this on a piece of paper just to remind yourself of what has been said. Any new contribution can then be related to what has gone before. It is still not an easy task to listen and concentrate. Nevertheless, it is a central social skill in management and therefore one to be developed by as much practice as possible.

Another decision you will have to make relates to your *behaviour towards fellow students*. In general you should try to maintain attitudes of respect, constructiveness, open-mindedness and support. This is more a statement about learning than morality. Your fellow students represent a major source of new learning for you. Evaluate the contribution, not its source or the way in which it was presented. Similarly, if you respect and support your fellow students, you are creating a richer learning situation. Everyone will feel free to contribute without fear of attack. This does not mean that debate should not take place, but the counter-position should be carefully and unemotionally stated. Not 'That's a stupid idea', but 'I see what you're getting at but isn't there a fairly major problem?

A number of positive ways in which you can *help the discussion along* have already been mentioned. Don't keep repeating your contributions. It is true that not everyone will have taken them in first time. However, those who have will not thank you for harping back on the same theme. If you feel it is absolutely necessary to do so, try a fresh approach and only introduce the idea again when it is relevant. Try to distinguish between controlled developments of the discussion and red herrings. If you feel that a particular topic has been exhausted, say so and introduce a new one with an original contribution. It is up to the rest of the class to decide whether to follow. Don't throw in the brilliant, but irrelevant, idea you have just had. Wait until the time is ripe and it becomes a relevant issue. In these and other ways you should see it as part of your task to

190

keep the discussion effective and interesting. To do so may mean subjugating your own needs to those of the group. Practice in this process is no bad thing, however.

Oral presentation of a contribution should be governed by the knowledge that it will be a transitory communication, difficult to follow and remember. The point should therefore be *simple, clear,* and as *precise* as possible. If you can add a simple structure ('I have two points to make'), so much the better. Try to avoid hedging bets and qualifying statements like this: 'I believe that, other things being equal, on the whole, taking everything into consideration, the product could, given the right conditions, be a qualified success'. The statement, 'This product will succeed' is more interesting and much easier to understand, and a statement like this will produce discussion as well as make an immediate and easily understood impact. The qualifications can emerge in the subsequent discussion. It is not necessary to make every statement self-contained and watertight. Attempting to do so results in stilted and long-winded discussions.

Case discussions provide an excellent example of the old adage, 'You only get out what you put in'. It is not difficult to 'hide' throughout a course which relies on discussion in a large student group, but the educational opportunity cost is very great. You can learn a great deal and develop skills quickly in the hothouse atmosphere of case discussions. It would be a pity to throw that chance away.

13.3 ORAL PRESENTATIONS

Oral presentations generally involve an individual, sometimes a group, taking most of a teaching period to deliver the results of a case analysis, often with visual aids. The rest of the class and the case instructor form the audience. Oral presentations are in many ways easier to plan for than classroom discussions. The structure of the discussion is under your control since you, or a member of your group, will be the only one speaking. This means that the emphasis moves from the execution to the preparation phase.

13.3.1 Oral presentations: preparation

Oral communications are essentially transitory in nature. They are delivered and then only partially heard or remembered. They are forgotten because it is impossible for most individuals to remember a long speech word for word. Only key points are remembered. In addition, these key points will vary from individual to individual, they may not be the key points the presenter would have liked to be remembered, or indeed they may not be the actual points made. The transience of oral communication gives rise to five problems which you must be aware of and do your best to avoid when planning a presentation:

1. First of all there is the problem of delivering the message. Written communications can be reviewed and rewritten by the author before giving them to an audience. This is not possible, at least to the same degree, when speaking. Who has not had that sinking feeling that there is no way to finish the sentence and still make sense? The act of speaking requires planning ahead. It is very difficult to do this and assess what one has just said.

2. If delivery of oral communications is difficult, listening is no less easy a task. An audience can re-read a written sentence or passage that they have failed to understand at the first pass. This luxury is not available in oral communication. The usual process is that the listener repeats the sentence which he or she has retained in short-term memory. This usually means that the next sentence or two is missed. The thread of the argument is broken. The listener struggles to catch up and misses or mis-hears much of what is said. He or she often gives up, returning to the fray at an obvious re-entry point, e.g. 'And now my third point'.

3. Comprehension is a short-term communication goal. But what of the longer term? Without mechanical storage much of what is said will be quickly forgotten. Most human minds have a rather limited storage capacity. If what is being said now must be related to something that was said much earlier, it may be based upon very shaky foundations. Audiences need to be given these foundations in some permanent form so that they can always relate to them. They need structure.

4. A related point has to do with the absolute memory capacity of an audience. This is usually much less than one thinks: it is easy to overestimate it. A presenter is, or should be, thoroughly familiar with the material. It is therefore difficult to judge how much members of an audience can take in when they are presented with a wealth of new material for the first time. In their eagerness to communicate their productivity, student presenters frequently overload their audiences.

5. The converse of this problem is that students often underestimate the time required for a presentation. They find themselves under pressure and in their haste they attempt to get a quart into a pint pot. The results are seldom edifying.

Much has been made of the problems of oral communication. However, it does have two important advantages:

1. Oral presentations can be very compelling: much more so than the written word. The presence of a living, talking human being, especially if he or she radiates interest and enthusiasm, is difficult to ignore. Attitude and emotion can add tremendously to the impact of a message.

2. Oral presentations also have the property, though it is used less often than it might be, of flexibility. Presenters can respond to the changing environment, human, physical, or temporal. They can also adapt their style, and even their material, as they sense the mood of an audience. This is a rather skilled accomplishment. Nevertheless, it is one which can be practised in everyday life, in conversation. It is also a very necessary skill for organizational survival.

Some rather specific *information* is required before you begin to prepare your presentation. The importance of knowing your audience has already been discussed in section 12.3.1. You must also find out what the case instructor's ground rules are. These may include length of presentation, structure and availability of resources such as overhead projectors, flip charts, etc. You may also want to find out what is negotiable. If you can make a good case for doing something different you will be listened to. If you just go ahead and do it the chances are you will be penalized. What I find surprising is that student presenters often fail to ask what the rules of the game are, or leave it until too late to find out.

Structure is of paramount importance in an oral presentation. This is due to the transitory nature of oral communication, as discussed earlier. In order for the audience to comprehend and remember the content a clear structure must be used and must be seen to be used. No single structure works best in all situations. Some alternatives are given in Table 13.1.

These are only three of the alternative general purpose structures that could be used for an oral presentation. The elements are not very different: some are at a more general level than others, but the major difference lies in the sequence. Broadly, there appear to be two alternatives: top-down or bottom-up. The top-down approach presents the solutions first, as in Alternatives 1 and 3, and then justifies those solutions. The bottom-up approach starts with the problems and reveals the solution at the end. Both have their merits. The top-down approach engages interest at the beginning but is difficult to present logically. The bottom-up approach follows a clear

Table 13.1 *Sample alternative structures for oral presentations*

Alternative 1	Alternative 2	Alternative 3
Recommendations	Attention-getting introduction	Outline
Why these?	Background	Conclusions
Why not others?	Problem	Recommendations
Supporting evidence	Analysis	Problems
	Alternatives	Alternatives
	Alternative chosen	Criteria for choice
	Implementation	Action plan
	Benefits/rationale	Summary

sequence but can prove long-winded and boring. Other more original structures are possible, and their creation and use is to be encouraged, but the audience should be left in no doubt about what the structure means and how it works. If the skeleton does not hang together, the flesh can never be put on the bones. An outline of the structure of the presentation will therefore usually form an early part of your speech. It is said that a tip for any instructors goes as follows:

- Tell them what you are going to tell them.
- Tell them.
- Tell them what you told them.

This is not bad advice. It establishes structure early on and reinforces it with a recapitulation at the end.

Simplicity is also important in communicating structure. Probably fewer than 10 headings will suffice. Any more than this and the audience will not be able to keep the whole shape of the presentation in mind. The headings should also be simple and almost self-explanatory. In any case, when outlining the structure of the presentation they should be explained in somewhat more detail: 'In the section on alternatives I will outline the four major alternatives as I see them, and what I expect might result from implementing each.'

One important structural variable that has already been discussed is length. In general you will be working to a time limit. It is worthwhile to allocate that time among the elements of the structure you choose to adopt. This helps to control the natural inclination to try to cover too much ground. It is better to have this discipline early so that the presentation remains in some sort of time balance. Sequence has already been mentioned as an important aspect of structure. A clear story line must be present at each level of the presentation. Thus it is important to structure the sequence within a segment as well as the overall sequence of the segments. For example: 'For each alternative I am going to look at the cash flow, organization and the impact on the local authority.'

To achieve continuity of the story line the best approach is to start at the most general level and work down until the right level of detail is reached. This ensures that the whole presentation is consistent, a very important attribute for any communication. An example of working down is given below.

Statement of major problems

1.1 Statement

1.2 Symptoms
    1.2.1 Cash flow (historic, forecast)
    1.2.2 Ratios

2.1 Statement

2.2 Symptoms
    2.2.1 Chairman's statement
    2.2.2 Appendix III analysis
    2.2.3 Graph 1

3.1 Statement

3.2 Symptoms
    3.2.1 Marketing manager's job description
    3.2.2 Share of advertising figures
    3.2.3 Chairman's statement
    3.2.4 Exhibits 1 to 3

Although structure must be described orally, this is not really sufficient. An audience cannot hold a structure in its short-term memory having only heard it once. It is, I believe, essential in any oral presentation to have the structure displayed in writing throughout or, if this is not possible, at each change of topic. It can then be referred to by the audience at any time. In addition, the presenter can easily refer to the structure, either to remind people of the point the presentation has reached or to refer back or forward to other segments. In summary, the structure of an oral presentation should be simple, compact, logical, self-explanatory and available at all times to the audience.

As a rule, presenters give too much rather than too little *detail* in oral presentations. They seem to want to demonstrate their productivity or else heavily buttress their position with data. But in an oral presentation detail cannot be comprehended: it adds enormously to the length of the presentation and it camouflages the main themes and arguments. In particular, it is important not to include a long recital of details already available in the case as 'background'. If the audience is fully prepared this is redundant, while if it is not, it will never be able to grasp the details sufficiently well to make sense of what follows.

What *visual aids* you use and how you use them should be decisions you make early on in your planning. Often they are considered only at the last moment. This means that they are badly executed and not integrated with the rest of the presentation. Nor is it effective simply to write out almost everything you are going to say on a flip chart or overhead projector slide. Visual aids should only be used when they add to the effectiveness of a presentation in one of the following ways:

1. To help the audience remember the structure of the whole presentation.
2. To provide the audience with the structure of a section within the overall presentation.
3. To emphasize key points clearly and dramatically (photographs, diagrams, graphs).
4. To show unavoidable detail.
5. To demonstrate the internal workings of a complex argument or calculation.
6. To break up a long section of speech.

In visual terms, the main fault with visual aids is to try to get too much on one slide or blackboard at a time. Too much visual information is confusing and lacks impact. If in doubt, put less on each slide and use more slides. My rule of thumb is: no more than 17 words on any slide or chart. Using a specific number seems to help students remember where more general exhortations fail!

Different visual aids have different characteristics. Blackboards and handouts both suffer from a major disadvantage. Since visual aids have to be prepared, the whole of the written side of the presentation is available to the audience before a word is spoken. This is distracting at the beginning of a presentation when the audience proceeds to glance at the material. It also leads to boredom and frustration because people know exactly what is coming and are longing for the presenter to get on with it. Flipcharts and other paper presentation methods are usually good and relatively inexpensive.

They are, however, somewhat difficult to use smoothly in the middle of a presentation. Projector slides are difficult and expensive to prepare, though they are of very high visual quality. However, the best medium for most oral presentations is the overhead projector slide. These can be prepared in colour, are easy to handle, have good visual qualities, and can be altered in the middle of a presentation. Preparation has been made much simpler by the development of processes which can convert images on paper to transparencies. Desktop publishing or even word processing programmes can produce hard copy slides which can be converted into slides or else directly, by means of chart plotters, to transparent media.

More recently, the advent of projectors capable of capturing the images from the visual display unit of a microcomputer allows the development of a much more flexible visual display. Simply by pressing a key the 'slide', in full colour, changes and can do so in various ways including dissolves and wipes. While the physical act of changing slides is made easier and the format and design of the 'slides' is much more impressive, there are dangers. In particular the technology tends to dominate the performance, both physically and organizationally. By all means experiment but remember to ask the question: does it communicate?

Oral information is difficult to grasp. *Repetition* is one solution to this problem. It has to be used carefully, however. Too much repetition is boring. Only key points bear repetition. One example of this is reminding the audience of the structure ('And now I want to move on to the third section and talk about the problems as I see them'). Another is the summary or recapitulation of the presentation that is given at the end ('To summarize, I think that Smith Ltd should build the new factory for these key reasons'). A third example might be a point that needs to be fully understood ('Let me repeat that this forecast is based on the assumption that there is no economic recession in the UK during the next five years'). Repetitions need not appear repetitious: saying the same thing in a different way helps to add variety to the presentation while still achieving the objective of reinforcement.

The most important issue concerning the *planning* of what you are actually going to say is the level of preparation. The alternatives are to read from a prepared text, to speak from brief notes, usually on index cards, or to work without notes relying on your visual aids. Few experienced teachers would recommend the first method to beginners. In the first place, it is very difficult to write a speech which will sound spontaneous and interesting. In the second, it is very difficult to deliver such a speech effectively. Some politicians never seem to manage it! The written and spoken word is very different: successfully transforming one form to another is a very difficult communication task and is best left to professionals. Thus there are strong arguments for adopting a more flexible, less structured approach. Having worked out the structure and content of your presentation, the next step is to convert them into a 'bridge' which will carry you easily and effectively into delivery. The usual procedure is to prepare a skeleton script with key words or phrases on index cards which will allow you to springboard into the actual presentation. An example is given below:

- Alternative 2 (repeat structure)
- Expansion: new factory
  new machines, old factory
  new products (but cut old)
  go for broke; motivation; excitement

These notes must be carefully laid out so that you will always know precisely where you are. You should also be thoroughly familiar with the link between the key word or phrase and what you actually want to say. There is nothing like the moment of panic that occurs when you read a key word and have no idea why you put it there!

Until recently, the index card method was the one that I asked students to use during their presentations. Unfortunately it has two related drawbacks. The first is that while the preferred method of use is to read the notes and then speak, some presenters find it difficult to endure the silences that result and proceed to read from the cards with their heads down. The result is that they cannot be heard and inspire little interest in their audience. The second problem is that it is often difficult to remember where you have got to on your cards, so you either hesitate or guess, leaving out some of what you wanted to say.

I have therefore experimented with forbidding presenters from using anything other than the visual aids that the audience will see. The results have been very impressive. Presenters now know what they want to say and say it more clearly and spontaneously. However, there is still the tendency to rely overmuch on the visual aids to read 'into' the overhead projector or flip chart rather than using them as cues.

It is asking for trouble to go into an oral presentation without *rehearsing*. You should attempt at least one full-scale dress rehearsal. If there is a high assessment mark attached to the presentation you may want to do more. Rehearsal is best done in front of a sympathetic audience. A classmate, or failing that a friend, are the most obvious choices. Rehearsing into a tape recorder is a good second best. Rehearsing by oneself is useful but not ideal: it is not easy to provide one's own feedback. Rehearsal should also cover the use of visual aids. Visual aids seem to cause more consternation among novice presenters than any other aspect of presentation. Carrying out physical acts in front of an audience when nervous seems to invite disaster.

One of the keys to good presentation is *confidence*. This stems largely from the knowledge that you know what you are going to be doing. Rehearsal helps, but it is also important to know your material so well that you can move from one part of a presentation to another without getting confused. The less you have to rely on outside stimuli, the more time you have to concentrate on delivery, assessing audience reaction, and enjoying yourself. Finally, it is important to repeat a point made earlier. The quality of an oral presentation, perhaps more than any other kind of presentation, is determined by the quality and quantity of the preparatory work. In my experience, 'It will be all right on the night' is not a good guiding principle.

13.3.2 Oral presentations: execution

There are some general rules of speaking which may help you in an oral presentation. But beware: expert communicators break them everyday, but still manage to communicate well. It would be best to treat them as suggestions rather than dogma.

1. Prepare your stage. Arrive early, make sure you know where everything is and familiarize yourself with the speaking position.
2. Make an interesting start. Set the tone for your presentation by saying something that grabs the audience's attention (e.g. 'I recommend that we close this company down').
3. Speak slowly. Your audience must have time to hear and think about what you say. Speak at the rate that the 'slowest' listener can cope with.
4. Pause. Allow time for the message to sink in and for you to marshal your thought for the next sentence. Don't be afraid of silence. Use pauses for dramatic effect.
5. Speak audibly. Sound carries most effectively in straight lines. Look up at the audience, not down into your notes or the overhead projector.

6. Introduce variety. Vary the length of sentences and pauses, the pace of presentation and the pitch of your voice (nothing is more boring than a monotone delivery).

7. Let the audience read the visual aid. Just because you know what's on it doesn't mean they do. Pause and let them take it all in before expanding on its content.

8. Use your eyes. Maintaining eye contact with your audience is important. It signals confidence, interest and concern and tells them that the message is important. It also keeps your head up!

9. Position yourself correctly. Stand centre, in full view with your head up and talk directly to all the audience. Don't stand bent over notes or hide behind the lectern or overhead projector.

10. Move, but not too much. Complete immobility suggests lack of confidence or interest. Hands are better than feet. Roaming around is distracting but excessive gesticulation conveys nervousness. Movement can be used creatively to suggest interest, excitement and commitment, but don't overdo it.

11. Think positively. Confidence feeds on itself – it can grow if you believe in yourself and are determined to succeed. If you approach the presentation tentatively and with doubts this will affect your performance and the audience's perception of that performance. Confidence will then disappear and the downward spiral will begin.

13.4 WRITTEN ANALYSES OF CASES

Written analyses of cases (known at Harvard as WACs) are usually used together with case discussions or oral presentations. They may be handed in at the time of the discussion or students may be allowed to include material from the discussion in their written presentation which is handed in at a later date. WACs are frequently required to take a management report format.

13.4.1 Written analyses of cases: preparation

Preparation for writing up a case analysis involves thinking mainly about its *structure* and its *audience*. The process will start with your virgin case notes and end with a detailed structural outline.

The audience for a written presentation is almost always confined to the case instructor. He or she will provide you with the formal parameters such as length, structure, style, submission date, assessment criteria, etc. However, there are also informal parameters which should govern your preparation. These are largely concerned with the case instructor's own likes and dislikes, preferences and requirements. These may be trivial (an aversion to green ink) or important (a requirement that all benefits and disbenefits should be quantified).

Trivial preferences can be met with a minimum of compromise. If you do not meet them you simply make the message more difficult to understand. However, if you do not share your case instructor's views about the case or how it should be written up then the problem is more difficult. You can choose to capitulate and write what he or she wants to read. Alternatively, you can choose to do it your way. You may, for example, wish to structure your report in a different way to that demanded by the case instructor. You may choose to recommend a course of action that values human freedom over economic advantage, knowing that your instructor believes otherwise. What you should do in these situations is to signal the differences where they become most apparent. You have to alert the case instructor to the fact that you may be disagreeing with him or her. This at least should help the case instructor assess your work using criteria like logic, creativity, presentation and so on, rather than those of philosophy or values. Whether you decide to compromise or confront, two points are vital. The first is to try to understand instructors as human beings rather than expect them to be totally rational and objective people. In practice, what we mean when we say 'The case instructor is not being objective' is 'He or she doesn't accept my values'. Every one has their own set of values and these values affect what we regard as good and bad. You simply have to accept that you may differ from the person who is assessing you in this respect and decide what you are going to do about it. The second, which follows from the first, is to make a conscious decision as to which alternative to choose in the light of what you seek to get out of the case course.

Structure

The development of a written document should, in my view, be essentially a top-down process: first the main headings, then the subheadings and paragraph descriptions and finally the actual writing. I know people who only manage to impose a structure at the end of the writing process. Doing it this way has been made much easier by the advent of word processors. However, it is clearly a less systematic and more time consuming process but, if you can't do it any other way, then so be it.

A written case analysis is rather like telling a story. A certain amount of character development or scenic description is helpful, even vital, but the story line must be maintained intact throughout if the reader is to understand. Working from the top downwards ensures that the story line is kept intact. You may not get the structure or content right the first time. You may decide to change the structure while actually writing. This is fine, provided that the whole structure is written out again and not just kept in your head, half-remembered and vague.

There are four decisions concerning structure which have to be made when writing a report. These are: structure visibility, headings, sequence, and length.

Structure visibility

The two extremes are the essay and the management report. An essay is a uniform piece of writing, with no headings or subheadings, maintaining structure by means of a logical thread. By contrast, management reports involve several nested layers of headings, categorizing small blocks of text which may themselves be simply numbered points.

Few case instructors allow students to write case analyses in essay form. On the other hand, there is usually still some choice about the amount of structure you wish to display. The decision should turn upon the type of case analysis you have carried out. If it requires long, interconnected, complex arguments, then less structure should show. The flow should be uninterrupted by headings or subheadings. If on the other hand there is a lot of detail and disparate material to communicate, then a typical management report style would be more appropriate. It should also be noted that it is easier to use a highly structured report as the basis for a case discussion since the analyses are neatly catalogued.

It is fairly clear that there is no universal agreement on what a written case report should contain or what order should be used. This is hardly surprising, but it needs demonstrating. There are some cases, for example Alternative 5 in Table 13.2, where it would be necessary, or even just more interesting, to develop a structure specifically for that case. An example of this might be to write an imaginary letter to the chief executive of the company described in the case. In some instances the case itself will suggest a structure. As always the criterion should be the effectiveness of the communication. If a specific and idiosyncratic structure makes the message clear and interesting, then use it.

Table 13.2 *Alternative written presentation structures*

=====

1. Summary
    Purpose
    Scope
    Conclusion(s)
    Recommendations
    Introduction
    Body
    Appendices
2. Problem statement
    Factors causing the problem
    The effects of the problem
    Examination of the possible solutions and their implications
    Conclusions
    Recommendations
    Appendices
3. Title page
    Table of contents
    List of exhibits
    Summary of recommendations
    Background material and facts
    Statement of problem
    Analysis
    Solution and implementations
    Appendices
4. Principal message
    Why it was chosen
    Why others not chosen
    Evidence supporting the analysis
5. The situation in the tool room
    What I would do
    Why I wouldn't close down the factory
    Action plans
    The future

=====

Headings and subheadings

Is there one ideal structure for all case study reports, or should the structure depend on the case? An examination of Table 13.2 is instructive in this respect. It compares a number of structures which have been recommended for the reporting of case results.

Sequence

In what order should the sections be placed? The obvious answer to this question is to place them in a logical order which carries a clear story line. As with presentations, it is argued that there are two major procedures which can be used in a report of this kind. The first is a sequential build-up of evidence until the denouement is reached in the final section. This is generally regarded as the academic model. The second is the reverse, starting with a clear statement of the outcomes of the analysis and then justifying the conclusions and/or recommendations in the rest of the report. This is a typical management report sequence. It is argued that managers need this kind of report because they are busy and need to know the 'bottom line' straight away. The 'academic' approach is easier to sequence since the logic is so much stronger. However, it is less interesting to read and it is difficult to keep the tension building up until the final section where all is revealed. The 'management' approach is more direct, exciting and punchy, but more difficult to sequence. The academic approach is probably better for complex, analytical cases. The management approach works best for simpler, more action-oriented, case situations.

There are other possible components of a case report which can only be described as 'housekeeping'. A clearly set out title page with all the relevant information on it can save the case instructor's time and effort. It also makes a good impression, both on the reader and the writer. For the writer it sets the tone for what will follow and makes him raise his eyes from the task of matching words to ideas towards the more important goal of communication. A contents page is also useful and performs a somewhat similar function. It conveys the structure of the report very quickly and gives an impression of where the emphasis, at least in terms of word volume, lies. It also allows the reader to find his way round the report at the second reading.

These components of a written report are by no means exhaustive or mutually exclusive. They merely represent a bank of ideas from which you can draw. You may in fact change the components as you get down to writing. The important point is that you consciously choose a way of breaking up the text which best expresses what you want to communicate with your primary audience: the case instructor.

Within the overall sequence there is also a finer level of sequencing to decide upon. The content of a report can largely be divided into points and arguments.

Points are self-contained ('one of the problems is cash flow') and may be conveyed in a single sentence. They can, in theory, be introduced in any order. In practice, an ordered sequence communicates better than an unordered one. Points may be ordered in terms of importance, relevance, cost, interest, time, etc.

Arguments have structure because they describe the relationship between things. When an argument is being developed the sequence almost decides itself. Consider the following example:

Argument – a recent increase in profitability is a problem, not a measure of success.

Profitability has improved from 13% to 16% in the last six months. This has been solely due to a reduction in investment in stocks following the stock reduction programme instituted by consultants. Sales have in fact been falling since availability is a key factor in this market. Stocks have fallen proportionately faster in the last few months, but this cannot continue indefinitely. In the near future sales will continue to fall and profitability will eventually slump.

If the same sentences were rearranged, the argument would simply make no sense. They have to be in this, or a very similar, order. A chain of logic is forged: sometimes the links are very obvious, sometimes they are not so obvious and extra links, which serve only the purpose of linking, have to be added.

Length

The length of a report is a major determinant of its content. The crucial decisions that have to be made are how many points, topics or arguments should be included and which they should be. The first task is to produce a draft outline. This means working through your rough case analysis notes, picking out points, topics and arguments and noting them down under the appropriate headings. An example might look like this:

Problems – auditor's report

> Benson's behaviour, effects of sacking, chief accountant's background, current position.

> – stock records

> discrepancies, methods of recording, workers' attitudes.

At this stage it is probably as well to ignore any length restrictions. The notes should be just explicit enough for you to know what they mean when you reread them. The next step is to make a rough estimate of how many words this draft outline will make when written up.

If you really have no idea of the likely relationship, it might be worthwhile to write up a short section from the outline. This can then be used to determine a rough conversion factor.

You may believe that you can comfortably fit within the word limit and so proceed to convert the points in the draft outline into prose. More likely you will discover that your report is going to be too long. Editing then becomes the order of the day. Firstly, you must be sure that there is no repetition in the outline. Secondly, you may be able to condense by moving material to an appendix or by using a graphic presentation. Thirdly, you may simply have to cut material, but beware that in this process you do not harm the logic, impact or readability of the report. In particular, leaving out lighter points can make the presentation turgid and difficult to read.

Controlling the overall length of a report is important. Allocating words between sections is not. Topics must be placed logically within one of the section heads that you have decided upon. This may produce sections of varying length but this is no great problem: at least it adds variety to the presentation.

13.4.2 Written analyses of cases: execution

The next stage is the conversion of a detailed structural outline into a finished report. This is achieved by the creation of paragraphs, sentences, graphics and presentation.

Paragraphs

Intelligent use of paragraphs can add enormously to the impact and readability of a report. Most of the time a paragraph should be confined to the discussion of a single topic. It is a useful discipline to name the subjects of a paragraph before you begin writing. With a highly visible structure these names correspond to the subheadings. In a freer format they will serve to remind you what message the paragraph must convey.

Paragraphs are needed because the reader's attention span is short. However, as well as encapsulation the reader needs continuity. He or she needs to be motivated to continue and to be shown the relationship between blocks of writing: links are necessary. Links can be provided by a numbering system ('The fourth reason ...'), by echoing the last sentence in the previous paragraph, or by contrast ('An altogether different aspect ...'). Missing links can be used to signal the end of a major topic or to add emphasis to a point. Variety is important. Too many linked paragraphs lead to a boring sameness. Too few links make a report episodic and difficult to read.

Sentences

Actually writing the sentences that will be read is the final act in creating a report. There are a number of excellent texts on the writing of English and it would clearly pay to study them. However, there are a number of errors that writers of case analyses are particularly prone to and it is worth briefly pointing out how to avoid these:

1. Write simply. Complexity of expression does not imply depth of thought. It often indicates poor communication skills, muddled thinking or a smoke-screen to hide a failure to understand.

2. Write briefly. Most case reporters persist with long sentences in the mistaken belief that they are more impressive. Occasional long sentences are necessary to convey ideas or to add variety, but the average length should be held down.

3. Avoid wordy phrases. For example, 'It is a fact that' or, 'There is no way that' are examples of this genre. They aren't really required: they simply add to your word count and blur the message.

4. Reduce qualifications. 'It is possible that' and 'If the present situation continues' are phrases that allow you to hedge your bets. They also make your writing more difficult to understand. Try to reduce qualification to a minimum.

5. Avoid evaluative language. Words like optimum, best, worst or even good and bad should be carefully considered before they are used. They imply you are making value judgements. This is fine if you are aware of the value basis for those judgements. Otherwise it is evidence of sloppy thinking or inadequate expression.

6. Add variety. Written case analyses require that a lot of work be levered into a small space. The process of rewriting and editing usually increases the denseness of the writing. If the result is to be at all readable, a little leavening must be added. This may be done in terms of structure or language. The effect should be one of creating contrast, interest or amusement.

7. Think of the audience. Above all keep in your mind the person for whom you are writing. Ask yourself continually, 'Will he or she be able to understand what I am saying and will they enjoy it?' It is so easy to commit yourself to getting your analysis on paper, and to forget why you are doing it.

207

Graphics

Graphics – diagrams, tables or graphs – can summarize or add impact to the written text. You should therefore judge whether points can be summarized better graphically or whether a point can be made with more impact as a graph or table before you decide to include them. You should not simply include them because you have done them. Knowing why you are including graphics also helps in their design. Graphs and diagrams are frequently too complex. They do not summarize, nor do they have impact. Decide what you are going to say and design the graphic to say it. Tables are frequently thrown into reports in their original crude form. The reader is asked to discover the treasure contained within. Frequently, the reader declines and the point is not taken. Constructing tables that communicate is one of the subjects of a useful book (Ehrenberg, 1975) on the analysis of data. Too many graphics break up the text and make it difficult to read, so be sparing. Too much variety is as bad as too little. Make sure that the graphics and the relevant text are close together, otherwise the point will be lost.

Presentation

The medium is the message. Illegible, badly spelled and scruffy reports on poor quality paper say something to the reader about the writer and his or her case analysis. It may be the wrong conclusion, but it is virtually unavoidable. Prepare a rough draft first and then convert it into something presentable, checking spellings and making sure your writing is legible. It is likely to be time well spent. On the other hand, it is not sensible to spend a great deal of time word processing and laser printing reports. If it is routine, then that is acceptable. But if it requires large amounts of effort, it might have been better expended on the analysis. From my experience I am tempted to conclude that the quality of the presentation is inversely correlated with the quality of the content.

13.5 CASE EXAMINATIONS

Although case examinations take a number of forms, the most common are seen examinations. These require students to answer questions in the examination room based upon a case study given out some time previously. Students are normally allowed to take their notes into the examination room, but the questions are not known in advance.

13.5.1 Case examinations: preparation

There are two kinds of activity involved in preparing for a case examination – predicting questions and organizing your case analysis notes so as to answer them.

Predicting questions

I disagree with examiners who argue that students should not attempt to predict questions, or rather areas where questions might be asked, because 'They are not taking in the full sweep of the syllabus'. It is the examiner's job to ensure that this occurs by setting appropriate questions. Students should be task-oriented and the task is to obtain good examination marks. Predicting questions, however, doesn't guarantee the outcome. Predicting questions can only be effective if the process of question setting is understood. For example, questions may be set by more than one examiner, or the examiner may have changed since the previous year. In general, case instructors do not try to deceive students. It is in their interest to make sure that examinees understand the questions. Most will be only too happy to discuss the process by which the case is chosen, the questions are set and the criteria by which answers will be judged. This information provides very good background against which more specific predictions can be made. More specific data come from past examination papers, past examinees or past examiners' reports. These data enable you to do two things. First of all they allow you to map out the territory covered and areas of concentration. This should influence you only at the most general level. Just because there was a specific requirement for a cash flow forecast last year doesn't mean that it won't be asked for again this year. There may, however, be a general preponderance of quantitative analysis and this may influence your preparation. The second function in analyzing past data is to discover the kind of question asked. Were they specific or general, theoretical or practical, all of one type or various? Understanding the style of questions helps you to organize the material when preparing for the examination.

Organizing case material

A case analysis for an examination may follow the stages suggested earlier in the book. However, it should be broader than that carried out for a case discussion or written case analysis. A comprehensive list of problems should be created. Generate a long list of alternatives

and evaluate them all. Develop implementation plans for each alternative, not just the preferred one. In this way you will be prepared to
move in any direction, to be ready for any contingency. In addition
to this very broad coverage you may wish to do more work in specific
areas which you judge are favoured by the question setter. Note that
this is in addition to, and not instead of, a complete broad analysis.
Do not attempt to prepare answers to specific questions in the hope
that they will come up. The chances are that they will not emerge in
the expected form, and that having prepared an answer you will be
tempted to use it even if it is off target. Worse still, it is difficult to
prepare new answers on the basis of old ones. The material is too
strictly ordered and specific, and you will not be able to reorganize
it in time. Instead you should organize your case material so that
relevant information can be quickly and effectively found, assembled
and structured into an answer to a question. It is also worthwhile to
convert your rough notes to something approaching final form. This
not only saves time in the examination room but prevents misunderstandings. In effect what you will be doing is creating a modular
answer kit.

13.5.2 Case examinations: execution

There are a number of pieces of advice which apply to any examination but which are particularly important in case examinations.

1. Analyze the question. Analysis means to break things up into
   their parts, in this case words and phrases. Ask yourself what
   they mean. For example:

   'Briefly set out the main reasons why the company is facing
   liquidation.'

   'Briefly' and 'set out' suggest that something less than a full
   discussion is required. Only the 'main' reasons are required, so
   you should not be tempted to pad out the answer with minor
   reasons. 'Reasons why' suggests that you should be able to link
   the causes with the effect – a company facing liquidation. This
   may seem a rather laboured exercise, but it forces you to confront
   the question.
2. Answer the question. Examinees, on the whole, do not misread
   questions by accident. They choose to misread them because they
   cannot answer the question set. A valiant attempt at an answer,
   however inadequate, should normally be given more credit than
   pages of off-the-topic waffle.

3. Prepare a timetable and stick to it. Allocate the time between questions in proportion to the marks they carry. Plan to use up to half your time preparing the answer, the remainder to actually answering it. Failure to stick to a timetable is the single biggest cause of exam failure. The first few marks on a question are easy to earn: the last few are very difficult. Allow time for checking – gross errors reduce credibility.

4. Structure your answers. This not only makes them easier and quicker to write, it also makes them easier to understand. Even if the detail is inadequate, a well-articulated structure indicates to the examiner that you have thought about and have attempted to answer the question.

Getting the Most out of Case Studies

In most spheres of human activity it is generally true that you only get out what you put in. This is particularly true of learning by the case method. Essentially, this is a group learning method and students have a responsibility to make the group experience a good and effective one. In addition I would like to give students some suggestions that might help them to get more out of case studies as individuals.

Group responsibilities

There is nothing more demoralizing for a case group than having a number of its members ill-prepared. It is certainly true that case preparation involves a large work load. It is also true that as the course proceeds it becomes easier to disguise the fact that you have done little preparation. Nevertheless, lack of preparation effectively sabotages the group's effectiveness and should be fought against. Try to put peer group pressure on students who are not pulling their weight. It is in their interests that you are doing so. Case groups usually comprise a rich mix of skills and abilities. It makes sense to draw on this variety and to use it to its best advantage. It also makes sense to help fellow students who are struggling: their difficulties in one area may be compensated by their strengths in others. A supportive and open case group is not only more effective, it is more enjoyable, which in turn makes it a better learning experience for all involved.

In a similar way it is important to recognize the difficulties inherent in the case instructor's role. Leading a case group requires a wide range of teaching skills which few case instructors have in full measure. Try to put yourself in your case instructor's place. Support his or her positive assets and tolerate his or her liabilities: intolerance or confrontation can only lead to an unsatisfactory learning experience. Case studies are only simulations of the real world. Yet they really only become capable of affecting behaviour if you suspend belief and treat them as the real thing. Try to throw yourself into the case situation and accept the occasional absurdities. Case studies allow you to explore feelings and emotions as well as thoughts and ideas.

Because case studies move into real-world situations they can raise ethical issues which more prosaic learning experiences do not. In particular, you must be careful to treat your fellow students' values with respect, even though they may be cloaked in the proposed solution to a particular problem. Cases allow individuals to explore ideas, roles, feelings, etc. Such explorations should be rewarded rather than punished. In some situations moral judgements may have to prevail over rational ones.

In a similar way you have a responsibility to the organization upon which the case is based. It is unlikely to co-operate a second time if hordes of students descend upon it with a view to abstracting further information: it has earned its right to privacy.

Individual development

Really getting involved in a case – whether it is a case discussion or an oral presentation – brings its own rewards. You have the chance of developing your skills and abilities by practice rather than by cerebration. You may occasionally make a mistake and look silly, but this is a small price to pay for accelerated individual development.

One of the themes of this book has been that case analysis, normally conducted, is a social process. As such it deserves as much attention as the content of the case. It is a great mistake to ignore this obvious point: it not only means a lost opportunity but it also constitutes a threat to effective case analysis. If you cannot learn from the real-life behaviour of the case group, how can you expect to learn from the dead world of the written case material?

Feedback has been mentioned before as a key element in learning, but it deserves emphasizing again. If you wish to learn you must get feedback on your performance. The greater the quantity and variety of feedback, the better. It is not easy to obtain, nor is it always easy to accept, but it is a very valuable commodity.

Too few students create a permanent record of the more cognitive aspects of case analysis. It is very valuable to take notes in case discussions or presentations. You may pick up interesting facts, ideas, concepts and principles which are worth remembering and even following up. Perhaps, more importantly, you may wish to record insights about how you or the group have behaved. In any case you should make your notes as soon after the session as possible. It is easy to put off the task and thereby forget it.

I hope that by reading this book you will have been made aware of the options open to you. In turn, therefore, you should be making conscious choices with regard to case analysis rather than being unaware of the variety of choices open to you. I hope you aspire to move beyond this stage towards developing an approach or style which, though it may draw on the procedures described here, will nevertheless be your own.

Finally, I would like to end on an upbeat. The case method is potentially one of the most exciting and interesting learning experiences available. That is why it is becoming more and more popular. It requires hard work and you have to be prepared to put in the hours. But it can also be a very stimulating and painless way to learn. Resolve to get the most out of it and you will be suitably rewarded.

Further Reading

Argyris, C. (1980) 'Some limitations of the case method: experiences in a management development program', *Academy of Management Review*, April, pp. 299–303.

An exposé of the way in which some top US case instructors go about teaching cases. In particular it points out how hidden agendas are used to control the process and the solutions reached.

Bromley, D.B. (1986) *The Case Study Method in Psychology and Related Disciplines*, Chichester: John Wiley.

An interesting book which looks at the nature of case studies both as research and teaching methodologies. Useful on thinking through problems.

Masoner, M. (1988) *An Audit of the Case Study Method*, New York: Praeger.

Report of some research into the effectiveness of the case method for particular learning outcomes. More useful for its review of the literature and bibliography. Strange writing style.

McNair, M. P. (1954) *The Case Method at Harvard Business School*, New York: McGraw-Hill.

Rather dated collection of papers about the case method generally, but it does include a number of worked case analyses and commentaries which might prove useful.

O'Dell, W. F., Ruppel, A. C. and Trent, R. H. (1979) *Marketing Decision Making: Analytical framework and cases*, Cincinnati, Ohio: Southwestern Publishing Company.

Not specifically about case analysis, but uses cases to illustrate a general problem-solving approach. Useful and interesting, if a little too general for case preparation.

Reynolds, J. I. (1980) *Case Method in Management Development*, Geneva: International Labour Office.

This book covers case analysis, case teaching and case writing as well as a number of organizational cases. The first section – around 30 pages – presents a very condensed approach to case analysis which is similar to the one outlined in this book.

Ronstadt, R. (1977) *The Art of Case Analysis: A student guide*, Needham, Mass.: Lord Publishing Company.

Should be subtitled 'How to survive a Harvard Case Course'. Down to earth, but deals with the detail of case analysis rather than the substance. Includes a worked case analysis example.

Tagiuri, R. (1968) *Behavioural Science Concepts in Case Analysis*, Cambridge, Mass.: Harvard.

A rather specialized book which provides examples of using theoretical concepts and frameworks in order to analyze case studies. Worth reading if you find application of theory to case material difficult.

Towl, A. R. (1969) *To Study Administration by Cases*, Boston, Mass.: Division of Research, Harvard University Graduate School of Business.

A classic report on a continuing investigation of the case method as practised at Harvard. Lots of very useful peripheral material, but mainly for case instructors.

In addition, books of case studies very often devote a few pages to case analysis guidelines. The Harvard Case Clearing House in Boston, USA, and the Case Clearing House at Cranfield, UK, hold master copies of many hundreds of case studies donated by case writers. In addition, the former has a collection of books and journal articles for those who wish to delve deeper into the subject.

Other useful books include:

Belanger, S.E. (1989) *Better Said and Clearly Written: An annotated guide to business communication sources, skills and samples*, Westport, Conn.: Greenwood Press.

The Americans put so much more effort into presentation than anyone else, it is hardly surprising that they publish so many books on all aspects of the subject. A very useful guide.

Ehrenberg, A. S. C. (1975) *Data Reduction*, New York: John Wiley.

This describes a particularly useful method of analyzing the kind of data met with in case studies.

Fletcher, J.A. and Gowing, D.F. (1987) *The Business Guide to Effective Writing*, London: The Institute of Chartered Accountants in England and Wales.

Written by accountants for accountants, but none the worse for that. Relatively broad but down-to-earth approach.

Jay, A. (1970) *Effective Presentation*, London: Management Publications Ltd.

A nicely presented (as one might expect) book about all sorts of business presentation including writing reports and making oral presentations. Dated but still rather good.

Pendlebury, M. and Groves, R. (1990) *Company Accounts: analysis, interpretation, understanding* (2nd edn), London: Unwin Hyman.

Any good book on finding your way around company accounts will have a section on financial ratio analysis. This one is particularly good.

Rickards, T. (1974) *Problem Solving Through Creative Analysis*, Aldershot: Gower Press.

Rickards, T. (1985) *Stimulating Innovation: A systems approach*. London: Frances Pinter.
Use these two Rickards books if you find you are stuck for creative ideas. They catalogue and describe a multitude of creativity techniques as well as a general approach to creativity in organizations.

Index

References to the case example are in italic type; location references to figures and tables are in bold type. In cases where an example of the use of a concept is taken from the case example the initials WDB are added. Individuals and companies mentioned solely in the case example are listed under the relevant heading.

alternatives, *see* outcomes; solutions
analysis
  frameworks of, 41–3, **43**
  morphological, 101–2, **103**
  multivariable, 49
    definition, 51
  restrictive form, 44–5
  techniques, 4
  see also presentation of case analysis
Argyris, C. (cited), 11

Banks & Co, 17, 21, 46
Brewers Society, 36
Brown, Matthew plc, *77*

Campaign for Real Ale (CAMRA), 23, 30
case studies
  'dead', 4
  definition, 1, 2–3, 5
  educational objectives, 148–9, 154
  function, xiv–xv, 4
  'live', 4–5
  method
    application, 14–15
    Harvard, 3–4, 7
    problems encountered, 10–11
    role-play, students', 73–5, 135, 143

  and skill development, 7–8, 9, 12, 94–5
  use of, 2–3, 4–6, **5**, 65
  see also presentation of case analysis
concept
  definition, 48
  example (WDB), 48
contingency planning, *see* decision–making
creativity, 8, 161
  importance of, 96–7
  techniques, 101–3, 115–17
  see also solutions
criteria
  definition of, 143
  examples (WDB), 145, 150–2, 154–8
  measurement of, 144, 149–50, **154**, **156**, **158**
  multiple, 147–58, **153**
  qualitative, 145–6
  see also values

data
  comparative, *77*
  qualitative (examples, WDB), *47–8, 49–50*
  quantitative (example, UK brewing industry), *46–7*
Davenport's Brewery (Holdings) plc, 17, 25–7, 48, 67

218